Edited by

WILLIAM A. DEMBSKI
& JAY WESLEY RICHARDS

UNAPOLOGETIC APOLOGETICS

MEETING THE CHALLENGES OF THEOLOGICAL STUDIES

InterVarsity Press
Downers Grove, Illinois

InterVarsity Press
P.O. Box 1400, Downers Grove, IL 60515-1426
World Wide Web: www.ivpress.com
E-mail: mail@ivpress.com

InterVarsity Press® *is the book-publishing division of InterVarsity Christian Fellowship/USA®, a student movement active on campus at hundreds of universities, colleges and schools of nursing in the United States of America, and a member movement of the International Fellowship of Evangelical Students. For information about local and regional activities, write Public Relations Dept., InterVarsity Christian Fellowship/USA, 6400 Schroeder Rd., P.O. Box 7895, Madison, WI 53707-7895.*

All Scripture quotations, unless otherwise indicated, are taken from the New Revised Standard Version of the Bible, *copyright 1989 by the Division of Christian Education of the National Council of the Churches of Christ in the USA. Used by permission. All rights reserved.*

Chapter eleven was previously published as "Jesus' Paradigm for Relating Our Experience to Our Language About God" in The Evangelical Quarterly *68, no. 1 (1996): 15-33. Used by permission.*

ISBN 0-8308-1563-5

Printed in the United States of America ∞

Library of Congress Cataloging-in-Publication Data

Unapologetic apologetics : meeting the challenges of theological studies / edited by William A. Dembski & Jay Wesley Richards.
   p. cm.
  Includes bibliographical references.
  ISBN 0-8308-1563-5 (alk. paper)
   1. Apologetics. I. Dembski, William A., 1960- II. Richards, Jay Wesley, 1967-

BT1102 .U52 2000
230'.071'1—dc21

                                            00-047173

20	19	18	17	16	15	14	13	12	11	10	9	8	7	6	5	4	3	2	1
17	16	15	14	13	12	11	10	09	08	07	06	05	04	03	02	01			

CONTENTS

Foreword

Phillip E. Johnson

I belong to one of the evangelical congregations in a mainstream denomination that has been dominated for many years at the national level by theological liberals who preach a very different gospel. Our First Presbyterian Church of Berkeley (PCUSA) nurtures many candidates for the ministry, and my wife, Kathie, is active on the candidate care committee. We worry every time we send these dedicated young (sometimes not-so-young) men and women off to seminary because we know they will be influenced there by teachers and fellow students who are committed to modernist and postmodernist concepts that change the Christian gospel into something else altogether.

It isn't that we want to protect future ministers from challenges to their faith commitments and their moral standards. On the contrary, it would be a poor education that failed to inform them that the prevailing view in religious as well as secular academic institutions is that the Bible is thoroughly unreliable as history, that the historical Jesus was no more than a fallible human teacher who was deified by his followers, and that the current moral agenda for the church should be to use all its influence against social evils like racism, sexism and homophobia. The problem is not that the case for modernist and postmodernist theology is argued but that the argument all too often goes unanswered. Indeed, the biggest problem is that the naturalistic assumptions that underlie both modernism and postmodernism often are assumed rather than explicit, so that they lie unobserved behind what is actually said instead of being brought forward for analysis and criticism. The student learns not to proclaim that naturalism is true but to avoid being stigmatized as a "fundamentalist" by saying or thinking anything that directly challenges modernist assumptions. Where naturalism is advocated, it is usually not under its own name but as an assumed component of "science" or just "rationality."

Kathie and I think it is stupid to try to protect people from dangerous ideas; we prefer to inoculate them. When a few years ago I found a copy of Martin Gardner's novel *The Flight of Peter Fromm*, then out of print, we decided we had the perfect vehicle and bought all the author's remaining private stock for use at seminar discussions with our church's seminarians. This novel of ideas tells the story of a young Christian fundamentalist, Peter Fromm, who enrolls in the University of Chicago Divinity School because he plans to convert the world and wants to start with the toughest audience. At Chicago Peter falls under the influence of a divinity school professor and Unitarian minister named Homer Wilson, who sets out to convert Peter step by step to his own agnostic liberalism. Homer's mephistophelean arguments are smoothly persuasive, and as Peter succumbs to them, he goes through one phase after another: a flirtation with Roman Catholicism; close encounters with Marx and Freud; intellectual immersion in the theologies of Barth, Bultmann, Niebuhr and Tillich; and finally a disastrous apprenticeship with a worldly minister reminiscent of Norman Vincent Peale. In the end Homer does not get Peter's soul, however; Peter somehow hangs on to a corner of his faith and asserts his own spiritual integrity at the cost of a mental breakdown in hilarious circumstances.

Gardner himself is thoroughly skeptical of orthodox Christianity, and his novel has since been republished by the vehemently anti-Christian Prometheus Press. What makes the book a wonderful teaching tool, however, is that it brings the basic issues to the surface and forces the reader to confront them through the eyes of both the sophisticated Homer and the initially innocent and increasingly bewildered Peter. Both men agree with each other and with the apostle Paul that the critical issue is whether Christ rose from the dead in the physical, empty-tomb sense, and both share a determination not to put up with the efforts of so many modern theologians and clergy to avoid committing themselves on this critical question. One thing we learn is that theologians who want to stay academically respectable while avoiding outright apostasy must become skillful at double talk. Homer Wilson divides the world of modernist clergy into "loyal liars" and "truthful traitors." Both assume that nature is all there is and that the methodological naturalism of scientific reasoning does not permit us to believe that a man who is truly dead can rise from the tomb and live again, much less live forever. The loyal liars reassure their congregations by pretending to believe, and the truthful traitors outrage them by spilling the beans. Seminarians who study the novel learn to recognize and criticize the ideas. More importantly, they learn to recognize how a teacher can escape addressing the inescapable issues without the class or congregation noticing.

Besides acquainting prospective seminarians with the ideas and evasions, it is important to furnish them with an effective support group. The occasional evangelical seminary professor who knows the score can be a helpful counselor, but there are limits on how far he or she can go without seeming to be disloyal to the seminary and to individual colleagues. What the student needs are mentors outside the institution and a peer group inside. In our church we try to provide the former in the form of elder advocates who help the future ministers maintain intellectual and spiritual contact with the lay people whom they will eventually be serving. William A. Dembski and Jay Wesley Richards have created what deserves to be called the mother of all seminary peer groups, an apologetics seminar where the tough issues are debated even in front of outside critics. Of course, this kind of forum has to be supplemented with more supportive prayer and fellowship circles, but the issue is whether those prayer groups are helping seminarians to confront the tough questions or to retreat from them. By founding their movement, and especially by (appropriately) seizing the banner of Charles Hodge as their flag, Dembski and Richards offended some faculty but did the only thing that could enable them to make a difference. I would like to think that Christian revolutionaries, following their master, will be charitable and loving. I would not like to think that they would be reluctant to step on a few complacent toes.

Behind this student movement is a more general intellectual movement that will bear fruit in the coming century. It is a bit thin on the ground for now, but so was the Christian faith in the first century. Materialism as a philosophy is superficially powerful but moribund, as we saw when the Soviet Union collapsed without a struggle a decade ago. Methodological naturalism is a branch on the materialist tree that will lose its power to intimidate when the tree is known to be hanging in midair. The Spirit moves when and where it chooses, and those who are moving with it are never afraid to perturb established branches and twigs that have lost sight of their own roots. That is the point of the intelligent design (or "mere creation") movement, to which Dembski and Richards have contributed much—to remind us of our roots, so we can carefully prune the branches.

We come from creation by God, not from unguided nature, and people who wish to be rational must recognize that fact. Show me a mainstream seminary that is unafraid to say that without equivocation, and dare the wrath of the scientific and academic establishments for doing so, and I will show you an institution that deserves your enthusiastic support.

Introduction

RECLAIMING THEOLOGICAL EDUCATION

William A. Dembski
Jay Wesley Richards

In 1943 Christian apologetics was still a required course at Princeton Theological Seminary. In 1944 apologetics was no longer offered even as an elective. Except for sporadic references to it, apologetics ceased to be part of the seminary curriculum. Princeton was not alone in abandoning apologetics. Indeed, a person would be hard-pressed to find a denominational seminary that includes it today. For post-Enlightenment liberalism the very idea of rational argument on behalf of the Christian faith is offensive.

And yet, throughout Scripture, Christians are enjoined to defend the faith through rational argument. Thus Peter urged, "Always be ready to make your defense *[apologia]* to anyone who demands from you an accounting for the hope that is in you" (1 Pet 3:15). Paul understands his own ministry as constituting a "defense *[apologia]* and confirmation *[bebaiosis]* of the gospel" (Phil 1:7). The Greek *apologia* denotes a legal defense, and the Greek *bebaiosis* means "verification" or "proof."

The Demise of Apologetics

Rational argument used to be regarded as an ally of the Christian faith, but this changed two hundred years ago during the Enlightenment. The father of liberal theology, Friedrich Schleiermacher, who came just after the Enlightenment, epitomized this change when he remarked, "We entirely renounce all attempts to prove the truth or necessity of Christianity; and we presuppose, on the contrary, that all Christians . . . have already the inward certainty that their religion cannot take any other form than this."

Karl Barth continued this negative attitude toward apologetics into our own day (cf. his *Church Dogmatics* 1/1).

Are Schleiermacher and Barth right? Throughout the book of Acts we find that Paul does not merely *proclaim* the gospel, hoping to score a conversion here and there. Instead he actively *persuades* people of the truth of the gospel, striving to convince both the hearts and the minds of his listeners. Indeed, it is instructive to trace the Greek *peitho*, the verb that means to persuade, through the book of Acts. Active persuasion, and not bald assertion, characterize Paul's ministry.

The failure of the mainline denominations to take Christian apologetics seriously is at least in part responsible for the steady decline of these denominations, not only in size but also in vision. At stake in apologetics is the question whether Christianity is true—objectively true. "Objective truth" is a dirty word these days. It is chic to relativize, contextualize and politicize the truth of the gospel. On the other hand, it is terribly gauche to cramp our free-swinging academic style by giving credence to objective truths, which by their nature are obligatory across the board and thus not subject to our control.

Lay people with the good fortune not to have been educated out of their good sense want to know whether the fundamental claims of Christianity are objectively true. A Christ who is merely a social or political or ethical construction does not interest them—and rightly so. Miguel de Unamuno's definition of belief in God is too thin a soup on which to nourish a vibrant Christian faith: "To believe in God is to long for His existence, and, further, it is to act as if He existed."[1] To desire that God exists and to act as though God existed express but a vague hope. Does God actually exist? And more to the point, Who is this God? and How can we know anything about this God? These are questions people need answered if their faith is to be sustained and strengthened.

By jettisoning apologetics from their seminary curricula, the mainline denominations have undermined the training of their ministers. Errors and confusions taught at seminary propagate not only up the denominational hierarchy but also down to the grassroots. Lay people these days scratch their heads at the theological disarray of their denominations. They are amazed because what was unthinkable only a few years back is

---

[1]Miguel de Unamuno, *The Tragic Sense of Life*, trans. J. E. C. Flitch (1913; reprint, New York: Dover, 1954), pp. 184-85.

now considered normal. They needn't be amazed—one semester at a mainline seminary is enough to dispel the amazement. What with Union Seminary in New York holding a voodoo chapel service, Harvard Divinity School offering a theology class in which students are taught that the Virgin Mary was raped by God, and Princeton Theological Seminary's gay-lesbian caucus stuffing the campus mailboxes with a flier showing two men in the Garden of Eden and with a caption reading "God created Adam and Steve," it is hardly surprising when today's pastors are more confused than their congregations.

In response to this theological malaise, a group of students at Princeton Theological Seminary, organized as the Charles Hodge Society, decided to offer a weekly seminar on Christian apologetics known as the Princeton Apologetics Seminar. These seminars began in the spring of 1995 and continue to the present. Semester themes for the seminar have included the authority of Scripture, Christian missions and Christianity's cultured despisers. The essays in this volume are largely taken from that seminar. We present these essays for two reasons: (1) to strengthen the faith of seminarians and other Christians who struggle with the theological disarray of our times, and (2) to provide an example of what a student group can do on a seminary campus to combat false and destructive ideas.

Besides starting an apologetics seminar, the Charles Hodge Society also reinstituted the *Princeton Theological Review*, a journal founded by Charles Hodge but disbanded by the seminary in the 1920s.[2] *The Princeton Theological Review* has published many of the papers presented at the Princeton Apologetics Seminar.

In adopting Charles Hodge's name, the Charles Hodge Society wished to recognize his towering presence in the early history of Princeton Theological Seminary. Charles Hodge was the premier American theologian in the nineteenth century. Unlike today, when theology is considered a second-class discipline readily ignored by the cultural movers and shakers, scientists and statesmen alike eagerly awaited Hodge's wisdom on everything from slavery to Darwinism. The Charles Hodge Society therefore wished to recognize his outstanding role in stimulating the intellectual and spiritual life of the seminary and of our nation.

---

[2]For subscription information write to the *Princeton Theological Review* at Princeton Theological Seminary, P.O. Box 821, Princeton, NJ 08542.

Fundamentalism and Accommodationism

Martin Luther once noted that "we can get along without burgomasters, princes, and noblemen, but we can't do without schools, for they must rule the world." If we take seriously that Christianity embodies humanity's chief truth—that God was in Christ Jesus reconciling the world to himself—then the most important school of all is the seminary. The seminaries teach our ministers who in turn teach their congregations about Jesus Christ. Whether they do so faithfully and truthfully depends on the training they receive at seminary.

The Roman statesman Seneca observed, "If you want a man to keep his head when crisis comes, you must give him some training before it comes." Seminary breeds many a crisis of faith. It is common for young men and women who are enthusiastic about serving God to go to seminary, lose their heads and turn away from the truth of Christianity. Since Christian symbols are easily reinterpreted within secular categories, often a form of Christianity remains. But once seminarians come to view orthodox Christianity as simplistic, biblicist or morally deficient—as is regularly taught at the mainline seminaries—loss of faith is inevitable. Students need to be equipped to handle the assaults on heart and mind that they encounter at seminary. For this reason apologetics is indispensable in the education of Christian ministers.

What will it take to reinvigorate Christian apologetics and thereby help reclaim theological education? We need to cultivate a certain attitude. Our work as Christian apologists must be of the highest quality and rigor to deserve the respect of the secular academic community (and this includes the mainline seminaries). Yet at the same time we must view any respect we actually receive from this community as inconsequential. Our attitude must combine two competing ideals: the desire to produce work worthy of respect, and a repudiation of any desire for actual acceptance or, respectability.

Why is this attitude so important? To transform mainline seminaries in particular and the secular academic world in general, the Christian apologist must steer clear of two obstacles. One obstacle is fundamentalism, which assumes all conceptual problems facing Christianity are easily resolved. The other obstacle is accommodation to the prevailing secular ideologies, which gives up so much ground as to lose any robust Christian witness. Fundamentalism prevents us from doing the quality work that's needed to deserve the respect of the secular world. On the other hand, accommodationism is so caught up in gaining the respect of the secular academic world that it loses its integrity as a Christian witness.

Consider an analogy. In earlier centuries actors were classified with thieves, prostitutes and pimps—the scum of society. Actors, and entertainers generally, make their living by pleasing an audience. As a result they are easily tempted to prostitute their art to the all-too-often debased tastes of their audiences. This temptation is so strong that many entertainers succumb, with the result that the profession has traditionally been viewed as scandalous.

The temptation to prostitute ourselves, which is so evident in the entertainment industry, is equally a danger to Christian scholars. There is only one way for Christians to resist this temptation and that is to accept fully the offense of the gospel. Christian apologetics must never be divorced from the offense of the gospel. The secular academy sets ground rules that doom Christianity from the start. For Christian apologists to play by these rules, whether in the name of ecumenism or pluralism, is to capitulate the faith.

That said, our response as Christian apologists must not be to stick our heads in the sand and mechanically repeat a creed. We are to engage the secular world, reproving, rebuking and exhorting it, pointing to the truth of Christianity and producing strong arguments and valid criticisms that show where secularism has missed the mark.

Will we be appreciated? Hardly. The Pharisees of our day—those who know themselves to occupy the moral high ground—reside preeminently in the academic world. The Pharisees killed Jesus and are just as ready to destroy our Christian witness if we permit it. Nevertheless, this is our calling as Christian apologists, to bear witness to the truth, even to the point of death (be it the death of our bodies or the death of our careers). The church has a name for this—martyrdom. The early church considered martyrdom the highest Christian calling. Martyrdom was counted an honor and privilege, a way of sharing in Christ's sufferings and living out the Christian life in its most logical and complete form.

Christian apologetics that's worthy of the name is a call to martyrdom— perhaps not a martyrdom where we spill our blood (although this too may be required) but a martyrdom where we witness to the truth without being concerned about our careers, political correctness, the current fashion or toeing the party line. We are not called to please the world; we are called to proclaim the truth within whatever context and conventions we find ourselves. This means we must have a thorough knowledge of our context and conventions. We must be informed. We must listen. We must know where we stand, and we must know where we are withstood. This requires effort.

Quietism, Imperialism and Engagement

There is another set of twin obstacles that the Christian apologist must avoid—quietism and imperialism. Quietism is the view that the proper response of the Christian toward the world is to wait things out. According to quietism this world is a bad place, in fact so bad a place that our best strategy is to sidestep the world as much as possible. Quietism tries to make it through life unscathed. This approach to the Christian life is a great temptation in our day. Feeling beleaguered by so many hostile forces in our society, we like nothing better than to retreat into a fortress. But this is precisely what the Christian may not do. Christian scholarship has no place in a ghetto.

We have Jesus' own example in this matter. Consider how Jesus began his ministry: "Jesus came to Galilee, proclaiming the good news of God, and saying, 'The time is fulfilled, the kingdom of God has come near; repent, and believe the good news' " (Mk 1:14–15). Jesus insists that people change the way they think and act. To a generation that regards religion as a harmless backwater having no real cognitive claims, this is the height of presumption. Jesus, never slow to place demands on people, enunciates here his two primary demands: repentance and faith.

It is important that we understand precisely what Jesus is demanding here. The repentance of which Jesus speaks denotes a fundamental reorientation of the human person and contains a strong cognitive element. Indeed the very word for repentance in the Greek New Testament refers primarily to cognition and has embedded in it the Greek word for mind. Repentance signifies a thoroughgoing change in mental outlook or perspective. Now there is only one way to change one's perspective and that is to move to a new vantage from which to see previously hidden things. The changed perspective that Jesus requires comes from believing the good news—the gospel. Through faith in this good news we reorient ourselves to see things as God means us to see them. This is the good news that God has loved the world and sent Christ to redeem it. The repentance and faith of which Jesus speaks are thus inseparable.

But what gave Jesus the right to demand of his listeners repentance and

faith? Even if we grant that quietism is not a valid Christian attitude, imperialism certainly does not fare any better. How can Jesus command us to
repent and believe? Isn't this the height of presumption? Religion is, after
all, a personal and private affair, isn't it? What business then does Jesus
have imposing his views on others? How can Jesus be so insensitive? How
dare he be so judgmental as to find fault with how other people are living
their lives. To paraphrase the gestalt psychologist Fritz Perls, we are not in
this world to live up to Jesus' expectations, and he is not in this world to
live up to our expectations.

Of course, these criticisms are utterly bogus. Jesus had every right to
express his views forthrightly, to find fault where there was fault, and to
demand change where justice was flouted. Unlike the crusaders of the
Middle Ages, Jesus was not putting the sword to anyone's neck. He was
straightforwardly speaking the truth. It is disingenuous to call this imperialism. Imperialism is always a matter of coercion, not a matter of discomfort. The deeper a lie is entrenched, the greater the discomfort when the
truth finally unmasks it. The Pharisees did not like it when Jesus
unmasked their hypocrisy. They did not like it when he showed them that
God's purposes for humanity were greater than their narrow, self-righteous
parochialism.

Our proper response in approaching the world is therefore neither quietism nor imperialism but engagement. This was Jesus' own attitude. God
is reconciling the world to himself through Christ. As Christians we are
the body of Christ and thus the instruments through which God reconciles
the world. We have a unique calling. Insofar as Christ is reconciling the
world today, it is through the lives of his people, the Christians who constitute his church. Our proper response therefore is one of engagement, to
engage the world with the truth of Christ.

As we engage the world with the truth of Christianity, we need to recognize how very high are the stakes. Not only does Christianity claim to possess humanity's ultimate truth, but it also claims that this truth is so
urgent that a person ignores it at his or her peril. At the heart of Christianity is the overwhelming truth that in Christ God has invaded space and
time, making it possible for humanity to take part in the divine life. The
opportunity to take part in the divine life is regarded by Scripture and
church tradition as good news—indeed, the best there is. But Christianity
also has a dark side: those who refuse to embrace this truth face separation
from that divine life. Again, the Scripture and church tradition are univo-

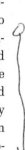

cal on this point; only this time the picture they present is incredibly bleak.

We need to remember that this is a fallen world. This is not the world God originally created. The world of Genesis 1 was, as the author of Genesis puts it, "very good." But the world that came into being after Adam's transgression is a different world. To be sure, there is continuity with the original creation. And it is this continuity that ensures God's love for this present, fallen world. But the present world is a different world from the original one. It is a world in which love and hatred, right and wrong, and good and evil coexist and commingle. It is also a world in which humans must decide their allegiances. There is in the end no straddling of fences. Jesus says that we are either for him or against him. There is no middle ground. This truth is the dark side of the gospel. For those who receive it, the gospel is the best news imaginable. For those who reject it, the gospel signifies sorrow and loss. The apostle Paul put it this way: "We are the aroma of Christ to God among those who are being saved and among those who are perishing; to the one a fragrance from death to death, to the other a fragrance from life to life" (2 Cor 2:15-16).

An urgency attaches to the Christian message. People's lives are in the balance. Not every story will have a happy ending. Everything is not going to turn out all right in the end. Only where God's grace is manifested will things turn out all right. But where God's grace is spurned, things will not turn out all right. There is a move afoot these days in theological circles to embrace a position known as universalism—that in the end everyone will be saved. This is the teaching neither of Scripture nor of church tradition. There is no universal safety net. Our feel-good pop psychologies urge us to think it more befitting of God to save everyone. Reality, however, is not ultimately determined by what we think fitting. Certainly we should be comforted in knowing that the God who decides human destinies is rich in love and mercy. But we must never neglect the holiness and justice of God.

Because the truth of Christ is humanity's chief truth, the truth of Christ is at once glorious and urgent. It follows that Christians have a mandate to declare the truth of Christ. This mandate consists of bringing every aspect of life under the influence of this truth. In an age of unbridled freedom and licentiousness, this no doubt will smack of elitism and intrusiveness. But in fact, unifying every aspect of life around the truth of Christ is the only hope humanity has to find true freedom and fulfillment. In the epistle to the Colossians, Paul writes that all things were created by and for Christ. To be united with Christ is therefore to fulfill a person's true purpose, whereas to be separated from Christ is to lose his or her way.

Rooting Out False Ideas

If we now grant that unifying every aspect of life around the truth of Christ is the ideal that ought to guide every Christian scholar, the question remains, How do we get there? Let us begin by acknowledging how far we actually are from attaining this ideal. Consider the words of J. Gresham Machen, a well-known Princeton theologian, who was active early in the twentieth century.

> False ideas are the greatest obstacles to the Gospel. We may preach with all the fervor of a reformer and yet succeed only in winning a straggler here and there, if we permit the whole collective thought of the nation or of the world to be controlled by ideas which, by the resistless force of logic, prevent Christianity from being regarded as anything more than a harmless delusion.[3]

These words have come true in our own day with a vengeance. Anything that hints at a Christian worldview is routinely discarded within our secular society.

Indeed, we have permitted the collective thought of the world to be controlled by ideas that prevent Christianity from being regarded as anything but a harmless delusion. It needs to be emphasized that we, the Christians, the church of Jesus Christ, have done this. Christianity has never held any illusions about the extent of evil and deception of which a lost humanity is capable. But if evil and deception prosper, part of the blame must inevitably be laid at the feet of those who can help prevent it.

Christians are called to be salt and light in the world, and in this way to stem and overthrow false ideas. Unfortunately we have not exercised our power as salt and light nearly enough. Through self-absorption, inattention and bad theology we have failed to act as salt and light. We have been careless. We have let false ideas prosper without challenge. False ideas have to be rooted out for faith to recover. This is not to say that Christians ought to form vigilante groups, set up an index of proscribed books as in the old days and condemn everything that strikes them as the least bit threatening. The inquisitorial method cannot fulfill God's redemptive purposes for the world.

---

[3]J. Gresham Machen, *What Is Christianity?* (Grand Rapids, Mich.: Eerdmans, 1951), p. 162.

Nonetheless, we are not to leave false ideas unchecked. False ideas must be rooted out, and to do so requires seeing them for what they are. Since Adam and Eve ate from the tree of the knowledge of good and evil, humans have known good and evil—the tree delivered what it promised. Indeed, we know good and evil not just abstractly but from experience—all of us have experienced good and evil in our lives. But to understand good and evil, to discern good and not confuse it with evil, this is a different matter entirely. This sort of knowledge eluded our first parents and, but for the grace of God, continues to elude us. Discerning between good and evil is a far different matter from simply having experienced them.

Now false ideas become a problem precisely when we lack such discernment. A false idea is harmless enough if we recognize it as such, if we understand its origin and history, if we untangle its partial truths, if we appreciate why the false idea seems plausible to its adherents, if we understand it better than its original proponents. Once we thoroughly understand a false idea, we need no longer be intimidated by it. Only then can we properly assess its place in the grand scheme of things and so bring it under the authority of Christ.

False ideas that undermine the Christian faith need to be exposed for what they are before they can lose their sting. Unfortunately, we have grown sloppy in exposing false ideas. We have refused to expend the necessary effort to bring the false ideas of our age under the authority of Christ. In the history of Christianity this is a recent development. From the sixth century up to the Enlightenment it is safe to say that the West was thoroughly imbued with Christian ideals and that Western intellectual elites were overwhelmingly Christian. False ideas that undermined the very foundations of the Christian faith (e.g., denying the resurrection or the Trinity) were swiftly challenged and uprooted. Since the Enlightenment, however, we have not so much lacked the means to combat false ideas as the will and clarity.

The will and clarity to combat false ideas comes from taking Jesus' promise to his disciples seriously: "I will give you words and a wisdom that none of your opponents will be able to withstand or contradict" (Lk 21:15). What is noteworthy about this promise is how perfectly it was fulfilled in the life of Jesus. Jesus was never at a loss for words. He always saw through the traps of his opponents. He had an uncanny ability for avoiding pitfalls. If this promise was fulfilled in Jesus' life, why should contemporary Christians expect less for themselves? The false ideas that undermine our faith today are no more insidious than the traps and snares that beset Jesus. Why should we not expect the same success in dealing with them that Jesus experienced? The threat that false ideas present is simply too great to be ignored. Jesus did not ignore them but addressed them squarely. How can we demand less of ourselves?

The remedy must be appropriate to the disease. Demons have to be cast out. Infections have to be drained. Cancers have to be surgically removed. And false ideas have to be analyzed, evaluated and refuted. Just as the word of God's truth is good seed that generates new life in Christ, so false ideas are bad seeds which, if allowed to grow, yield bitter fruit. The only way to get rid of seeds once planted is to dig them up. Recovery of faith is the art of cultivation. Weeding is as much a part of gardening as are planting and nurturing. False ideas need to be weeded out. This requires work, patience and diligence. Above all, it requires a willingness to listen and inquire into ideas that oppose the faith. We must be willing to learn from the world. We must grasp what the world is saying even better than it does itself. Only in this way will Christ's authority over the life of the mind be reestablished and the doors of faith reopened.

What is the goal of all our intellectual exertions as Christian apologists? Certainly our goal is not to make a name for ourselves. Nor is it simply to glorify God with our minds by probing the wonders of God's creation. The goal is rather to restore a simplicity of faith to a generation that has grown cold and cynical. As Jesus put it, "Unless you change and become like little children, you will never enter the kingdom of heaven" (Mt 18:3).

The great fault of secularism—and there's plenty of secularism at our seminaries—is that it actively hinders us from coming to such a simplicity of faith. By simplicity of faith we mean a belief in the unqualified goodness, wisdom and trustworthiness of God—that God always has our best interests at heart, that God knows exactly what he is doing, that God is actively involved and interested in our lives and that in spite of circumstances God is always worthy of our praise, gratitude and adoration.

The goal of Christian apologetics is to clear the way for a simple, childlike faith. Indeed, once our doctrines of God and salvation become so encrusted with qualifications, nuances and doubts that we can no longer run to God as a loving father, we're probably better closing up shop. This is not to say that there's no room for sophistication in theology. But the goal of all such sophistication must again be to restore us to the simplicity of the faith.

Quarantine Versus Inoculation

The tendency among evangelical Christians has been to (1) retreat, not simply from the world but also from those portions of the church that have assimilated "worldly" standards and ideas, and (2) build fortresses. This strategy has its own logic: false ideas tend to corrupt and whoever engages such ideas risks corruption. Ideological purity, however, has its own risks. A quarantine maintains safety only as long as one can prevent exposure. Preventing exposure may be possible when combating physical toxins. But when the toxins are false ideas, isolation is difficult to maintain.

The proper model for handling exposure to false ideas is not quarantine but inoculation. Inoculation exposes a person to a disease, but in measured doses so that the destructive effects of the disease are mitigated. The person inoculated against a disease ceases to be at risk, even when exposed to it. The inoculated individual is immune. Similarly, the student who has been inoculated against false ideas is far less likely to succumb to them than the student who has been cloistered from them. Precisely because they have already been exposed to falsehood, inoculated students become convincing critics of falsehood and defenders of truth. For this reason, Christian apologetics needs to stress inoculation.

The mainline and liberal seminaries can be a dangerous place for a student's Christian faith. Those who surrender their faith at seminary typically lack adequate exposure to the false ideas they encounter, as well as the critical-thinking skills for analyzing those ideas. For students who were previously "quarantined," a liberal seminary education can constitute overexposure and result in infection. Take, for instance, students whose undergraduate education was at a Bible college. Such students will arrive at seminary with extensive knowledge of the Bible's content, yet may know little about mainstream biblical studies. So when they arrive at seminary and learn of, say, the documentary hypothesis (i.e., that the first five books of the Bible were not written by Moses but rather are a patchwork of different source traditions closer to the time of the Babylonian exile in 587 B.C.), they lack the tools for evaluating it.

At a mainline seminary, students will hear neither a thorough defense nor a thorough critique of the documentary hypothesis. In all likelihood professors will present a brief sketch of the hypothesis and thereafter simply presuppose it. This is not necessarily because seminary professors seek to indoctrinate students. In most cases professors teach what they think is correct and, because of time constraints, avoid treating alternative theories. Consequently, students either reflexively reject what they hear without benefit of cogent argument or surrender to it wholesale since everyone around them seems to assume its truth. More insidiously, young seminarians may suspect that their former "fundamentalist" teachers and pastors intentionally kept them in the dark about this "newfound knowledge." This suspicion can have devastating effects.

What's the solution? Students must be exposed to the documentary hypothesis so that not only its claims and presuppositions are presented as fairly as possible (e.g., the role of philosophical naturalism in its formation and defense) but also the reasons for and against it. This approach inoculates students against the destructive power of false ideas while at the same time enabling them to appropriate elements of truth that the idea may contain. Ideally, this should be the task of any good Christian education. Thankfully, there are still Christian institutions that aspire to such a balanced and intentional educational philosophy.

Puncturing the Myth of Invincibility

But what about mainline or liberal seminaries where this educational philosophy is lacking? Should students simply avoid such places altogether? Is it better to go to an evangelical seminary than risk spiritual meltdown? Certainly, some seminaries are so hostile to the Christian faith that it is impossible to acquire a sound education there. Nonetheless, to abandon the large, influential and well-endowed institutions because they are in trouble makes poor strategic sense. The unstated assumption here is that when a seminary's leadership becomes subverted, all hope is lost—time to pack up and move out. This assumption even comes with its own proof text: "Therefore come out from among them and be separate" (2 Cor 6:17).

Although this text is important for maintaining the integrity of the church, it remains equally important that the church act as salt and light in difficult situations. Yes, the mainline and liberal seminaries are in a tight spot. But that is hardly a reason for abandoning them. Even if their leadership is corrupt, what is to prevent reform and renewal coming from the bottom up—from the students themselves?

The leftist students and campus agitators of the 1960s have become the tenured faculty, political leaders and opinion-makers of the nineties. Similarly, the theological left has successfully employed an incrementalist strategy of gradually displacing orthodox Christianity and replacing it with liberal Christianity. So why isn't the ideological converse possible?

Why should evangelical students be incapable of similar aspirations? Our own experience at Princeton Theological Seminary made it clear that evangelical students are the key to renewing the mainline seminaries and churches. The faculty and administration of these institutions are typically too entrenched and hidebound to accomplish significant change. The enthusiasm of youth, on the other hand, is wonderfully capable of upsetting the status quo.

What we are urging, then, is an intentional activism by evangelical students directed at the mainline seminaries both to renew and to reclaim these institutions. What should evangelical students do? Some activities are obvious and essential: They should seek like-minded students for spiritual and psychological support, maintain a vigilant prayer life, read Scripture, participate in the sacraments and worship God. But there's more: Evangelical students need to take up the mantle of public apologist.

But isn't this presumptuous? How can we expect mere students to defend ideas publicly when their professors, who enjoy more education and experience, are daily dismissing those very ideas? Is this not sending sheep to the slaughter? Not at all. We speak from experience when we say that the heterodoxy of the mainline seminaries is far from invincible. Fashion tends to rule the day and is easily upset by students bold enough to challenge it. What the Charles Hodge Society accomplished at Princeton Theological Seminary ·is possible at every other mainline seminary, provided that a handful of committed evangelical students are willing to put their necks on the ideological chopping block.

Here is what we did: Since Princeton Theological Seminary offered no course in apologetics and was unlikely to reinstate apologetics in the curriculum at our request, we decided to supplement the curriculum. Specifically, we decided to conduct apologetic seminars on campus, open them to the public and lead them ourselves. This might seem onerous given that we were already full-time students. But in truth, running an apologetics seminar can be done without a great deal of extra effort. What is required, initially, is that a group of students, say six to ten, be willing to lead one or two seminars per semester.

We held the seminars every Tuesday at 8:00 p.m. in a seminary classroom. We chose a semester theme and divided up relevant topics. The bulk of the labor for seminar leaders therefore went into writing an extra paper per semester (approximately 6,000 words for a 45 minute presentation, which was then followed by questions and answers). Typically we also had a designated respondent to analyze and critique the paper that had just been presented. After the paper was presented, it was put on reserve in the seminary library.

As semester themes we chose those that were of particular concern to the seminary community. The first semester of the apologetics seminar was devoted to the discipline of *apologetics:* its history at Princeton Seminary and elsewhere, its different types, its value and also several case studies of apologetics in action (e.g., the challenge of the biological and human sciences). The following semester we tackled the doctrine of *Scripture:* inerrancy, inspiration, aberrant treatments of biblical authority (such as Paul Tillich's), different evangelical doctrines of Scripture and so on. We had a local priest come and defend the Roman Catholic doctrine of Scripture. We also had a convinced Barthian present Barth's view of the inspiration of Scripture. Friendly and even not-so-friendly adversaries were always welcome at our podium.

The next semester we treated *missions* (an unpopular topic in many mainline seminaries these days, except as a surrogate for leftist political activism). Although our preference has been to keep the apologetics seminar "owned and operated" by students, we broke with tradition that semester and invited a retired evangelical professor of missions, Samuel Moffett, to speak on the continued need for evangelistic missionaries from the West. The next semester we examined *orthodoxy* and treated the main themes of the Apostles' Creed such as the Fatherhood of God, the virgin birth, Christ's human and divine natures, the resurrection, the atonement and the definition of the church. Again students did most of the speaking, but one week the director of InterVarsity for Princeton University graduate students, Gary Deddo, defended Christian language of God as Father (his essay is included in this volume).

Our theme the next semester was Christianity's Cultured Despisers (a takeoff from Schleiermacher's *On Religion: Speeches to Its Cultured Despisers*). We treated specific arguments against Christianity from famous historical figures like Hume, Darwin, Marx, Freud and Bertrand Russell. The story continues, and the Princeton Apologetics Seminar is active to this day. Its great strength is its ownership by Princeton students. We do not depend on speakers outside the seminary community. We do not look for the esteem of faculty and administration. Those of us who participated in the apologetics seminars received a broader and more liberal education (in the true sense) than those who limited themselves to the seminary curriculum. There is no reason that students at other seminaries cannot do the same.

Students at today's mainline seminaries are more conservative than their faculties (at least at the beginning of their studies). This contrasts with the situation in the 1960s, in which students were much more liberal and radical than their professors. There are now far more students from evangelical congregations than from liberal ones that attend seminary. In contrast, liberal Christianity has great difficulty regenerating itself. Hardly anyone converts from agnosticism to liberal Christianity. Many liberal Christians started out as evangelicals. Indeed, liberal Christianity is parasitic. To survive it must recruit evangelical Christians. What's more, the key recruiting ground is the theological seminary.

What we are proposing, then, is to exploit the theological disparity between students and faculty at mainline seminaries through focused and intentional student activism. To succeed, such activism requires that a few committed seminary students be willing to risk their status, security and popularity. Additionally, it requires the help and encouragement from faithful people in the pews—this includes spiritual, emotional and financial support. Financial support is especially important. Seminary students tend to be poor. What's more, apologetics remains sufficiently unpopular at the mainline seminaries that funding, which is readily given to other campus groups, tends to get diverted from evangelical students engaged in apologetics. For instance, the *Princeton Theological Review* would long be defunct were it not for subscriptions by supporters outside the seminary as well as for donations by the students themselves (donations we could ill afford to make).

Standing up for Christian orthodoxy at a mainline seminary is a quick way to lose friends and alienate people. Members of the Charles Hodge Society were threatened with two lawsuits for their work on the *Princeton Theological Review*, threatened with physical violence, accused of racism and sexism, denied funding that other campus groups readily received, had posted signs destroyed and removed, and were explicitly informed by faculty that membership in the Charles Hodge Society jeopardized their academic advancement. Nonetheless, we also met with approval and encouragement from some faculty and administrators, from lay people in the churches who heard of our efforts, and from fellow students who saw us as giving them a voice.

In retrospect our hardships were minor—even trivial—and do not merit comparison with the sufferings of Christians throughout history and in many parts of the world today. Nonetheless, we mention them because students at other institutions who want to take a similar stand need to do so with their eyes open. Although every institution is unique, the response we received at Princeton Theological Seminary is likely to be typical. There is a price to be paid. But there are also rewards to be reaped. The liberal Christianity of the mainline seminaries is not invincible. But it is up to seminary students to puncture that myth of invincibility.

PART 1

FOUNDATIONS

1

THE TASK
OF APOLOGETICS

WILLIAM A. DEMBSKI

W HAT IS THE TASK OF APOLOGETICS? ACCORDING TO THE NEW TESTA-
ment writer Jude it is this: "Contend for the faith that was once for all
entrusted to the saints" (Jude 1:3). I want in this essay to flesh out Jude's
characterization of apologetics. Jude urges us to contend for the faith.
What does this mean? The very idea of contending for the faith rings foreign to our modern and postmodern ears. To contend for something, after
all, presupposes we have something worth contending for—that the faith
is something definite and precious, all too easily lost, and therefore in
need of being vigorously preserved. I want therefore to begin this essay by
showing that it is legitimate to think of the faith in these terms, that is, as
something definite, precious and worth fighting for.

The Stability of the Faith
The idea of contending for the faith rings foreign to our ears because we
have become accustomed to viewing all our beliefs about God and the
world as in flux. Evolution and revolution are the dominant metaphors
of our age. Nothing stays the same. Either a thing so changes with the
times that we can't recognize it after a while, or it doesn't keep up with

the times, in which case it becomes obsolete and has to be replaced. In other words, things either evolve or get overthrown. Our throwaway society mirrors this state of our minds.

In contrast, Jude affirms that the Christian faith is stable and unchanging. Christians are to contend for a faith that has been entrusted to them *once for all*. The metaphors of evolution and revolution are thus implicitly rejected. We are not called to contend for a sociologically constructed faith or a historicized faith or a demythologized faith or a politicized faith or any other enculturated faith. We are called rather to contend for the faith that Christ entrusted to the apostles and which the apostles in turn entrusted to us through the intervening generations of Christian witnesses.

This faith is grounded in the truth of the gospel, a truth that must itself be stable and unchanging if the faith that it grounds is to be stable and unchanging. Though the idea that truth can be stable and unchanging is foreign to our contemporary mindset, it is an idea that nonetheless prevails throughout Scripture. The unchanging quality of truth is at the heart of how the Scriptures characterize God and God's word. For instance, we read in Isaiah 40:8: "The grass withers, the flower fades; but the word of our God will stand forever." Similarly, we read in the epistle of James that with God "there is no variation or shadow due to change" (Jas 1:17). God does not change. God's truth does not change. To be sure, our knowledge of this truth will always be partial. Yet insofar as it is knowledge at all, it must be accurate. And where this knowledge is accurate, it must not change.

This conception of truth as something stable and unchanging has few advocates in the academic world these days. The very idea that truth can be immune from the vagaries of sociohistorical contingency is problematic for contemporary thinkers. Why is this? The past two hundred years have witnessed a series of intellectual and sociological revolutions in which many of the things we thought were solid have been swept away. In physics, Newtonian mechanics had to give way to relativity theory and quantum mechanics. In biology, the view that biological systems are designed gave way to the view that biological systems are solely the product of naturalistic mechanisms. Marx showed us that economic forces govern history. Freud showed us that unconscious psychic forces beyond our control govern our personalities. In the arts, the absence of any stable reference points has become a cause célèbre. It has become increasingly difficult to chart continuities over time. What continuities there are invariably exhibit dramatic variation. And no continuity continues indefinitely. Once again evolution and revolution show themselves as the dominant metaphors characterizing the growth of knowledge.

The question remains, however, whether these metaphors should continue to dominate our understanding of the growth of knowledge. Granted, we are fallible creatures. We've made plenty of mistakes in the past and will continue to make plenty of mistakes in the future. How dare we then be dogmatic about having gotten anything right? But turn the question around. Have we gotten nothing right? Is there nothing about which we can assert with confidence, *This is the way it is—period?* Or is the only thing about which we can say, *This is the way it is—period*, that nothing ever stays the way it is? If so, we've committed a fallacy of self-referential incoherence.

I regard myself as blessed for having been at one point in my career research mathematician. Though the appeal to human fallibility has become a trump card for contemporary skeptics and relativists, the card loses its magical appeal quite quickly in mathematics. Despite Morris Kline's ill-titled *Mathematics, the Loss of Certainty*, mathematics remains a fully cumulative enterprise, whose practitioners are refreshingly unconcerned that the edifice they are building will suddenly collapse on them, much less that it has already collapsed. Pythagoras' theorem, though first demonstrated 2,500 years ago, remains just as valid and compelling today—not merely in its statement but also in its proof. Once a mathematical result has been demonstrated, it is here to stay.

Mathematics therefore is a field where we do seem to get unchanging truths. Is mathematics unique in this regard? Not at all. For the evolution and revolution metaphors to do their dirty work, they must trade in high degrees of generality, where human thinking becomes fuzzy and uncertain, and thus must employ heuristic aids that by their very nature cannot be reliable. In other words, for the evolution and revolution metaphors to do their dirty work, they must studiously avoid the concrete and particular. In science, for instance, general scientific frameworks (theories, as they're called) are notorious for being overturned. But who seriously questions the efficacy of the smallpox vaccine in controlling smallpox or the capacity of morphine to suppress pain? And who thinks that our judgment about these matters is likely to change in the future? A little thought ought to convince us that there are plenty of low-level scientific claims that we take to be perfectly secure and without danger of being overturned. The same is true for concrete historical claims—for example, that Abraham Lincoln was president during the Civil War. Indeed, any discipline worthy of the name will make low-level concrete claims that we may take to be perfectly secure and without danger of being overturned.

On closer inspection the fallibility objection to unchanging truth is therefore hardly persuasive. No one is denying that humans make mistakes. Indeed, as a general rule it is healthy to regard all our claims as potentially fallible in the sense that they can always be scrutinized, criticized and overturned in the light of new evidence. But the mere possibility of being wrong neither precludes the possibility of being right nor the possibility that we can be thoroughly justified in thinking we are right and will continue to be right. Still, it is one thing to assert with full confidence that we are right, another to assert that we cannot be wrong. The absolute certainty that denies the possibility of being wrong is by its nature beyond the reach of finite, rational agents like ourselves. Yet our inability to attain absolute certainty in itself provides no grounds for thinking that our knowledge of the world is shaky or arbitrary or wrong, especially when we are dealing with the concrete and particular.

Thus in the face of innumerable claims that continue to stand the test of time, the mere possibility of being wrong hardly constitutes a good reason for doubting the stability of a truth claim. Ludwig Wittgenstein, for instance, allowed no room for a skepticism based solely on the possibility of being wrong. He wrote, "I am sitting with a philosopher in the garden; he says again and again, 'I know that that's a tree,' pointing to a tree that is near us. Someone else arrives and hears this, and I tell him: 'This fellow isn't insane. We are only doing philosophy.' "[1]

If the fallibilism card doesn't succeed in undermining the stability and unchangeability of the faith, the contextualism card is likely to be employed next. This card is extremely common at the mainline seminaries. Unlike the fallibilism card, the contextualism card allows that you might be right and even affirms that in many cases you are indeed right. But the contextualism card doesn't leave it there. Having admitted that you are right in many cases, the contextualism card immediately adds that when you are right, it is because you have acted in accord with the norms, practices and beliefs of the community of discourse to which you belong.

---

[1]Ludwig Wittgenstein, *On Certainty* (New York: Harper & Row, 1969), p. 61e, no. 467.

Having identified your context with the community of discourse in which you happen to find yourself, contextualism asserts that your context determines what is true.

Contextualism leads easily to bizarre conclusions. If, for instance, your context happens to be a tribe of cannibals, then it is right for you to feast on missionaries because this action is consonant with the norms, practices and beliefs of the community to which you belong. If contextualism can lead to such absurd conclusions, what is its appeal? Contextualism's appeal consists in rightly acknowledging that our contexts *condition* what we can know to be true. But having rightly observed that, the contextualist goes on to assert that contexts also *determine* what is true. It's this last point that doesn't hold water (for more on this, see chapter two).

In sum, skeptics and relativists oppose the classical view of the Christian faith as something definite, stable and precious by playing either the fallibilism or the contextualism card. Neither of these cards is a trump card. Indeed, when we leave the realm of generalities and concentrate on the concrete and the particular, we find that many claims about the world are stable and unchanging. Neither fallibilism nor contextualism therefore undermines the stability of the Christian faith.

The Core of the Faith

Since I am attributing to the Christian faith stability and unchangeableness, you may well ask, What, pray tell, is stable and unchanging about it? Haven't I heard of doctrinal development? And don't Christians fight over just about everything? Vincent of Lérins, a fifth-century theologian, stated a rule of faith known as the Vincentian Canon: *quod ubique, quod semper, quod ab omnibus creditum est* (what has been believed everywhere, always, and by all).[2] As we shall see, this rule of faith tells us where to locate the stability of the Christian faith.

Does this rule of faith make sense for the present day? Is there anything about which the church stands in universal agreement? The Vincentian Canon was criticized as far back as the twelfth century. In his widely cited *Sic et Non (Yes and No)*, Peter Abelard noted how on question after question the early church fathers disagreed. You may therefore contend: "Okay, so the fallibilism and contextualism cards don't work. But you, Bill Demb-

---

[2]"Vincentian Canon," in *The Oxford Dictionary of the Christian Church*, ed. F. L. Cross and E. A. Livingston, 2nd ed. (Oxford: Oxford University Press, 1983), p. 1443.

ski, have yet to establish what about the Christian faith is stable and unchanging. So far all you have shown is that arguments against the stability of the faith have proven less than decisive."

I accept the challenge. Thankfully, the challenge is easily met. To identify what about the Christian faith is stable and unchanging, we need but look in the right places. Certainly we won't find the stability of the Christian faith by, in the first instance, concentrating on such controversial topics as homosexuality, double predestination or the ethics of a just war. What is stable and enduring about the Christian faith must be located at a more fundamental level.

To understand what is stable about the Christian faith, it will help to draw a distinction. In analyzing a worldview, a theoretical system, an economy of thought, a way of grasping the world, a paradigm (à la Thomas Kuhn), a research program (à la Imre Lakatos), a research tradition (à la Larry Laudan) or an episteme (à la Michel Foucault)—call it what you will—you need to identify three components: (1) its physical content, (2) its theoretical content and (3) its regulative principles. Because the Kuhnian term *paradigm* continues to be in vogue, I'll use it.

The physical content of a paradigm is what the paradigm tells us specifically about the state of the physical world. Any change in the physical content of the paradigm corresponds to a change in the physical world. To take the Darwinian paradigm as an example, its physical content includes the claim of *common descent*, that all organisms trace their genealogy back to a common ancestral stock. You have parents, they in turn had parents, and so on. When you trace your genealogy back far enough, do you get to a single-celled organism? Common descent says yes. Common descent has physical content because it is compatible with only certain states of the physical world and not with others. To take a silly example, if, like Aphrodite, your parents originated from the froth of the sea, common descent would have to be ruled out, and the physical content of the Darwinian paradigm would be wrong.

Next let us turn to the theoretical content of a paradigm. The theoretical content of a paradigm is what the paradigm employs to explain its physical content. To use the Darwinian paradigm again as an example, since the Darwinian paradigm includes within its physical content the claim of common descent, the obvious question is how common descent ought to be explained? Our usual experience, after all, is that organisms exhibit only limited variation. It's not as though a mouse gives birth to a cat or vice versa. Like seems to beget like. How then can one account for a single-celled organism being the ancestor of the human race? To account for common descent, the Darwinian paradigm posits that a *mutation-selection mechanism* governs the slow, gradual development of organisms over vast periods of time. It's the mutation-selection mechanism that belongs to the theoretical content of the Darwinian paradigm, and that explains its physical content.

It needs to be stressed that though this mechanism helps explain the physical content of the Darwinian paradigm, the mechanism itself is not part of its physical content. Theoretical content is always underdetermined. Unlike physical content, theoretical content can be changed without logically compelling a change in physical content. In place of a mutation-selection mechanism, for instance, a person can substitute a Lamarckian mechanism, according to which acquired characteristics are inherited. Though this mechanism could, at least in principle, also account for common descent, it is at variance with the Darwinian mechanism. Nevertheless, while physical content never uniquely determines theoretical content (or as philosophers of science would say, theories are underdetermined by data), physical content can provide evidence or support for theoretical content. For instance, Lamarck's theory of the inheritance of acquired characteristics has been strongly disconfirmed in experiments with laboratory animals, whereas Darwin's mutation-selection mechanism has been confirmed, at least to a limited degree, in experiments with bacteria and fruit flies.

Finally, let us turn to the regulative principles of a paradigm. The regulative principles of a paradigm are those that govern how the paradigm is to be applied in practice. To take the Darwinian paradigm again, one of its regulative principles is a commitment to naturalism, or what may be called *methodological naturalism*, the commitment to explaining the facts of biology through purposeless, purely naturalistic mechanisms. Thus when some novel structure is observed in an organism that is more complex than we ever imagined, this principle will be invoked as a way of keeping the Darwinian paradigm on track and not veering into vitalist or teleonomic explanations. The use of regulative principles requires discernment. Methodological naturalism constrains the Darwinian naturalist to employ naturalistic categories in explaining a novel structure. But just which naturalistic explanation is preferable or even right is something methodological naturalism cannot decide. Regulative principles limit our options but do not tell us which of the remaining options is best.

Common descent, the mutation-selection mechanism and methodological naturalism thus belong respectively to the physical content, theoretical
content and regulative principles of the Darwinian paradigm. More is true.
They also belong to the core of the Darwinian paradigm. The *core* of a paradigm is the part of the paradigm that is nonnegotiable, which cannot be
modified without destroying the paradigm. Whether life evolved over a
period of three billion years or three-and-a-half billion years is negotiable
within the Darwinian paradigm. Nothing stands or falls with the precise
time period over which evolution occurred. The duration of the evolutionary process therefore does not belong to the core of the Darwinian paradigm. On the other hand, common descent, the mutation-selection mechanism and methodological naturalism do. Tinker with any of these and
you are no longer working within the Darwinian paradigm. To use Thomas
Kuhn's phrase, if you change any of these, you'll be introducing a "paradigm shift." Note that the core of a paradigm includes physical content,
theoretical content and regulative principles—all three. Thus we may
speak respectively of the physical core, the theoretical core and the regulative core of a paradigm.

Having analyzed the concept of paradigm and delineated the core of a
paradigm, we are now in a position to understand wherein the stability of
the Christian faith consists. The *once-for-all* character of the Christian
faith consists in its nonnegotiable core that must be maintained lest the
faith fall into ruin. This core divides into a physical core, a theoretical
core and a regulative core. Though in general a precise delimitation of the
core of a paradigm is not possible (sometimes it doesn't become clear
whether some aspect of a paradigm is nonnegotiable until someone starts
monkeying with it), there are always clear cases that stand out and must
be included in the core. For the Christian faith the following constitute
such clear cases (Protestant, Roman Catholic and Eastern Orthodox con-
fessions traditionally have been united on these cases): To the physical
core of the Christian faith belong the virgin birth, the crucifixion and the
resurrection. To the theoretical core belong the incarnation, the redemption through Christ and the Trinity. To the regulative core belong the reliability of Scripture, the preeminence of Christ and a commitment to truth.
These elements certainly do not exhaust the core of the Christian faith, but
they suffice for the purposes of illustration.

Let us consider these elements briefly. First the physical core. The virgin birth, the crucifixion and the resurrection all clearly constitute physical claims. In conceiving and giving birth to Jesus, either Mary was inseminated by a human being or she wasn't. Note that simply as a physical claim the virgin birth does not invoke the category of miracle. For all we know, an incredibly improbable thermodynamic accident may have occurred in Mary's womb, giving rise to Jesus. In merely affirming the virgin birth we are not committing ourselves to any explanation of it. Emil Brunner's pooh-poohing of the virgin birth by saying it constitutes an unwelcome intrusion into Mary's gynecology misses the point. You don't have to be a gynecologist to understand whether someone has had sex. So too the crucifixion and resurrection constitute physical claims. Either Jesus was crucified or he wasn't. Either Jesus' corpse went on rotting (whether in Joseph of Arimathea's tomb or somewhere else), eventually to decompose, or Jesus' corpse revived. A video camera focused continually on Jesus from Good Friday through Easter Sunday would be quite capable of confirming or disconfirming the resurrection. Again the category of miracle need not be invoked. In affirming the resurrection we are not committing ourselves to any explanation of it.

Next let us turn to the theoretical core. Unlike the physical core, with the theoretical core we actually are committing ourselves to certain explanations of events like the virgin birth and the resurrection. The incarnation, the redemption in Christ and the Trinity all constitute theoretical claims that explain the physical core of the Christian faith. How is it possible for Mary to conceive without being inseminated by the sperm of a male human being? Answer: it was God who caused her to conceive. Moreover, God did this in order to assume human form. Why was Jesus crucified and resurrected? Answer: this was God's way of redeeming sinful humanity. How is it that Jesus, though God, can pray to God as Father and promise God as Holy Spirit to his disciples? Answer: God is not an undifferentiated unity but a threefold unity. Note that I'm not saying the physical core of the Christian faith logically entails the theoretical core. There are other conceivable ways of interpreting the physical core of the Christian faith. Nevertheless, to offer alternate interpretations that contradict, say, the incarnation, the redemption in Christ and the Trinity is to violate the theoretical core of the Christian faith and thus to violate the Christian faith.

Finally, let us consider the regulative core. The reliability of Scripture, the preeminence of Christ and a commitment to truth all constitute regulative claims. The Christian faith is not an algorithm that spits out precisely what humans are to do and think in every conceivable circumstance. Rather, the Christian faith provides us with regulative principles that in the light of its physical and theoretical content help us navigate through the circumstances of life. Navigation is not a precise science but always involves risks and discernment. Anything that treats Scripture as less than a marvelous gift of God must be repudiated. Anything that in any way minimizes the importance or scope of Christ and his work at the cross must be repudiated. Anything that compromises truth must be repudiated.

Christians must always affirm these principles. To deny them is to deny the faith. Yet how to apply these principles in practice is not always straightforward. Take the following example. The Gestapo knocks at your door. They ask, "Do you have any Jews in this house?" Does a commitment to truth require answering, "Yes, up the stairs, second door on the right"? Clearly no. Similarly, is it impugning the preeminence of Jesus to admit that Jesus got angry, sick and tired like the rest of us? The Gnostics would say yes, for all these things represent human weakness and are thus beneath God's dignity. The Gnostics, however, got it wrong, whereas the church fathers got it right. What Christ has not assumed is not healed. It is to Christ's glory that he assumed human frailty, not that he evaded it. So too with Scripture. Is it impugning the reliability and worth of Scripture to take certain passages figuratively or to ask as a matter of human construction how the Scriptures came together? Augustine's *On Christian Doctrine* answers no.

In identifying a core to the Christian faith, all I have done is refine the Vincentian Canon and bring it up to date. The stability and universality of the faith that is implicit in the Vincentian Canon (recall, *what has been believed everywhere, always, and by all*) receives a precise formulation in terms of paradigm, core, physical content, theoretical content and regulative principles. To assert that the Christian faith contains a stable core that is at least in part explicitly specified is a way of making precise the Vincentian Canon. Note that this reformulation of the Vincentian Canon leaves plenty of room for doctrinal development as well as plenty of room for controversy in all departments of the Christian faith.

The perpetual virginity of Mary, for instance, is a physical claim but does not belong to the physical core of the Christian faith. It continues to be a point of controversy between Protestants and Roman Catholics. The addition of the *filioque* to the Nicene Creed by Roman Catholics is a theoretical matter that continues to be a sticking point in negotiations between Roman Catholics and Eastern Orthodox. The question whether Christians should be pacifists is a regulative concern that continues to divide Protestants in the Reformed and Lutheran traditions from Protestants in the Anabaptist tradition. If a stable core of Christian belief does not stop Christians from fighting among themselves, much less does a stable core stifle theological inquiry. Theologians committed to a stable core of Christian belief have spilled barrels of ink writing about the implications of that core. A commitment to a stable core of Christian belief is therefore compatible with vigorous theological inquiry and multifarious doctrinal development.

Contending for the Faith
Given that the Christian faith has a stable core, the general task of apologetics is now clear enough, to wit, defending that stable core. All the same, the question remains how to defend the core in practice. Are we simply to mouth the claims that constitute the core of the Christian faith, repeating them like robots programmed to handle repetitive tasks? An apologetic of the form "You deny X, but X belongs to the core of the Christian faith, and therefore you are wrong to deny X" hardly constitutes a persuasive argument. Typically when someone attacks X, it is not simply by claiming that X is false or unimportant or in need of reimagining. Some such claim will of course be made. But in addition to the claim there will be an argument supporting it. When someone attacks X, it is to persuade others that there is a problem with X. The challenge facing the apologist, therefore, is not simply the assertion that X is problematic but the argument employed to show how X is problematic. To defend X it is therefore not enough simply to keep reasserting X. Rather, one must in turn challenge the argument that is being used to attack X.

It is for this reason that theologians have traditionally linked apologetics and polemics. Apologetics connotes a defensive posture, whereas polemics (from the Greek word for war) connotes an offensive posture. Yet in practice, the two cannot be separated. The adage that "the best defense is a good offense" holds true in Christian apologetics. Invariably the apologist finds him or herself in the following situation: an antagonist has targeted X, where X belongs to the core of the Christian faith. The antagonist has also advanced an argument Y, which in some way undermines X. The antagonist may, for instance, use Y to explicitly deny X or to minimize the importance of X or to reinterpret X inconsistently with how X has traditionally been understood. For example, X might be the virgin birth, and Y might be an argument to the effect not that X is false but that X is irrelevant to the faith (this was Emil Brunner's move against the virgin birth). Confronted with an attack on X, the apologist must now carefully identify the argument Y that is being used to justify the attack on X. It's here that all caricaturing and misrepresentations must be avoided. The apologist needs to know exactly what are the antagonist's grounds for attacking X.

Having carefully analyzed Y, the apologist's next order of business is to formulate a counterargument Z that refutes Y. Such a refutation can take any number of forms. Z may simply note a rather obvious logical error in Y. Alternatively, Z may be an argument that confirms X better than Y disconfirms X. The possibilities are limitless. Just how the apologist formulates Z will depend not only on Y but also on the audience that the apologist is trying to persuade. Typically the antagonist, in attacking X and offering Y as an argument to undermine X, is trying to influence a certain audience. It is this audience that the apologist will in turn want to influence, this time on behalf of X. If, for instance, Y is an argument presupposing certain premises that the audience does not agree with, then it will be fairly easy to refute Y—simply point to the offending premises. On the other hand, if the audience is already hostile to the Christian faith and assumes many propositions at variance with the core of the Christian faith, refuting Y may be more difficult. In general, to persuade an audience the apologist must work as far as conscience permits on the audience's own terms. If the audience is already hostile to the Christian faith, the apologist will share little common ground with the audience, so that finding a persuasive counterargument Z may require diligence and ingenuity.

To sum up, the task of the apologist is to find counterarguments to the arguments being used to attack the faith. It follows that Jude's exhortation about contending for the faith appropriately characterizes the apologetic task. Passivity has no place in Christian apologetics. We do not sit idly by while the faith gets trashed. When an attack is directed against the core of the Christian faith, the attack's power invariably resides in an argument. The apologist's task is then to find a counterargument that disables the argument. Until the audience is persuaded that the apologist's counterargument has indeed disabled the antagonist's original argument, the apologist's work is unfinished. Sometimes we have to chalk up the failure to convince an audience to the stubbornness of people's hearts. These days, however, the fault is more likely to lie with ourselves—that we haven't done the necessary conceptual work to carry an effective counterargument through to completion.

Apologetics is not an exact science but an art that requires ingenuity, skill and rhetorical sensibility. Though apologetics appears to place undue weight on logic and rhetoric, it is serious theological business. Most of the great doctrines of the church have been forged in the fires of controversy by theologians adopting the stance of apologists. Marcion's rejection of the canon of the Old Testament, the Gnostic's denial of the full humanity of Christ, Arius's denial of the deity of Christ and Nestorius's separation of Christ's two natures—all of these constituted attacks on the core of the Christian faith. In repulsing these attacks apologists have, among other things, given us the canon of Scripture, the doctrine of the Trinity and the Chalcedonian formula.

In closing this essay I wish to leave you with two thoughts, one about heresy, the other about seeking truth. Within late twentieth-century North American Christianity, *heresy* has become an unpopular word. Can't we all just get along and live together in peace? Unfortunately the answer is no. Peace cannot be purchased at the expense of truth. In 1 Timothy, Paul writes that we are to pay close attention to ourselves and the doctrine and to continue in it, for in doing so we shall save both ourselves and those who hear us (1 Tim 4:16). There is an inviolable core to the Christian faith. Harsh as it sounds, to violate that core is to place ourselves outside the Christian tradition. This is the essence of heresy, and heresy remains a valid category for today. This is not to endorse a McCarthyism that finds heretics under every rock. Nor is it to deny the action of God's grace in anyone's life. But it is to own up to the fact that truth is never supplemental but always fundamental to Christian community.

The second point I wish to make is this: The Christian apologist is a contender for the faith, not merely a seeker after truth. Seeking after truth certainly seems a less combative and more humble way of cashing out Christian apologetics. Unfortunately, it is also an inadequate way of cashing out apologetics. The question I would ask of any seeker after truth is this: Have you found any truth lately? And if so, is it worth fighting for? If you are a seeker after truth with the misfortune of not having found any, then it may be time to redirect your efforts. Alternatively, if you are a seeker after truth who has found some but do not think it is worth fighting for, I can only assume that the truth you have found is insignificant and that you are probably wasting your time. Only if you have actually found truth worth fighting for can your search for truth be regarded as worthwhile. And if this is the case, you are called to be not merely a seeker after truth but an apologist for the truth.

2

THE FALLACY
OF CONTEXTUALISM

WILLIAM A. DEMBSKI

IN THE LAST FEW DECADES PHILOSOPHY AND THEOLOGY HAVE INCREASINGLY taken a "contextual turn." The contextual turn begins with the observation that all human inquiry occurs within contexts. By itself this observation is innocuous. It is obvious that each of us thinks and moves within certain social, linguistic and epistemic contexts. There are people we associate with, places we live, ways we express ourselves, things we believe and modes of behavior we are expected to observe. Together these aspects of our life make up our context. We are not disembodied spirits living in a Platonic heaven but flesh and blood people living at certain concrete times and places. This view of contexts is innocuous. Let's call it *moderate contextualism.*

Moderate contextualism, the view that all human inquiry occurs within and is constrained by contexts, is uncontroversial. Nevertheless, controversy arises when we move beyond this simple observation and embrace the dogma that contexts fundamentally determine what is true, good and right. It is one thing to admit that inquiry occurs within contexts and therefore that contexts constrain what we can know to be true, good and right. It is quite another to assert that contexts so completely control inquiry that they also determine what is true, good and right. This more extreme view of contexts is not innocuous. Let's call it *hardcore contextualism.*

Hardcore contextualism leads quickly to some rather bizarre conclusions. If, for instance, your context happens to be a tribe of cannibals, then it is right for you to feast on missionaries because this action is consonant with the norms, practices and beliefs of the community to which you belong. Sad to say, this example does not misrepresent hardcore contextualism. Hardcore contextualists, good pragmatists that they are, typically comfort themselves with the thought that there will be progress and that people won't remain cannibals forever. But the hardcore contextualist is in no position to impose universal ethical principles on the cannibals—the very idea of universal ethical principles that cut across all contexts is absurd to the hardcore contextualist. For the hardcore contextualist a missionary may not go to the cannibals and say, "What you are doing is morally reprehensible and violates the divine intention for creation." That would be imperialist. The cannibals are, after all, being true to their context.

If hardcore contextualism leads to such absurd conclusions, what is its appeal? Hardcore contextualism's appeal consists in rightly acknowledging that our contexts constrain what we can know to be true, good and right. For instance, if we don't know about telescopes, we won't know that Jupiter has moons. Our ability to know depends on what our contexts enable us to know. This, however, seems hardly a deep insight. And indeed, hardcore contextualism would not be the big deal it is in philosophy and theology if this were all it claimed. Having rightly observed that contexts constrain what we can know to be true, good and right, the hardcore contextualist goes on to assert that contexts also determine what is true, good and right. It is this last point that doesn't hold water, constituting an invalid jump from epistemology to metaphysics. If by contexts we mean the norms, practices and beliefs according to which a community of discourse operates, then no, contexts do not determine what is true, good and right.

Although the distinction between what can be known and what is the case is obvious to anyone who hasn't imbibed inordinately at the well of contemporary philosophy, it is nonetheless a distinction that hardcore contextualism refuses to make. Almost invariably what underlies this refusal is an idealist commitment to seeing the world as a human construction. Once the world is seen not as God's creation but as our own human construction, we are indeed lost. As Etienne Gilson puts it in *Methodical Realism*,

> Most people who say and think they are idealists would like, if they could, not to be, but believe that is impossible. They are told they will never get outside their thought and that a something beyond thought is unthinkable. *If they listen to this objection and look for an answer to it, they are lost from the start*, because all idealist objections to the realist position are formulated in idealist terms. So it is hardly surprising that the idealist always wins. The very questions the idealist raises invariably imply an idealist answer. Realists, therefore, when invited to take part in discussions on what is not their own ground, should first of all accustom themselves to saying No, and not imagine themselves in difficulties because they are unable to answer *questions which are in fact insoluble, but which for them do not arise.*[1]

Thus we see the contextual turn taking two forms: one moderate, the other hardcore. Of these I am entirely in sympathy with the moderate turn. Moderate contextualism, as we may call it, uncovers the pretensions of positivism, which in line with the Enlightenment vision of reason, claims the ability to settle all our questions at the bar of disembodied reason writ large. Against this inflated view of reason, moderate contextualism affirms that all human inquiry occurs within contexts and must therefore acknowledge the role of contexts in shaping how we view the world. Reason functions within contexts and cannot be divorced from contexts. According to moderate contextualism, reason is to context as soul is to body. Objectivity is not lost by acknowledging the role that contexts play in shaping how we learn about the world. Moderate contextualism, while acknowledging the obvious, does not open the door to unbridled skepticism or relativism.

Moderate contextualism as the view that all human inquiry occurs within and is constrained by contexts is unproblematic. Even what Christians regard as humanity's chief truth, that God in Christ assumed human form to redeem the world, cannot be divorced from the time, place, history and culture within which Jesus lived. Jesus was not a Platonic ideal being but a Jew. If we fail to understand Jesus' Jewish roots, we fail to understand the gospel. The problem with the contextual turn, however, occurs

---

[1]Etienne Gilson, *Methodolical Realism* (Front Royal, Va.: Christendom Press, 1990), pp. 127-28, emphasis added, gender rendered inclusive.

when this moderate contextualism is transformed into hardcore contextualism by being universalized and absolutized in the same way that reason was itself absolutized in the Enlightenment. It is the absolutization of context that constitutes hardcore contextualism and results in what I call the "fallacy of contextualism." It is against this absolutized form of contextualism that I am arguing in this essay.

What is wrong with hardcore contextualism? Hardcore contextualism asserts that context alone determines what is true, good and right. In so doing, hardcore contextualism makes a universal claim, which therefore can be applied to itself. Yet when applied to itself, hardcore contextualism strips itself of any claims to universality: If context alone determines what is true, then there can be no universal truths that hold across contexts. Yet by speaking for all contexts at once, hardcore contextualism claims itself to be a universal truth. Hardcore contextualism tries to pass off as the universal truth that there are no universal truths. This is the fallacy of contextualism.

The fallacy of contextualism commits what philosophers call a fallacy of self-referential incoherence. Self-referential incoherence arises whenever a universal claim is applied to itself and thereby contradicts itself. Fallacies of self-referential incoherence are blunders. Usually they get rooted out as soon as they are discovered. But not so the fallacy of contextualism. It is amazing the variety of forms this fallacy takes and the vast number of reputed thinkers who continue to take it seriously. The next thing I want to do, therefore, is present a few concrete examples of this fallacy in action. Having presented these examples, I then want to draw several conclusions both about the proper place of moderate contextualism in theology and philosophy, and the proper way to safeguard theology and philosophy from the fallacy of hardcore contextualism.

Let us begin by considering a book endorsement by William Placher that appears on the back cover of Ronald Thiemann's *Constructing a Public Theology:*

> In a pluralistic society . . . no set of theological *or* philosophical first principles provides a starting point on which everyone can agree. . . . Thoughtful Christians in particular want to make their voices heard in public debate without opening themselves up to charges of trying to impose their agenda on everyone else.[2]

---

[2]William Placher, back cover endorsement of Ronald F. Thiemann, *Constructing a Public Theology* (Louisville, Ky.: Westminster John Knox, 1991).

Prima facie, this statement appears innocuous—even tolerant and gener-
ous. In our pluralistic society we have grown accustomed to the notion that
everything is up for grabs. Indeed, for any claim made, someone else seems
ever ready to advance a counterclaim. Cicero's dictum has come home to
our generation with a vengeance, to wit, "there is nothing so ridiculous but
some philosopher has said it."[3] And in our day, everyone is a philosopher.

Now while it is perfectly true that our society no longer adheres to any
common first principles on which a consensus exists, it does not follow
that society should abjure the search for a common set of first principles or
consider it somehow progressive that first principles are now regarded as
passé. A society's search for or adherence to first principles does not entail
a return to classical foundationalism in epistemology, to positivism in science or to the glorification of reason à la the Enlightenment. Presumably
our society itself constitutes a context within which common purposes
and goals can be worked out. For this reason it seems artificial to pro-
scribe, prior to any discussion or analysis, the search for such principles
by the society. Without such a discussion and analysis, we simply don't
know whether a society's search for first principles is doomed to fail.

In this light let us reconsider Placher's claim that "in a pluralistic society . . . no set of theological *or* philosophical first principles provides a
starting point on which everyone can agree." Placher is making more than
a simple statement of fact. Indeed, he is not just claiming that the members
of our pluralistic society do not agree on any theological or philosophical
first principles. The latter claim is certainly true but holds little philosophical interest since our society contains many criminals and mentally
deranged individuals to whom philosophers and theologians will not, at
least in their academic writing, give the time of day.

At issue is not the obvious fact that the members of our society don't agree
on anything. Rather, it is the claim that we are in principle barred from reaching agreement. In this way our *inability to agree* is itself elevated to a first
principle. If you will, this becomes a first principle: *societies are, properly
speaking, pluralistic and therefore cannot have first principles.* Such a first
principle is of course self-referentially incoherent. If a society accepts that "no
set of theological or philosophical first principles provides a starting point on
which everyone can agree," then that society does indeed have such a first

---

[3]*De Divinatione* II 119, in *Bartlett's Familiar Quotations,* ed. John Bartlett and Justin
Kaplan 16th ed. (New York: Little Brown, 1992).

principle. If an individual claims that any search for first principles is doomed to failure, then this individual has already found such a first principle. (The claim itself becomes a first principle.)

Self-referential incoherence is typically greeted with amusement once it is exposed. Nevertheless, we need to recognize that whenever an argument founders on self-referential incoherence, there is a serious problem with that argument. Indeed, whole schools of philosophy have crumbled under the weight of self-referential incoherence. Among these I would point out the failure of Frege's logicism for mathematics as a result of the Russell paradox, the failure of Hilbert's program for showing that every mathematical claim is decidable as a result of Gödel's theorems, and the failure of logical positivism as a result of its unsalvageable verificationist theory of meaning.

If Placher is asserting that the search for theological or philosophical first principles is a doomed enterprise, then Placher is guilty of self-referential incoherence. Such an assertion has no logically compelling force, and any conclusions drawn from it are unsupportable and suspect. Thus when Placher concludes, "Thoughtful Christians in particular want to make their voices heard in public debate without opening themselves up to charges of trying to impose their agenda on everyone else," this conclusion must be evaluated on its own merits and not as a consequence of a self-referentially incoherent first principle that by fiat bars first principles *tout court*. On its own merits, however, Placher's conclusion carries little weight. The references to "thoughtful Christians" and "impose their agenda" are rhetorical moves designed to distinguish the good guys from the bad guys, that is, those who respectively embrace and eschew pluralism.

Perhaps I'm being a bit obsessive, working to death a mere blurb of endorsement on the back of a book cover. Nevertheless, as a blurb of endorsement it indicates to what extent the theological community is prepared to accept the fallacy of contextualism and with it the relativism and radical skepticism entailed by hardcore contextualism. Placher's blurb is not saying anything that Thiemann does not espouse and develop in the body of his book. For instance, on the question of pluralism, Thiemann comments:

> Political and cultural diversity is a gift to be nurtured and celebrated. The freedom upon which such diversity is based is particularly precious and must be preserved and extended to those who have been excluded from full participation in a free society.[4]

---

[4]Thiemann, *Constructing a Public Theology*, p. 47.

Here again pluralism is elevated to a first principle. Question: Where in this pluralism is there room for "singularists" like myself who think Christianity makes exclusive truth claims that are binding on the world at large?

Next, let us consider a contextual fallacy that occurs all too frequently in contemporary literary theory. Once again Ronald Thiemann lays out the fallacy, though this time without giving his assent to it. Thus he describes the following views that have become commonplace in literary circles:

> (1) Literary texts are indeterminable and thus inevitably yield multiple, irreducibly diverse interpretations.
>
> (2) There can be no criteria for preferring one reading to another and [thus we are] cast into the darkest of hermeneutical nights in which all readings are indistinguishably gray.[5]

I find it helpful to set claims like this apart in the way I have done here. Indeed, if one reads claims like this within the flow of a paragraph, their self-referential incoherence is likely to be lost. But set apart as they are here, their self-referential incoherence becomes strikingly evident.

Although (2) is supposed to make a more radical claim than (1), both quickly run into difficulties when we turn the hermeneutic questions they raise back on themselves. Is the hermeneuticist who asserts either (1) or (2) ready to admit that what he or she is asserting is itself indeterminate? Do (1) and (2) admit no semantic boundaries? In all likelihood a hermeneuticist who asserts claims like (1) and (2) wants to be taken seriously and wants the semantic range of (1) and (2) narrowly constrained. Thus for a philosophical subversive like me to come along and interpret these claims differently from their plain sense would be deemed unacceptable. But what if I choose to interpret claims (1) and (2) as saying respectively the following:

> (1') Literary texts are determinable and thus yield a single, univocal interpretation corresponding to the original intention of the author.
>
> (2') There are sharp criteria for preferring one reading to another and thus we can always avoid the darkest of hermeneutical nights. All readings are either black or white.

Let me emphasize that I'm not endorsing (1') or (2'). My point is simply that if one starts out by taking (1) and (2) seriously, then (1') and (2')

---

[5]Ibid., pp. 45–46.

become *legitimate readings* of (1) and (2) respectively, with the result that it becomes impossible to take (1) and (2) seriously. In this way deconstruction becomes a tool not just for deconstructing texts but also for deconstructing itself.

And this is why deconstruction is at base an intellectual subterfuge. The key theoretical problem facing the literary theorist is to characterize the relation that obtains between the reader of a text and the text itself. In the classical conception, meanings inhere in texts, and the reader's job is to dig out the meaning from the text, the meaning of the text typically being tied to the intention of the author.[6] Deconstructionists, on the other hand, start by assuming that any meaning associated with texts is so underdetermined as to issue in "endless labyrinths of possible meanings."[7] Deconstruction therefore "invites readers to approach texts creatively and to appreciate their ability to generate an unlimited plurality of meaningful effects."[8]

The key word in the last sentence is *creatively*. Because the meaning of the text is so unconstrained, the reader must create the meaning rather than discover it. Nonetheless, the writings of deconstructionists do themselves constitute texts that can be read deconstructively. But of course Derrida and his disciples do not want the texts they write deconstructed in the way they are advocating that other texts be deconstructed (i.e., something like what I was doing above when I reinterpreted sentence [1] as sentence [1']). Rather they want their texts taken seriously and read nondeconstructively. Only after their own work is taken seriously and read using a classical hermeneutic do they enjoin the reader to read everything else deconstructively.

The fallacy of contextualism is frequently tied to a faulty view of language. This faulty view of language comes up repeatedly in feminist theology, where it is used as a tool for systematically transforming traditional God talk. Let us therefore turn to a particularly apt expression of this faulty view of language as stated by the feminist theologian Elizabeth Johnson:

There has been no timeless speech about God in the Jewish or Christian tradi-

---

[6]Compare Umberto Eco, *Interpretation and Overinterpretation* (Cambridge: Cambridge University Press, 1992).

[7]Mark A. Powell, *What Is Narrative Criticism?* (Minneapolis: Fortress, 1990), p. 17.

[8]Ibid.

tion. Rather, words about God are cultural creatures, entwined with the mores and adventures of the faith community that uses them. As cultures shift, so too does the specificity of God-talk.[9]

Certainly languages are evolving, living entities—a reader has only to compare the King James Version of the Bible with more recent translations into English to see how much our language has changed in the last four hundred years. Words change their meanings over time. Grammar changes over time. Even logic and rhetoric change over time. What's more, language is conventional. What a word means depends on convention and can be changed by convention. For instance, there is nothing intrinsic about the word *automobile* that demands the word denote a car. If we go with its etymology, we might just as well have applied *automobile* to human beings, who are, after all, "self-propelling" also. There is nothing sacred about the form a word assumes. For instance, *gift* in English means a present, in German it means poison, and in French it means nothing at all. And of course, words only make sense within the context of broader units of discourse like whole narratives.

No one who reflects on the matter thinks language is in any way fixed or ossified. But then again this is not Elizabeth Johnson's point. Her aim is to develop a feminist theology in which she can be justified referring to God in the feminine, that is, as "she." The very title of her book leaves no doubt on this point: *She Who Is*. But how can Johnson justify such a change in our language about God? It certainly isn't enough to say that language evolves, that words are conventional and that the meaning of language depends on context. Rather, Johnson needs the much stronger notion that language is incapable of conveying enduring senses that are expressible over time and translatable from the past into the present.

Where then is the fallacy of contextualism in all this? In denying that there is "timeless speech about God in the Jewish or Christian tradition," Johnson certainly does not mean that her own pronouncements about the nature of language and the impossibility of timeless speech about God are not to be taken in a timeless sense. The problem is that if language is incapable of expressing "timeless senses," then any claim that language cannot express timeless senses becomes uninterpretable and meaningless. Language is evolving. The publication date of Johnson's book is 1992. As of this writing it is now 2001. At least seven years have elapsed since

---

[9]Elizabeth A. Johnson, *She Who Is* (New York: Crossroad, 1992), p. 6.

Johnson wrote the above passage that denies such a thing as timeless speech. How then can I know what Johnson meant seven years ago if language cannot convey timeless senses?

But that was only seven years ago, you say. Then please explain what distinguishes the seven years since the publication of Johnson's *She Who Is* from the two thousand years since the publication of the Gospels. Why should we not attach the same disclaimer to Johnson's writings that she seems to attach to the Scriptures, namely, that her writings have no timeless sense? Is it because Johnson and we are part of the same culture? But she is a feminist theologian, and I am an evangelical mathematician. What then does it mean to say we are part of the same culture? Johnson's denial that language can convey timeless senses is incoherent. If language cannot express timeless senses, then speech occurring two seconds ago or two millennia ago are equally incapable of speaking to the present.

Having now described the fallacy of contextualism and given a few examples of it, I want in the final portion of this essay to turn to a somewhat different question; namely, What keeps this fallacy alive? As a strictly logical matter the fallacy of contextualism represents an egregious blunder that once noted can be duly dismissed. Nevertheless, the persistence with which this fallacy rears its head, and the multiplicity of guises that it assumes, should lead us to ponder why this fallacy keeps being reincarnated.

Once Aristotle formulated his logic, there was no longer any question about whether a given syllogism was valid or invalid. Moreover, anyone who proposed an invalid syllogism was henceforth laughed to scorn and considered an uneducated boor. Not so the purveyors of the contextual fallacy. They remain some of the brightest lights on the literary, philosophical and theological landscape. How is it that they manage to keep their reputations intact despite committing what on closer examination is an inexcusable error?

To be sure, the error is often concealed, being cloaked in a morass of terminology and notation. Yet at other times the contextual fallacy is not so much concealed as proclaimed and celebrated. This is likely to occur in those theologies that revel in contradiction and think faith cannot be faith unless it embraces the absurd, as though logical clarity and precision were somehow inimical to faith.

A thoroughgoing pragmatism often underlies the fallacy of contextualism. If all that is interesting is happening in my own little context, and if no one outside my context is entitled to rebuke or correct me, then the fallacy of contextualism serves to affirm my way of life and give me the autonomy to do as I please. Autonomy and self-determination are the watchwords of our age. They are the principal goals of self-realization. They are psychological desiderata to which the American psychiatric and psychological associations give their seal of approval. Pragmatism, as it were, tells us, "Yes it is a logical fallacy, but it feels so good. It lets me do what I want. It is liberating. So what if something that feels so right and works so well is logically wrong?" And so we are encouraged not to take the fallacy too seriously. It does useful work. It encourages pluralism and diversity. It keeps us in step with the times.

It seems, however, that there is a deeper issue at stake here, deeper than the rationalizations offered by pragmatists on behalf of the fallacy, and deeper also than the logical critique offered against the fallacy earlier in this essay. The deeper issue concerns both the nature of contexts and the nature of human rationality. Hardcore contextualism and the fallacy of contextualism that it engenders view contexts as essentially bent in on themselves. According to hardcore contextualism, contexts are autonomous little worlds alienated from other contexts and incapable of interacting coherently with them. Hardcore contextualism takes the alienation humans experience on account of sin and corruption, and elevates it to a philosophical principle. For Augustine the sin and corruption of the self consisted in the self being bent in on itself. Hardcore contextualism elevates, glorifies and transfigures this corruption, taking the contexts in which humans live, move and have their being and turning them in on themselves.

This is bad. As Christians we live, move and have our being in God. We are therefore not to have our vision focused on our own little contexts but rather to open our contexts to God and the world. In short, we are to be in communion with other contexts. The Christian view of contexts and human rationality is therefore quite different from the view advanced by hardcore contextualism. On the Christian view, contexts are not bent in on themselves, but are fundamentally open, embracing the world and seeking to learn from it. Yes, we operate within contexts, but we are able also to reflect on our contexts and broaden the scope of our contexts to embrace and enter other contexts. Reinhold Niebuhr referred to this ability of ours as "self-transcendence."[10]

---

[10]See Reinhold Niebuhr, *The Nature and Destiny of Man,* vol. 1 (New York: Scribner's, 1949), chap. 1.

There is no context that God does not simultaneously inhabit and transcend. At the root of the fallacy of contextualism is the notion that we can have our own little worlds, into which no one else can intrude, not even God. Pride undergirds this thirst for autonomy, this desire to be masters of our own little worlds. Curiously, though this thirst for autonomy is almost always advertised as setting us free, it invariably accomplishes the opposite. For the autonomy that bends contexts in on themselves is an autonomy of isolation and solitary confinement. This sort of autonomy is wholly incompatible with the freedom offered to humanity by God in Christ. Instead of imprisoning us in our contexts, God has created us so that we can interact with and learn from other contexts.

Christianity has never been a religion of the self. The first commandment is a commandment to worship God. Corrupted as it is by sin, the self, when it turns in on itself, discovers nothing of enduring hope or value. To see this, one has only to consider the logical outworkings of religions that do make the self rather than God the center of their attentions. In both Hinduism and Buddhism "the chief end of man" (to use a phrase from the Westminster Catechism) is not "to glorify God and enjoy him forever" but to have the self absorbed into Brahman or annihilated in the Void so that it can escape the weary cycle of reincarnation. In either case the goal is to do away with personal identity.

To this the Westminster Catechism responds that "the chief end of man is to glorify God and enjoy him forever." But how is this goal to be accomplished? The eighth chapter of Mark's Gospel begins to answer this question: "If any want to become my followers, let them deny themselves and take up their cross and follow me. For those who want to save their life will lose it, and those who lose their life for my sake, and for the sake of the gospel, will save it" (vv. 34-35). Our first step then is not to turn in on ourselves but to turn outward and to God.

But once we have turned outward and toward God, where do we go? To this Gregory of Nyssa responds that we go on to perfection. Nevertheless, the form of this perfection is dynamic and progressive rather than static. For Gregory of Nyssa perfection is identified with ever-increasing growth in the knowledge of God. Indeed, as finite beings perfection is never something we attain once and for all. Rather, perfection is a matter of continuing growth in the knowledge of God. Now this view of Christian perfection is incompatible with any view of contexts that treats them as isolated, mutually inaccessible compartments.

In conclusion, let me offer a few predictions about what we can expect from the fallacy of contextualism in the future. First, I predict that this fallacy will not go away, despite refutations of it like the one you have just read. The practical benefits of this fallacy are simply too great for people to let mere trifles like *logic* and *truth* get in the way and prevent them from enjoying its benefits. Second, we can expect ever more sophisticated versions of this fallacy, which are so richly ornamented in terminology, notation and all manner of scholarly appurtenances that the job of exposing the fallacy of contextualism will require increasing care and diligence. Third and last, I predict that hardcore contextualism will be employed with increasing vigor as a weapon against traditional Christian thinking. The attack will come chiefly in the name of pluralism, diversity and tolerance, and will challenge Christianity at every point where Christianity stands in opposition to the secularization of culture and society. To put the matter in a by now familiar idiom, the goal will be to transform the Christian context into the secular context. In this respect Romans 12:1-2 provides a decisive corrective.

3

HISTORY OF APOLOGETICS AT PRINCETON SEMINARY

RAYMOND CANNATA

T HE YEAR 1815 WAS ONE THAT THE TOWN OF PRINCETON WOULD NOT soon forget. Something was happening on the college campus, something explosive. The college president, Ashbel Green, had labored earnestly for this for the past three years, and it appeared that God was answering his prayers. A great revival had come to Princeton. This was the genuine article. It was more than "enthusiasms"; it was not just shouts and tears. One after another, young students had evidenced real conversion. They were passing from spiritual death into new life by the grace of God. As Green described it, "The divine influence seemed to descend like the silent dew of heaven; and in about four weeks there were few individuals in the college edifice who were not deeply impressed with a sense of the importance of spiritual and eternal things. There was scarcely a room—perhaps not one—which was not a place of earnest secret devotion!"[1]

Green knew that the source of this wonderful work was the Holy Spirit, but he also knew that God used human instruments. Since his inaugura-

---

[1]Ashbel Green, *A Report to the Trustees of the College of New Jersey, Relative to a Revival of Religion Among the Students of Said College, in the Winter and Spring of the Year 1815* (Philadelphia, 1815), p. 6.

tion three years earlier, he had set out to be faithful in the task he believed God had called him. He had reintroduced into the curriculum John Witherspoon's published *Lectures on Moral Philosophy*, he developed his own set of lectures on Christian evidences, and he brought in William Paley's *Evidences* and *Natural Theology* as the basic texts in religion. Beyond that, he preached and taught and prayed.[2]

He enlisted some assistance as well. In addition to his staff at the college (a professor and two tutors), he recruited a friend named Archibald Alexander. Alexander had more than enough items on his plate already, organizing and operating a new seminary down the street. But he also had a heart for soul winning, so he took the time to give a hand. And God blessed his work abundantly. Alexander, a consummate evangelist and apologist, had emerged from his own youthful struggles with doubt with an able command of what he termed "Christian evidences."[3] By his careful and impassioned teaching and preaching he helped lead forty men, nearly all of the unconverted on the college campus, to Christ in less than a month. Many of these men were profoundly transformed by this experience, and several of them began eminent ministries by enrolling in Princeton Seminary upon graduation. Among the ranks of the converted was a bright young man, later the valedictorian of his class, who had previously been preparing to become a physician. His name is Charles Hodge.[4]

This episode in the opening days of the seminary's history is but one instance of an impulse that surged powerfully through this campus for many years. Apologetics was a central focus in its life and thought.

This is clearly evident from its founding constitution in 1811, *The Plan of the Theological Seminary*. It sets forth a capsulized theological encyclopedia[5] listing the characteristics of its hoped for "Calvinist War College," which would specialize in the learned defense of the faith. This document is long and complicated. Here are a few excerpts from it:

> It [the Seminary] is to form men for the Gospel ministry, who shall truly believe, and cordially love, and therefore endeavor to *propagate* and *defend* . . . that

---

[2]See Mark A. Noll, *Princeton and the Republic* (Princeton, N.J.: Princeton University Press, 1989), p. 275.

[3]Lefferts Loetscher, *Facing the Enlightenment and Pietism* (Westport, Conn.: Greenwood, 1983), p. 244.

[4]See Noll, *Princeton and the Republic*, p. 280.

[5]See Loetscher, *Facing the Enlightenment*, p. 152.

system of religious belief and practice which is set forth in the Confession of Faith, Catechisms, and Plan of Government and Discipline of the Presbyterian Church; and thus to perpetuate and extend the influence of true evangelical piety. . . .

It is to provide for the church an adequate supply and succession of able and faithful ministers; workmen that need not be ashamed, being qualified to rightly divide the word of truth.

It is to unite, in those who shall sustain the ministerial office, religion and literature; that piety of the heart which is the fruit only of the renewing and sanctifying grace of God, with solid learning: believing that religion without learning, or learning without religion, in the ministers of the Gospel, must ultimately prove injurious to the Church. . . . It is to provide for the Church, men who shall be able to defend her faith against infidels, and her doctrines against heretics.

It is to furnish our congregations with enlightened, humble, zealous, laborious pastors, who shall truly watch for the good of souls, and consider it as their highest honor and happiness to win them to the Savior. . . .

It is to found a nursery for missionaries. . . .

Every student . . . must be able to explain the principal difficulties which arise in the perusal of the Scriptures, either from erroneous translations, apparent inconsistencies, real obscurities, or objections arising from history, reason, or argument. . . . He must have read and digested the principal arguments and writings relative to what has been called the deistical controversy. Thus he will be qualified to become a defender of the Christian faith.[6]

Such was the mandate of Princeton Seminary. It was highly ambitious and to some even foolhardy. For one thing, it set a course through uncharted waters. At this point in time only a handful of seminaries existed in America, and the only one of any significance was the four-year-old Andover Seminary in Massachusetts. There was also opposition to Princeton from within the Presbyterian Church, as many believed that numerous small regional centers would serve better than a single national school.

Nevertheless, Archibald Alexander gave up the presidency of Hamden-Sydney College in his native Virginia to start a school in Princeton with no facilities, little money and no students. By August of 1812 he had three

---

[6]*The Plan of a Theological Seminary Adopted by the General Assembly of the Presbyterian Church in the United States of America, in Their Session of May 1st, A.D. 1811; Together with the Measures Taken by Them to Carry the Plan into Effect* (Philadelphia: Aitken, 1811).

pupils, twelve Hebrew Bibles and permission to use space in Nassau Hall.

It was not very long, however, before his little venture exceeded the wildest of expectations. Even as other seminaries began to sprout across the country, Princeton Seminary soon became, and long remained, the indisputably leading institution of its kind in America. I won't subject you to a litany of dry statistics here, but as Mark Noll has ably demonstrated in his article for the *American Presbyterians* journal, Princeton soon was without peer in terms of its size, prestige and denominational and regional diversity, and remained so for over one hundred years. In a day when travel was expensive and difficult, Princeton Seminary attracted students from around the world, including literally hundreds from Europe and Asia. It trained not only Presbyterians but leaders of all the major denominational families, including numerous Episcopal bishops, the founder of the NAACP and the founder of the Southern Baptist Theological Seminary in Louisville.[7]

What were the major features of this institution? What were all these students flocking to? What system were they being trained in? Was there a discernible core of convictions that constituted a coherent "Princeton theology?"

Despite considerable development over time, a rapidly shifting cultural context and a rotating cast of characters, it can be said that there existed a common set of beliefs and emphases that identified the Princeton approach from its beginnings in 1812 well into this century. There are four major convictions that I will try to briefly list before we more specifically unpack the development of the seminary's apologetic enterprise.[8]

The first Princeton trait is a pronounced *Reformed confessionalism.* The old Princetonians were all deeply committed Calvinists, without exception. They viewed this as nothing more than the most faithful reading of Scripture. God's grace, proclaimed most forcefully and consistently in Reformed thought, was the plain teaching of Holy Writ. Thus we find them expressing powerfully the chief emphases of that tradition: the Fall, original sin, God's sovereignty, election and Christ's sacrificial atonement.

---

[7]Mark Noll and Peter Wallace, "The Students of Princeton Seminary, 1812-1929: A Research Note," *American Presbyterians* 72, no. 3 (1994): 203-15. See also *The Princeton Theology: 1812-1921,* ed. Mark Noll (Grand Rapids, Mich.: Baker, 1983), p. 19.

[8]Mark Noll lists these four Princeton traits in *The Princeton Theology,* ed. David F. Wells (Grand Rapids, Mich.: Baker, 1989), pp. 18-24.

Sinners, turning from God by their rebellious hearts, are "bound" to sin and utterly unable to come to faith except by God's grace. Faith is a gift of God, to which we contribute nothing. God alone, with no qualifications, is given all credit and glory for our salvation. God changes hearts by the work of the Holy Spirit mediated by Scripture, preaching of the Word, sacraments and Christian nurture. The redeemed sinner, while always hindered by the lingering effects of the Fall, yet is quickened and moved by the Holy Spirit for joyful service to God. When the Princetonians looked for kindred spirits in the church's rich tradition, they most frequently found affinity with Augustine of Hippo, Luther, Calvin, Zwingli, the Puritans, the Westminster divines and Jonathan Edwards.

The second Princeton trait is a high view of *scriptural authority*. Alexander gave his inaugural sermon in 1812 on John 5:39, "search the scriptures," and made it clear from the start that Princeton would establish its witness on the sure foundation of God's Word. Though the growing criticism of this position caused the Princetonians to clarify their formula of biblical inspiration over time, their doctrine of Scripture remained remarkably consistent.

The third Princeton trait is the so-called *Scottish Common Sense Realist philosophy*. This is an epistemological approach that arose in the Scottish Enlightenment in answer to Hume and Kant; however, its exponents rightly argued that it was no novelty. It was not simply a contingent attempt to rescue the British moderate Enlightenment of Locke and Newton from the skepticism of Hume. Rather, its roots are very deep, a point missed by many modern observers. In some ways, it was a modern reassertion of classic Christian realist approaches and much of the thought of Greek antiquity. For example, all of its elements are present in the seventeenth-century Genevan Reformed theologian Francis Turretin, whose Latin work was the basic textbook at the seminary for most of the nineteenth century.[9]

Reduced to its most basic thrust, it simply asserted that the common sense of humanity could be shown to verify the reliability of the physical senses and of intuitive consciousness (i.e., the "moral sense"), while the skeptical attacks on rationality (represented most recently by Kant and Hume) were self-refuting. It upheld the crucial nature of classic epistemo-

---

[9]See chapters 9-11 of Francis Turretin, *Institutes of Elenctic Theology,* vol. 1 (Phillipsburg, N.J.: Presbyterian and Reformed, 1992).

logical "first principles" as the necessary foundation for all intelligible discourse. These "laws of logic" were properly basic and universal to all thought.[10]

This Common Sense Realism was asserted in the mid-eighteenth century by Thomas Reid and Francis Hutcheson among others and gained wide acceptance, not only at Princeton but at Harvard, Edinburgh, Belfast and elsewhere. John Witherspoon was a particularly ardent exponent of Common Sense Realism. When he left his native Scotland in 1768 to take the presidency of Princeton College, he made it a great center for this philosophy. One of Witherspoon's star pupils, William Graham, later trained his own star pupil, Archibald Alexander, in this system. A century later this philosophy became unfashionable but was steadfastly maintained by the Princetonians.

The fourth Princeton trait was an emphasis on *religious experience and the work of the Holy Spirit*. This served as a complement to the highly rigorous academic side of the Princeton enterprise. The reasoned, orderly approach to theology was uplifted by a passionate emphasis on warmhearted piety. These men were not the dry as dust, bloodless old scholastics that some superficial contemporary commentators assert against all testimony. While emphasizing the objective works of God, the Princeton divines also stressed the importance of religious experience and the mysterious work of the Holy Spirit. This came through clearly in their published works (see, e.g., Charles Hodge's book *The Way of Life*, recently reprinted in a series of classics in Western spirituality, or Archibald Alexander's book *Thoughts on Religious Experience*).[11] This impulse is also clearly evident in the testimony of the students who witnessed God's overpowering grace poured out on the Sabbath Afternoon Conferences held weekly in the Alexander Hall oratory. The Princeton divines strongly emphasized the importance of genuine religious experience, though they insisted that this could never be opposed by the propositional testimony of Scripture.

To sum up, Princeton Seminary was committed to (1) Reformed confessionalism, (2) the authority of inspired Scripture, (3) Scottish Common Sense Realist philosophy and (4) stress on religious experience and the

---

[10]See Gordon Clark, *Logic* (Jefferson, Md.: Trinity, 1985).

[11]See also Andrew Hoffecker's excellent *Piety and the Princeton Theologians* (Phillipsburg, N.J.: Presbyterian and Reformed, 1981).

quickening work of the Holy Spirit. This is a hasty glimpse of the Princeton landscape from forty thousand feet. Considering that some seminaries have recently offered three credit courses devoted entirely to the Princeton theology, this is almost unpardonably sketchy. But as we turn to look at the Princeton apologetic enterprise more carefully now, I hope that we will see how these all fit together.

*   *   *

As we have previously observed, Princeton Seminary was founded on a mandate that included a reasoned defense of the Christian faith as a key element of its mission. This mission was well served by Archibald Alexander, whose official title was professor of didactic and polemic theology. Besides being one of the most effective preachers of his age and, by all accounts, a truly remarkable mentor and warm-hearted pastoral counselor, Alexander was a highly competent philosopher. He read the classic works with great enthusiasm. His son estimated that Alexander had probably read more works in Latin than he had in English during the last fifty years of his life![12]

Alexander believed strongly that the truth claims of the Christian faith were objective in nature. Jesus either rose from the dead or he did not rise from the dead. And we cannot believe such a truth claim if we are not first committed to the truth enterprise itself. This involves establishing very basic but hotly contested rules that govern our reasoning. For example, the "law of noncontradiction" (that something cannot be *A* and *not-A* in the same time and in the same relationship) and the "law of identity" (that something is itself). A person must also hold that reality itself is real, and that cause-and-effect relationships are valid. For Alexander these first principles were unquestionable, foundational starting points from which all arguments were rooted. An individual cannot refute skeptics or defend or even explain the existence of God or the trustworthiness of Scripture without them.[13]

Alexander's views on this subject are clear from a talk that he gave before the General Assembly of the Presbyterian Church during the sum-

---

[12]See James W. Alexander, *Life of Archibald Alexander* (1854; reprint, Harrisonburg, Va.: Sprinkle, 1991).

[13]See also Clark, *Logic;* Peter Kreeft, *Fundamentals of the Faith* (San Francisco: Ignatius, 1988).

mer of 1812, just a few months before the start of the seminary's very first session, on the nature and evidence of truth.[14] In that talk he stated his belief that first principles are rooted in the nature of all humans and are provided by intuition and common sense. They are as beyond questioning as are the axioms of mathematics. You cannot prove that $2 + 2 = 4$ unless you first assume the basic laws of mathematics as a starting point. So also with first principles; they cannot be demonstrated. However, we know that these laws of logic are true for a number of reasons.

First of all, first principles are impossible to escape. A person can claim that they are not valid, but he or she cannot really believe that to be the case. Alexander says, "Those philosophers who in their books have pretended to call in question the existence of a material world, they have, nevertheless, in common life acted upon the same principles, with other men. They have as cautiously avoided running into the fire, or striking their heads against a post."[15] Skeptics must *use* first principles to *refute* first principles and therefore have already lost the argument. As soon as skeptics say, "First principles are not valid *because* . . ." they have already embraced what they are trying to refute. Thus, Alexander says, "No man can consistently assert that he is a universal skeptic; for if he doubts of all things he must of course doubt about the reality of this act, and therefore must be uncertain whether he doubts or not."[16] The laws of logic may not be articulated by all. Undoubtedly most people who have lived in history have never even heard of such things as the "law of the excluded middle." However, the reasoning of all people in all ages and in all cultures has by necessity operated under such laws. Alexander concludes that these foundational principles are to be affirmed, despite sophistical attacks against them, because "the best reason which anyone can have for believing any proposition is that it is so evident to his intellectual faculty that he cannot disbelieve it."[17]

The early students at the new Princeton Seminary wrestled with these concepts in their studies. They covered some of this material in the required first-year course of study entitled "Evidences of Natural and

---

[14]Archibald Alexander, address to the General Assembly of the Presbyterian Church, summer 1812, reprinted in Noll, *Princeton Theology*, pp. 61-71.

[15]Ibid., p. 66.

[16]Ibid., p. 63.

[17]Ibid., p. 64.

Revealed Religion." This course involved topics dear to Alexander's heart. As a young man he had been delivered from an anguishing time of doubt through the reading of a certain Soame Jenyns's book titled *A View of the Internal Evidences of the Christian Religion*. Alexander went on to provide replies to the arguments against the Christian faith made by William Godwin, Thomas Paine and Elihu Palmer.[18] Much of this material went into the production of Alexander's first two published books, *A Brief Outline of the Evidence of the Christian Religion*[19] and *Evidences of the Authenticity, Inspiration, and Canonical Authority of the Holy Scriptures*.[20]

In these books and in the lectures that he gave to first-year seminary students, Alexander contended for the importance of evidences for the Christian faith. Here we find a classic case of natural theology directed in service of the defense of the biblical faith. So while he argued that the unregenerate sinner can never be converted by mere exposure to the proofs, and that saving faith involves more than assent (it also involves the will, which is converted only by a supernatural special work of the Holy Spirit), Alexander also argued that a person cannot have faith in anything apart from facts. An individual cannot possibly believe that Jesus rose from the dead to save sinners if he or she does not first believe that such a resurrection is even possible. While a person ought not to seek to "prove" anyone into the Christian faith, he or she is commanded to give a reason for the hope that lies within his or her self. What's more, God uses these reasons as a vehicle for drawing his elect to himself.

Alexander was strongly committed, then, to the concept of God's Word shown forth in two books: the specially revealed, inspired book of Scripture and the generally revealed book of nature. All truth is one. There could be no contradiction between what humans, by God's grace, learn from the natural world, and what they learn, by God's grace, from the spe-

---

[18]See John De Witt, "Archibald Alexander's Preparation for His Professorship," *Princeton Theological Review* 3 (1905): 583, 586; Raleigh Don Scovel, "Orthodoxy in Princeton, N.J.: A Social and Intellectual History of Princeton Theological Seminary, 1812-1860" (Ph.D. diss., University of California, Berkeley, 1970), p. 49; Noll, *Princeton and the Republic*, p. 285

[19]Archibald Alexander, *A Brief Outline of the Evidence of the Christian Religion* (Princeton, N.J.: D. A. Borrenstein, 1825).

[20]Archibald Alexander, *Evidences of the Authenticity, Inspiration, and Canonical Authority of the Holy Scriptures* (Philadelphia: Presbyterian Board of Publications, 1826).

cial revelation of Scripture. Both books were by the same author and were equally true, though only the special revelation of Scripture was fully salvific. In any case, salvation is impossible apart from faith in Christ, which comes only by God's gift.

Alexander, as a Reformed theologian, knew that the Fall had left humans utterly unwilling to follow God's Word, yet our natural ability to reason was still partly intact (much as our mortal bodies, while weakened, remained partly intact after the Fall).

With such an epistemology, Alexander was open to whatever could be learned about God from the natural world. "Evidences" drawn from reason and from Scripture were a helpful tool for the apologetic task, both as an offensive means of driving unbelievers to see the credibility of the Christian truth claims and as a defensive means of staving off attacks on the faith and reinforcing the believers' certainty. So philosophy, whether yielding the classic arguments for God or showing the illogic of infidelity, is useful for apologetics.

Alexander's tenure at Princeton Seminary lasted almost forty years. He was not alone in his efforts. Samuel Miller, one of the country's great social historians, joined the faculty in 1813 and remained Professor of Ecclesiastical History for more than thirty-five years. The most significant faculty addition with respect to apologetics, however, came in 1822. Charles Hodge, as I noted, was converted under the ministry of Alexander while still a student at Princeton College. His talents were such that not long after graduating from the seminary he was invited to become an instructor and soon thereafter the seminary's third professor. Here he began what was arguably the most distinguished career of any nineteenth-century theologian in America. In 1825 he founded a journal known as the *Biblical Repertory*, later renamed the *Princeton Review*, which soon became a powerful organ for transmitting the Princeton message not only to its large student body but to the church and academy around the world. At the time that he passed the editorial duties on to a younger colleague in 1871, this journal was identified by the *British Quarterly Review* as "the oldest Quarterly in the United States . . . [and] beyond question the greatest purely theological Review that has ever been published in the English tongue."[21]

After four years of teaching at the seminary, Hodge realized that he was

---

[21]Quoted in A. A. Hodge, *Life of Charles Hodge* (New York: Scribner, 1880), p. 257.

ill equipped to engage the new German biblical criticism that was being introduced in America. Thus in 1826 Hodge began a two-year period of study in Germany, at a time when very few Americans had done this. He did work under some of the most significant theologians of his day, including Friedrich Schleiermacher, Johann Neander and August Tholuck. After grappling with this troubling new world and learning from it, Hodge returned to Princeton more committed and better equipped to articulate the Reformed, orthodox faith. For the next fifty years Hodge did just that and did it as well as anyone of his generation. The three thousand students he taught, more than any other theological educator in nineteenth-century America,[22] were joined by the legion of others who read his published works. His commentaries on Romans, Ephesians, and 1 and 2 Corinthians were widely used and are, interestingly enough, still in print and being purchased today. His devotional book called *The Way of Life* was actually a best seller in its day and was quickly translated into Spanish, German, French, Hindi and Japanese. He wrote a two-volume constitutional history of the Presbyterian Church, an early critique of Darwinism and a massive 2,500 page systematic theology in three volumes (which is still a basic textbook in some evangelical seminaries, both in America and South Korea). By far his most winsome and lively writing is found in the 142 long articles, totaling nearly 8,000 pages, that he contributed to the *Princeton Review.*

Through all this work, whether in the classroom or in the oratory for his famous Sabbath Afternoon Conferences, addressing the Presbyterian General Assembly or Protestant ecumenical gatherings, writing in the *Princeton Review* or in his rich commentaries, Hodge exuded that marriage of "piety of the heart" and "solid learning" that was sought after in the 1811 Plan of the Seminary. For this reason one modern commentator has labeled Hodge the exemplary "kneeling theologian."[23] Hodge addressed himself to a remarkable range of issues, from slavery to politics to exegesis to theological controversies, always with a burden for bringing glory to God.

Hodge brought his considerable charm, wisdom and intellectual powers to bear in service to the apologetic mandate that he believed was an

---

[22]Noll, *Princeton Theology,* p. 19.

[23]David F. Wells, "The Stout and Persistent Theology of Charles Hodge," *Christianity Today* 10 (1974): 1276-79.

essential part of the theologian's job. This often involved evidences from Scripture and from observing the world around him. This is *not*, however, to say that Hodge was a bare evidentialist.

Hodge, in the introduction to his *Systematic Theology*, lays out his intentions to forge a *via media* between the two extremes of what he terms the "speculative philosophers" (that is, the pure rationalists, such as the deists and atheists) and the "mystics" (that is, those that make the subjective primary, such as Schleiermacher and Finney). He believed that a true faith is a reasonable one and to scorn evidence of God's handiwork is bad stewardship. He did not, however, reduce Christianity to the sum of its data. Only the testimony of the Spirit can ultimately give rise to true faith. He said, "The most important of all evidences of Christianity can never be properly appreciated unless the heart be right in the sight of God. The same exhibition of truth which produces unwavering conviction in one mind leaves another in a state of doubt or unbelief. . . . No amount of mere external evidence can produce genuine faith."[24] As he points out, the very same people who saw Christ perform great miracles later cried out "Crucify him! Crucify him!"

Faith for Hodge was not intellectual assent to a set of propositions but trust in a living Person. Growth in grace is not simply an increase of cognitive knowledge about God but a growth in heart knowledge, trusting faith in the mystical union, which binds the believer, by the Holy Spirit, to Christ.

As Mark Noll points out, Hodge was not criticizing Bushnell, Finney or Nevin for trusting their hearts but rather reproving them for letting their hearts move their head in the wrong direction![25] For Hodge, what a believer subjectively feels and experiences is founded in what is objectively true. Thus he says that "though the mode of the Spirit's influence is often inscrutable, it is still the influence of a Rational Being on a rational subject."[26] All this is to say that reason is a gift of God and should be put to use in the Christian life.

This posture of Hodge and the other Princetonians promoted an honest interest in the work of the nontheological disciplines. They looked to their cultural surroundings as a good (though sin-corrupted) gift of God, which

---

[24]Charles Hodge, *The Way of Life* (1841; reprint, Grand Rapids, Mich.: Baker, 1977), p. 10.

[25]Noll, *Princeton Theology*, p. 108.

[26]Hodge, *Way of Life*, pp. 333-34.

could yield truth useful for their apologetic arsenal and which might even help guide their theology in some qualified sense.

This is most obvious when we look at the Old Princeton attitude toward the natural sciences. They believed they had nothing to fear from the natural sciences as long as the scientists conducted themselves properly. A large portion of the *Princeton Review* articles covered scientific topics with enthusiasm. Hodge and the Princeton divines were certain that any conflicts that arose between theology and the natural sciences would eventually work themselves out.

Within the Princeton scheme, theology had both the privilege and the limitations of reigning as queen of the sciences. This meant that it was the proper role of theology to determine the ultimate meaning of scientific discoveries. It also meant, however, that theology looks to science for data.

So this model cut both ways. On the one hand, truth is not served by an arrogant intrusion of the natural sciences into the domain proper to theology. There are segments of reality that bare natural science as science cannot address. Science must not become burdened by false materialist presuppositions, or attempt to draw metaphysical or religious conclusions from its data.

On the other hand, as one Princetonian confessed, "The Church is willing that the Bible should be interpreted under the guidance of the facts of science."[27] The Bible cannot err nor can unprejudiced science, but our human interpretations of both can. Thus science may uncover data that will aid the church in correcting a traditional but flawed reading of Scripture.

Thus, Hodge notes, as the new geology of the nineteenth century uncovered evidence of this planet's great antiquity, previous interpretations of the dating of the Genesis account must be readjusted, though in such a way as to not attribute error in the biblical account. Thus Bishop Ussher's old 6,000 year chronology was discarded by the Princetonians in favor of "day/age" or "gap" readings of the Genesis account.

Hodge also cites the example of Galileo. Theologians used to contend that the Bible taught a geocentric solar system until seventeenth-century scientific discoveries helped adjust their faulty interpretation of Scripture. For this the church ought to be grateful to the scientists.[28]

---

[27] *Biblical Repertory and Princeton Review* 31 (1859): 106.

[28] See letter to *New York Observer*, March 20, 1863, in *What Is Darwinism?* (Grand Rapids, Mich.: Baker, 1994), p. 55.

This attitude was tested by the Darwinian theories that emerged following the publication of *Origin of Species* in 1859. While most of America, including the theological community, was slow in recognizing the importance of these new developments, Hodge provided significant commentary in 1862 on what he referred to as "this remarkable book from a very high authority."[29] Hodge eventually came to view Darwinism as bad science, as he expressed in an 1874 book on the subject, because he thought that Darwinism was too influenced by personal materialist biases to be valid. Some of his Princeton colleagues who shared an identical epistemology and systematic theology with Hodge came to more positive appraisals of evolutionary theory. Thus James McCosh, whom Hodge handpicked while chair of the college trustees to be president of the college (now Princeton University), as well as Hodge's son, A. A. Hodge, and successor at the seminary, B. B. Warfield, all acknowledged that if evolution was ever to prove correct beyond all reasonable doubt, they would adjust their exegesis to reconcile the Genesis account and some form of theistic evolution.[30]

Not everyone shared Princeton's enthusiasm for science and for harmonizing Scripture and science. Some in the theological world began to reject the classic Princeton approach in favor of a separation of theology from culture—into a fideism undergirded by a new epistemology. Faith was set in stark contrast to reason to avoid the difficulties of Kantian philosophy, Darwinian science or biblical criticism. Here the direct engagement of the church to culture on culture's own terms was deemed either undesirable or impossible, or later in the case of the Barthians, even sinful. Princeton did not choose this route. Instead it chose the more difficult and increasingly unfashionable course of engaging the culture faithfully and vigorously with the truth of Christianity.

The apologetic task of the seminary was given additional aid by a new chair of apologetics and Christian ethics, first filled by Charles Aiken in 1871, former president of Union College in New York. Students were required to take several courses in this field to complete the seminary program. The passing of Charles Hodge at age eighty in 1878 created a vacuum that could hardly be filled, but Francis Landey Patton was recruited

---

[29]*Biblical Repertory and Princeton Review* 34 (1862): 462, reprinted in *What Is Darwinism?* (Grand Rapids, Mich.: Baker, 1994), pp. 50-51.

[30]See David Livingstone, *Darwin's Forgotten Defenders* (Grand Rapids, Mich.: Eerdmans, 1988), as well as Bradley Gundlach's excellent M.A. thesis at Trinity Evangelical Divinity School, "The Evolution Question at Princeton, N.J.: 1845-1888" (1988).

to take the Stuart Chair of the Relations of Philosophy and Science to the Christian Religion in 1881. An able philosopher and theologian and one of the great orators of his generation, Patton was forced to reduce his teaching load at the seminary in 1888, however, in order to assume the presidency of Princeton University, before returning to the seminary as its president in 1902. A. A. Hodge, a fine thinker, taught systematic theology with a decidedly apologetic interest from 1877 to 1887. And William Brenton Greene ably filled the chair of apologetics for over thirty-five years starting in 1892.[31]

Each of these individuals made unique contributions to the seminary and to the academic and ecclesial world as a whole, which are worthy of full treatments in themselves. But to save time, I will skip to an even more significant figure: Benjamin Breckinridge Warfield. Following his graduation from Princeton Seminary and graduate studies in Europe, Warfield returned to his alma mater in 1887 as the professor of didactic and polemic theology rather than apologetics proper. Nevertheless, his impact on apologetics was considerable.

Though lacking the immense pastoral gifts of Hodge and Alexander, Warfield more than matched them in intellectual prowess. It would be difficult to overestimate the academic talent of Professor Warfield. At the height of what Sydney Ahlstrom calls the "Golden Age of Liberal Theology," B. B. Warfield was a spoiler. Both the skeptics and the exponents of the rapidly multiplying new theologies had a formidable foe in Warfield. Lefferts Loetscher, by no stretch a proponent of Warfield's theology, nevertheless identified him as "second to none in learning among American scholars. . . . He was the country's most scholarly—and most unyielding—opponent of the so-called Liberal Theology."[32]

In literally hundreds of scholarly articles, books, pamphlets and reviews Warfield devoted himself to the disciplines of history, historical theology, biblical studies, apologetics and theology. He was a highly reserved man, and partly due to the needs of his wife (who was infirm and housebound for the duration of their marriage), his personal presence and

---

[31]*Biographical Catalogue of Princeton Theological Seminary* (Princeton, 1932).

[32]Sydney Ahlstrom, *A Religious History of the American People* (New Haven, Conn.: Yale University Press, 1972), p. 763; Lefferts Loetscher, *Broadening Church* (Philadelphia: University of Pennsylvania Press, 1954), p. 136; Cf. James S. McClanahan, "Benjamin B. Warfield: Historian of Doctrine in Defense of Orthodoxy, 1881-1921," *Affirmation* 6 (fall 1993): 89.

involvement beyond campus was limited. Yet his influence could hardly be overstated. Even today, nearly seventy-five years after his death, a ten-volume set of his works, another five-volume set and at least a half-dozen individual volumes of sermons and theological discourses remain in print.[33]

Warfield's contribution to Princeton apologetics began at his inauguration. In his address titled "The Idea of Systematic Theology Considered as a Science," Warfield emphasized the apologetic mission of the church. This set the tone for his entire thirty-five year ministry at Princeton.

To say that Warfield continued the Princeton theology of Alexander and Hodge is not to say that he was not his own thinker. For example, while he never wrote his own comprehensive systematic theology because he found Hodge's to be sufficient, he was not afraid to criticize Hodge's work at points. Warfield's politics also differed sometimes from his colleagues. Though a son of Southern aristocracy, Warfield silenced an instructor who objected to a black student being roomed next to the instructor's suite in Alexander Hall. Warfield wrote a moving piece of poetry about the good Samaritan, where the last line reveals that the reason the victim is neglected by the passing priests is because his skin is black.[34] It was Warfield who recommended that his star student John Mackay do his postgraduate training under the then obscure, heterodox, Spanish existentialist mystic philosopher Miguel de Unamuno. Warfield was a remarkable individual who defied all efforts to stereotype him.

As did his predecessors, Warfield believed that, difficult as it was, the responsible theologian needed to constantly contextualize the form of his message in order to speak to the secularists on their own terms. He stated, "Christians of today must state their beliefs in terms of modern thought. Every age has a language of its own and can speak no other." However, this was not a call to syncretism. Warfield warned: "Mischief comes . . . when, instead of stating Christian belief in terms of modern thought, an effort is made, rather, to state modern thought in terms of Christian belief."[35] In a secular realm, whose leaders were becoming increasingly emboldened and powerful, it became harder for the faithful Christian to address skepti-

---

[33]See McClanahan, "Benjamin B. Warfield," pp. 88-111.

[34]Hugh T. Kerr, lecture on Warfield at Princeton Theological Seminary, March 1, 1982, audio tape transcribed by author.

[35]Benjamin B. Warfield, *Critical Reviews* (Grand Rapids, Mich.: Baker, 1991), p. 332.

cism's errors while remaining open to criticisms and to the lessons they bring. Nevertheless, the holy call must not be abandoned. Warfield reminded his frustrated readers and students that criticism is good for theology. He was personally grateful for the way that recent criticism had, he said, "Correctingly affected the details and modes of presentation of the old evidences."[36] He reminded them that Arianism prompted the church fathers to clarify the doctrine of the holy Trinity. Have the efforts of heightened criticism vanquished Christian belief? he asked. "A thousand times no!" he replied. "Criticism has proved the best friend to apologetics a science ever had."[37]

Warfield also believed that a strategic retreat was generally not feasible. The idea of giving up the historicity of a person's truth claims for a faith that is metaphorical or that resides only in his or her heart meant winning the battle in order to lose the war. He said, "We all desire a Christianity which is secure from assaults of the unbelieving world. . . . What folly it is to seek it rather by yielding to the assault all it chooses to demand, and contracting Christianity into dimensions too narrow to call out the world's antipathy and too weak to invite its attack. Such an eviscerated Christianity may no longer be worth the world's notice, and by that same token is no longer worth the Christian's preservation. It has reduced to a vanishing point and is ready to pass away."[38]

Most disturbing for Warfield was the quarters from which this call was coming. By the turn of the century it was no longer only the watered-down orthodoxy of the Arminians or the liberals that sought to limit or end the apologetic enterprise. The orthodox, evangelical Calvinists were equally at fault. And here we encounter a very contemporary difficulty that Warfield and his colleagues encountered. Many of the conservative Dutch Calvinists, including Abraham Kuyper, with whose dogmatics Warfield was in almost complete agreement, insisted on what one modern observer has called (in the case of the modern Barthians and Christian existentialists) a "retreat to commitment."[39] For example, Kuyper believed in an inerrant scriptural text, but he said that no intellectual attempts are able to or even ought to be made

---

[36]Richard Gardiner, "In Favor of Apologetics," unpublished manuscript.

[37]Benjamin B. Warfield, *Shorter Selected Works* [hereafter referred to as *SSW*] (Nutley, N.J.: Presbyterian and Reformed, 1972), 2:131.

[38]Warfield, *SSW*, 2:252.

[39]W. W. Bartley, *Retreat to Commitment* (London: Open Court, 1984).

to defend the Bible's authenticity. Warfield sensed the beginnings of this move, and it horrified him. He said, "The mystical tendency is showing itself in our day most markedly in a widespread inclination to decline apologetics in favor of the so-called *testimonium Spiritus sancti*. The convictions of the Christian man, we are told, are not the product of his reasons addressed to his intellect, but the immediate creation of the Holy Spirit in his heart. Therefore, it is intimated, we can not only do very well without these reasons, but it is something like a sacrilege to attend them." He called such a move an "empty irrationalism of the heart."[40]

So when Warfield wrote the introduction to the English translation of Kuyper's monumental *Encyclopedia of Sacred Theology* in 1898, he praised the work for both its substance and its form. Yet he differed sharply on the process whereby a person comes to knowledge of God. In the introduction to Francis Beattie's famous 1903 study of apologetics, Warfield expresses this sentiment succinctly. He wrote: "It is easy, of course, to say that a Christian man must take his standpoint not *above* the Scriptures, but *in* the Scriptures. He very certainly must. But surely he must first have Scriptures, authenticated to him as such, before he can take his standpoint in them."[41]

Warfield died in 1921 at the age of sixty-nine, just a few hours after giving one of his regular class lectures. At the funeral President Patton lamented that old Princeton might die with him.[42] That did not happen immediately. The remaining faculty was still as able and accomplished a collection of scholars as any in the country. But problems did arise, which were not unrelated to apologetics. William Brenton Greene retired from the chair of apologetics in 1925 after thirty-five years of service. The faculty's nomination of their New Testament scholar J. Gresham Machen as his replacement, however, was set aside by the General Assembly of the Presbyterian Church in a move completely without precedent. This was largely due to reasons other than apologetics, but in 1929 the General Assembly chose to step in and reorganize the personnel and the structure of the seminary's board of directors and board of trustees. Machen, three other faculty members, an instructor and about a third of the students left

---

[40]Warfield, *SSW*, 2:94-95.

[41]Warfield, "Introduction to Beattie," in *SSW*, 2:98.

[42]Francis L. Patton, "Benjamin Breckinridge Warfield: A Memorial Address," reprinted from *Princeton Theological Review*, July 1921.

Princeton to found Westminster Seminary in Philadelphia, with the sympathy and support of many faculty and students who remained.[43]

The individual who the new trustees appointed as Greene's successor in the chair of apologetics was a basically orthodox Kuyperian named John Kuizenga. Kuizenga's systematic theology was not very far removed from that of his predecessor, but his outlook on apologetics was. In 1940 he was given the Hodge Chair of Systematic Theology, and his apologetics chair went dormant. Apologetics continued to be taught by Kuizenga, and it even continued to be a required course for graduation, but in 1944, with the rise of Barthian and Dutch Reformed influences on the faculty, apologetics was removed from the catalog altogether. While certain courses in the last fifty years have occasionally had apologetic aspects or covered topics in apologetics, apologetics proper was never again offered at Princeton Seminary.[44]

What can we learn from all this? My intention was not to build up "household gods" at Princeton—this is not about ancestor worship. This was not supposed to be an exercise in antiquarianism or nostalgia. The Princeton experience has something to say to us today. If not in the details of its apologetics (which I personally recommend), at least in its basic approach. To many Christians today a reasoned defense of the faith is viewed as a hopeless waste of time. To others it is a sub-Christian, or even an anti-Christian, elevation of reason over faith, of nature over revelation. Barth said that to embrace contradictions was a mark of Christian maturity and that classic apologetics was actually in some ways a sin. Some fundamentalists have also rejected rationality in theology as "carnal." Peter Kreeft, a contemporary Thomistic philosopher at Boston College, says that such Christians "fear that human reason is a leftist tool, something invented in pagan Athens or in pagan Boston—the Athens of America— probably Harvard."[45]

---

[43]See D. G. Hart, *Defending the Faith: J. Gresham Machen and the Crisis of Conservative Protestantism in Modern America* (Baltimore: Johns Hopkins University Press, 1994) for a thorough, modern treatment of the events surrounding the seminary. Also Edwin H. Rian, *The Presbyterian Conflict* (Grand Rapids, Mich.: Eerdmans, 1940; reprinted most recently by the Orthodox Presbyterian Church, Horsham, Penn., 1993).

[44]Modern Princeton professors who have approached the subject in the classroom or in print include Richard S. Armstrong, Diogenes Allen (*The Reasonableness of Faith*, 1968), and Max Stackhouse (*Apologia*, 1988). Still none have taught a full course on apologetics proper.

[45]*Fundamentals of the Faith* (San Francisco: Ignatius, 1988), pp. 13-14.

But the problem remains for such Christians: Without rational argument and engagement, how does an individual counter the modern and postmodern belief that every theological claim is at base a provisional guess, an unfounded opinion? Is theological truth really just a greased pig that can never be finally grasped? The Christian truth is objective truth. The Christian truth is not "true for me" and at the same time "*not* true" for someone else. Christ either did really give himself up on a cross and rise in triumph over sin, or he did not. As Paul states, "If Christ has not been raised, then our proclamation has been in vain and your faith has been in vain. . . . If for this life only we have hoped in Christ, we are of all people most to be pitied" (1 Cor 15:14-19). How can the modern fideist believe Christ resurrected and yet does not follow the mandate of Peter: "Set apart Christ as Lord. Always be prepared to give an answer to everyone who asks you to give the reason for the hope that you have" (1 Pet 3:15 NIV). The Greek word translated "to give an answer" is the one from which we derive the English word *apologetics.* Part of what it means to have Christ as our Lord is to defend what we believe.

I have not dwelled on the details of the Princeton apologetic, for example, what they thought about the classic theistic proofs of God, the ontological argument, arguments from design, evidence for the authenticity of Scripture, the moral arguments and so forth. These are difficult topics taught to highly disciplined students over a three-year course of study and could hardly be squeezed into this brief essay. I strongly urge that you investigate further and let the old Princetonians speak for themselves. They are rarely unclear. You may find that their arguments are unconvincing, unuseful or outdated. I hope not. I do believe, in the very least, however, that we can learn much from the basic Princeton approach. In the midst of contemporary Barthianism, Kuyperianism, evangelical pietism, Kierkegaardian existentialism, bare rationalism and postmodern skepticism, there is a Princeton *via media* that is not a pure novelty of the nineteenth century or a wooden-headed return to the seventeenth century Reformed scholasticism but which stands in the long, Spirit-inspired, catholic tradition of bringing all reality to testify to the glory of God.

PART 2

SCRIPTURE

4

THE PROBLEM OF ERROR IN SCRIPTURE

WILLIAM A. DEMBSKI

Great is the profit of the divine Scriptures, and all-sufficient is the aid
which comes from them. And Paul declared this when he said,
"Whatsoever things were written aforetime, were written aforetime
for our admonition upon whom the ends of the world are come,
that we through patience and comfort of
the Scriptures might have hope." (Romans 15:4, and 1 Corinthians 10:11)
For the divine oracles are a treasury of all manner of medicines,
so that whether it be needful to quench pride, to lull desire to sleep,
to tread under foot the love of money, to despise pain, to inspire confidence,
to gain patience, from them one may find abundant resource.

JOHN CHRYSOSTOM, *HOMILIES ON THE GOSPEL OF JOHN*

THE BIBLE HAS TAKEN A SEVERE BEATING IN THE LAST ONE HUNDRED years. Increasingly viewed as a hodgepodge of historical and literary curiosities with little hold on truth or fact, the Bible is said to be riddled with inconsistencies, moral monstrosities and, above all, errors. To take a high view of the Bible is to risk being called a fundamentalist. Are these attitudes toward the Bible warranted? Is it possible to steer clear of a wooden literalism on the one hand and a hypercritical approach to the Bible on the other? My aim in this chapter is to present a view of Scripture that is faithful to the Christian tradition and at the same time takes into account the legitimate findings of modern scholarship. I take the debate over biblical inerrancy as my point of departure.

Most of the contemporary debate over the inerrancy of Scripture assumes we all know what error is and then examines Scripture to determine whether and to what extent Scripture contains error. In this chapter I want to change the terms of this debate. Instead of throwing the Scriptures into question and holding our notion of error fixed, I want to throw our understanding of error into question. Once we do this, we see that error is not nearly as transparent a notion as we might at first have imagined. Once we clarify what is meant by error, it becomes apparent that error is not a property blithely attributed to Scripture. Indeed, we shall find that attributing error to Scripture is itself highly problematic—indeed, more problematic than holding to an inerrant Scripture.

The first thing we need to examine then is error. Only after we are clear about the nature of error does it make sense to consider what it means for Scripture to contain error. Let's therefore start by massaging our intuitions about error. Our natural inclination is to think that error is a perfectly straightforward notion. For example, you get your monthly bank statement. It shows that you have less in your account than is recorded in your checkbook. You investigate the matter and find that when you paid your phone bill two weeks ago and entered the amount into your checkbook, you didn't carry a one when computing your new balance. The error is discovered and rectified. What could be simpler than that?

Now it's true that errors can be as simple as that. But they need not be. And as we shall see, when it comes to Scripture, they are never as simple as that. In massaging our intuitions about error, let us therefore begin by considering an example where error is not quite so straightforward as in the checkbook example. Consider the following problem. Nine dots are arranged in the form of a square as follows:

      •   •   •

      •   •   •

      •   •   •

What is the minimum number of line segments needed to join all nine dots if they are joined continuously? Many of you have probably seen this problem, but if you have, try to imagine how you approached this challenge when it was first presented to you.

For my part I was about twelve years old when my dad presented it to me. We were on the beach in Italy when my dad arranged the nine dots in the sand and then challenged me to connect the dots with four continuous line segments. I stared at this problem for fifteen or so minutes, trying many different ways to connect the dots, but found I couldn't connect all of them in less than five line segments. Because I figured my dad had a trick up his sleeve, I didn't tell him that he had committed an error in claiming the dots could be joined with four continuous line segments. But privately I doubted whether it could be done with that few segments. As far as I was concerned, the minimum number of line segments needed was five. Five was the *correct* answer; four was an *erroneous* answer. Finally I gave up trying to solve the problem with only four continuous line segments and asked my dad for the solution.

When he showed me the solution, the light immediately went on. I had *assumed* that the line segments joining the dots had to be confined to the square implicitly outlined by the dots. But of course this assumption was entirely gratuitous. My dad had said nothing about confining the line segments to this implicit square. Once the assumption of confining the line segments to this implicit square was discarded, and the possibility of drawing line segments outside the implicit square was taken seriously, the solution to the problem became perfectly straightforward, as is apparent:

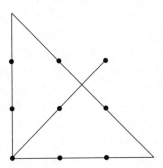

There is an important lesson to be learned from this example and one that is particularly relevant to the problem of error in Scripture. Ordinarily

when this nine-dot problem is presented, it is to illuminate human prob-
lem-solving abilities. To be sure, this problem illuminates our cognitive
ability to solve problems. Yet for our purposes it does much more, pointing up a fundamental difficulty whenever we attribute error. On the beach
in Italy my dad challenged me to connect nine dots arranged in a square
by means of four continuous line segments. Given my assumption that
those line segments had also to be confined to the implicit square outlined
by those dots, I was perfectly right in attributing error to my dad. Indeed,
how could he be so stupid to think those dots could be connected with
four line segments—at least five were needed! Given my assumption, I was
perfectly correct in attributing error to my dad.

But my assumption was itself ill conceived. I myself was in error for
holding an assumption that was not required, and that prevented me from
solving the problem in the way my dad had set out. There is an irony here:
in attributing error, I was myself committing an error. I could of course
stick pig-headedly to my assumption that the lines had to be confined to
the implicit square outlined by the dots. But only when I became willing
to relinquish this faulty assumption could I understand the solution that
my dad had intended. Error is thus a two-edged sword. In attributing it we
risk committing error ourselves.

Error is a matter of perspective. In giving me the nine-dots problem my
dad viewed the problem from one perspective and I from another. For me
to charge my dad with error in claiming the dots could be joined with four
continuous segments meant that from my perspective my dad had committed an error. But did it therefore follow that my dad had in fact committed an error? Not at all. If my dad's perspective was the same as mine, and
if I could demonstrate that joining the dots with four lines is incompatible
with his perspective, then my dad would have been right to admit error.

But this is hardly the only possibility. I might be employing a perspective nothing like my dad's and therefore missing the truth of what my dad
was claiming. So long as my perspective is the only one in question, I can
rightly attribute error to my dad. But once I am shown that my perspective
is itself in error, my charge of error evaporates. Whose perspective then do
we pick, my dad's or mine? To resolve this dilemma my dad and I need to
communicate with each other, share each other's thoughts, learn from one
another, check out where our background assumptions agree and disagree—in short, we need to enter each other's perspectives.

But this raises an obvious question: How does one person enter another's perspective? Despite all the talk these days of knowledge being perspectival and distinct perspectives being incommensurable and truth being relative to perspective (or context, cf. chapter two), the fact remains that we are capable of moving quite freely among diverse perspectives. The following analogy illustrates this point. Near where my parents have a home in Arizona are two adjacent mountains. Depending on your perspective, one mountain will look taller than the other. What's more, changing perspectives is simply a matter of changing location. But note that not all perspectives are created equal. One of the mountains actually is taller than the other. A perspective from which the shorter of the two mountains seems the taller is therefore deceptive. Note also that there are privileged perspectives from which it is possible to tell which mountain actually is the taller of the two. Thus if I were to get into a helicopter and fly between the two mountains, the perspective of flying between the two mountains would allow me to decide conclusively which of the two mountains is indeed taller.

But of course in treating the subject of error, we are concerned not with physical perspectives but with epistemic perspectives. Physical perspectives are physical locations from which we view a scene. Epistemic perspectives are conceptual frameworks from which we examine the world. All the same, the preceding remarks about physical perspectives carry over to epistemic perspectives quite nicely. In practice we move quite freely between distinct epistemic perspectives. To return to the nine-dots problem, when my dad presented me with the problem initially, I was operating from a perspective in which any continuous set of line segments connecting the dots had to be confined to the implicit square outlined by the dots. My dad, on the other hand, was operating from a perspective in which the line segments were allowed to protrude outside this implicit square. Once my dad pointed this out, I immediately entered his perspective. Moreover, it's clear that my dad had also entered into my perspective, for he knew precisely why I was having such a hard time solving this problem.

The problem of error in Scripture is first and foremost the problem of what perspective to adopt in viewing Scripture. Is there a "right" perspective for viewing Scripture and from which Scripture does not have any errors? Before examining the various perspectives available to us for viewing Scripture (our perspectival options, if you will), I need to stress—indeed overemphasize—that we can and do move quite freely among distinct perspectives. The reason I cannot stress this point strongly enough is because all too frequently in our day we are led to imagine ourselves inescapably imprisoned within our perspectives. Thus we are led to believe that our perspectives are unalterably fixed and that whatever we see is solely a function of the perspective where fate has stuck us. The fact is, however, that much as God has given us mobile bodies with which to change our physical perspective, so too God has given us mobile minds with which to change our epistemic perspective. To change our physical perspective we simply have to move our bodies, an activity to which all normal bodies are ideally suited. So too, to change our epistemic perspective we have to move our minds, an activity to which all normal minds are ideally suited. Of course, we don't typically speak of "moving our minds." We have another word for that, and it is called *inquiry.*

We move our minds, or alternatively change our epistemic perspective, through inquiry. Inquiry has two components. One is the gathering of new information. The other is the sorting of previously gathered information by holding certain pieces of information fixed and throwing others into question. Consider once again the nine-dots example. When my dad initially presented the problem to me, I was operating from the perspective that the continuously joined line segments had to be confined to the square outlined by the dots. Operating from this perspective I was unable to solve the problem with only four line segments. But when my dad presented me with the crucial information that the line segments did not have to be confined to the implicit square, I appropriated this information and at the same time questioned my old assumption about confining the line segments to the implicit square outlined by the dots. By doing this, that is, by gathering new information and throwing old information into question, I was able to change my perspective and solve the problem as my dad had initially indicated, namely, with four continuous line segments.

Our minds are ideally suited for inquiry, for changing perspectives and looking at things from different perspectives. Inquiry is not passive learning in the sense of passively adding to one's stock of knowledge. Nor is inquiry strictly cumulative. As the writer of Ecclesiastes puts it, there is "a time to keep, and a time to throw away" (Eccles 3:6). The gathering of information is certainly a part of inquiry. But inquiry also has a critical aspect. Any information that forms part of one perspective may be thrown into question and rejected when examined from another perspective (and here by information I don't just mean factual claims about the world but any claims, beliefs, assumptions or presuppositions whatsoever).

Let's summarize where we are in the argument. First, I have argued that we always attribute error in relation of a given perspective. Thus whether we attribute error to a claim depends crucially on the perspective adopted. Note that this is not to endorse relativism, the view that what's true or false depends on a person's perspective. A perspective does not *determine* what is true or false but only what the person *regards* as true or false. Second, I have argued that perspectives are not all created equal. Some may be much better for generating fruitful and trustworthy insights than others, and still others may be downright deceptive. Thus, for example, the perspective of modern molecular biology is extraordinarily fruitful for biological research, whereas the four humors theory of the Middle Ages has proven scientifically sterile. Third and last, I have argued that we can and do move freely among distinct perspectives by means of inquiry, which I characterized in terms of gathering and critically examining information.

One final observation about error needs to be made before we examine error in relation to Scripture. As I have characterized error thus far, error is merely the flip side of truth. Thus a given claim is in error just when it is false. Error, however, has an additional, personal component that is not shared by falsehood and that does not make falsehood a synonym for error. Whereas statements may be false, it is only people—rational personal agents—who can be in error. To be sure, we speak of a statement as being in error, but only by extension, in the sense that the person making the statement claims to know what in fact is not the case.

Error always consists in overextending yourself, in claiming more than is warranted from the perspective you have adopted. Error is therefore not the same as lying. The liar is intent on perpetrating a falsehood; the individual who commits an error hopes to hit the truth but unfortunately fails to hit it. Nor is error ignorance. "Ignorance," as Adler and Van Doren aptly put it, "is simply a privation of knowledge unaccompanied by any pretension to know."[1] Error, on the other hand, always entails such pretensions. It is always people who commit errors and not impersonal detached statements. Moreover, when people commit errors, it is by claiming to know what is not the case, by failing to acknowledge their ignorance, by pretending to knowledge, by presuming competence where they lack it.

---

[1]Mortimer J. Adler and Charles Van Doren, eds., *Great Treasury of Western Thought* (New York: Bowker, 1977), p. 434.

Errors may be excusable, but once discovered are not permitted to stand. Whenever they are discovered, errors are rooted out, unmasked and rectified. The proper response to error is not rationalization but eradication.

Error always signals a lack of competence. Consequently we hesitate to attribute error to highly competent individuals when they are speaking in their area of expertise. It is one thing to be told by someone just coming off a hallucinogenic drug that space is curved. It is another thing to be told by Albert Einstein that space is curved. Our ordinary experience is that lines through space are straight. Ordinary experience seems to confirm that old Euclid got it right. To claim that space is curved is counterintuitive. We are therefore inclined to dismiss as erroneous the claim that space is curved when coming from someone just off a hallucinogenic drug. A physicist of Einstein's stature making the same claim, however, is a different story. We may scratch our heads, but we probably wouldn't want to charge him with error.

To recap, people commit errors when despite intending to assert truth, they actually assert falsehood. Committing an error is not the same as lying or ignorance. The person who commits an error has overextended him- or herself, exhibiting some degree of incompetence. In committing errors, people always operate from a given perspective. In charging people with error, we must enter their perspective so that we may know precisely what they are claiming. Finally, having entered someone else's perspective, we must ask, Is the claim being made compatible with that person's perspective? and Does that person's perspective warrant the claims he or she is making? Any charge of error requires an answer to these questions.

With these observations about error in hand, let us next examine the different perspectives from which theologians view Scripture. Contemporary theologians typically adopt one of three basic perspectives for viewing Scripture. For brevity I shall refer to these as the *divine-inspiration perspective*, the *human-response perspective* and the *human-constructivist perspective*. I'm not saying that these perspectives logically exhaust the perspectives from which Scripture can be viewed. Yet in practice these perspectives constitute the three main polarities from which theologians orient themselves. Here is a brief summary of these perspectives.

The *divine-inspiration perspective* is the classic orthodox perspective on Scripture. It assumes that Scripture constitutes the very words of God—the *ipsissima verba Dei*. The divine-inspiration perspective allows that the human writers of Scripture expressed themselves in the full integrity of their humanity, without the slightest diminution of their wills or intellects, but that God, in tandem with their wills and intellects, moved in and through the human writers to express precisely what God intended. The divine-inspiration perspective is encapsulated in 2 Peter 1:21, where the writers of Scripture are described as being moved by the Holy Spirit. According to the divine-inspiration perspective God is fully capable of expressing himself in human language and of doing so without embarrassing himself. According to this perspective God is not silent; God speaks Hebrew, Aramaic and Greek—and all other human languages for that matter. God has thoughts expressible in these languages, and more particularly for our purposes, God can and does express claims that have the possibility of being in error—that is to say, in the revelatory act God puts his neck on the line.

As for what I'm calling the *human-response perspective*, it is also known as the neo-orthodox perspective on Scripture and is associated most prominently with the name Karl Barth. According to this perspective the human writers of Scripture do not so much experience the divine revelatory act as communication, rather they get hit over the head with it and then try to figure out what happened. God acts, and the human writers record their response (or "witness" as it is usually called) to the divine acts. From the classic orthodox perspective what's acceptable about the human-response perspective is that the human writers of Scripture are responding to a real revelation by a real God. Thus the human-response perspective does not reduce Scripture to a merely human construction but retains an ineliminable transcendent element in Scripture—the human writer of Scripture is responding not to some internal psychological state but to the revelatory activity of a God whose existence does not depend on whether we like it or not.

Nevertheless, as a human response to a divine revelatory act, Scripture no longer constitutes the very words of God. Rather Scripture constitutes a fallible human witness to what God has done in salvation history. Accordingly, Scripture contains errors, factual and otherwise. Within the human-response perspective any errors in Scripture are not regarded as crucial since Scripture, as a human witness to divine revelation, is not the Word of God in itself (the Word of God in itself being Christ) but rather a vehicle by which the Word of God comes to us. And what's important about a vehicle is that it gets the job done, not that it be error-free. Thus when we hear Scripture read from a neo-orthodox lectern, we do not literally hear the Word of God but rather a witness to the Word of God. For this reason we are told to "listen for the Word of God" inasmuch as what impinges on our eardrums is not the Word of God per se but the vehicle that conveys the Word of God.

Last, we come to the *human-constructivist perspective.* If the divine-inspiration perspective sits on the ideological right and the human-response perspective sits in the ideological middle, then the human-constructivist perspective sits on the ideological left. Whereas the divine-inspiration and human-response perspectives assume there is a real God who delivers a real revelation to humanity, the human-constructivist perspective assumes none of this. According to the human-constructivist perspective Scripture is a purely human construction conditioned entirely by sociological, polit-ical, cultural, biological and environmental factors. The human-construc-tivist perspective is thoroughly reductionist. Human beings have a religious impulse, yes, and they regularly give expression to that impulse. But that impulse and its expression are to be understood not by appealing to a transcendent personal God who acts in people's lives but as a human idiosyncrasy. The Scriptures of the Old and New Testaments constitute but one expression of that idiosyncrasy. À la Freud we construct our gods to serve our needs. The fact that Christians study Scripture is thus more or less accidental. Religion is important not because it is true but because people find it important. Similarly, Scripture is important not because it is true but because a lot of people have made and continue to make a fuss about it.

With this brief summary of the three basic perspectives from which theologians view Scripture in hand, let us next examine these perspectives critically, specifically with reference to how they handle the problem of error in Scripture. Because I am critiquing these three perspectives, the question of perspectives may be turned back on me. Someone may ask, What, pray tell, is the perspective from which you, Bill Dembski, are oper-ating and from which you are going to tell us which of these three perspec-tives on Scripture to adopt? The intent behind this question is of course to point up that I am not operating from a privileged, neutral perspective and thus cannot properly decide among the three perspectives I've just laid out.

This objection is easily dispatched. The question concerning what per-spective I am operating from is a valid one but hardly does the damage it seeks to do. The perspective from which I'm operating is, not surprisingly, my own personal worldview, the one I've hammered out upon reflection over the course of my life. In the grand scheme of things this worldview may be inadequate or even ill-conceived, but it is *my* worldview, and it is one I believe is substantially correct. In critiquing the three perspectives on Scripture that I've just laid out, I'm inviting you, the reader, to hear me out, listen to my concerns, study my arguments and thereby enter my perspective (if not fully then at least to some extent). Perhaps you'll be convinced, perhaps not. My aims are modest. I'm not seeking to coerce you. I won't charge you with being ignorant, wicked, stupid or insane (as the evolutionary biologist Richard Dawkins is apt to do) if at the end of the day you don't see things my way.

First then, let us turn to the human-constructivist perspective. From the human-constructivist perspective the problem of error in Scripture simply does not arise. According to this perspective Scripture is a purely human production that admits no transcendent element. Those who adopt this perspective may disagree violently with Scripture, charging it with androcentrism, logocentrism, patriarchy, misogyny, homophobia, hierarchy or what have you—the list goes on. But the charge of error in and of itself will not come up among these charges. To be sure, those who currently hold to the human-constructivist perspective typically see Scripture as riddled with logical inconsistencies, as well as scientific and factual errors. But all such errors are beside the point. The truth of the Scripture is not at issue. Conditioned by their context, the writers of Scripture simply wrote what they wrote. Within the human-constructivist perspective, critical, hermeneutical and literary methods have but one aim—not to determine the truth in Scripture but to appropriate the Scripture for the present day so that it may serve the contemporary context by either advancing or challenging its ideals. Yes, I say advancing *or* challenging. Thus we'll find process theology baptizing the secular paganism of our age, whilst liberation theology challenges its capitalist ideals. The point to realize is that whether furthering or challenging the status quo, the Scripture is used as a pragmatic tool and not as an authority to which we are required to bow the knee.

The chief problem with the human-constructivist perspective is, of course, that it is non-Christian. In making this claim I am not being uncharitable but simply asserting a fact. Just as Naugahyde is not leather and never can be leather, so all the various theologies that take a human-constructivist approach to Scripture are not Christian and never can be

Christian. To be sure, we can artificially stipulate the meaning of words and make the word *Christian* mean something it doesn't mean. But Christianity has always presupposed a realist metaphysics in which a real God does real things in the world—one of those things being to reveal himself in Scripture. But the human-constructivist perspective has no place for this fundamental presupposition of Christianity. The fact that there are process, liberationist and feminist theologies that appeal to the Bible and appropriate its terminology is simply not enough to make their theologies Christian. Christian theology, properly so called, is impossible within a human-constructivist perspective.

Next let us turn to the human-response perspective. At first blush the problem of error in Scripture does not seem to arise for the human-response perspective either. Indeed, one will find Barth in his headier moments claiming that the more radical and disturbing the results of critical studies of the Bible, the better. Nevertheless, error does remain a problem for the human-response perspective. To see this, it is not enough to consider some minor historical glitch about the life of Jesus. The human-response perspective is ever ready to accommodate small errors, but it is incapable of accommodating massive error. Perhaps it doesn't matter whether Jesus performed this or that miracle attributed to him in the Gospels. But if Jesus never lived at all, then there is no Word of God incarnate to which the Scriptures, as the Word of God written, can bear testimony. Thus we may safely conclude that while small, niggling errors are not a problem for the human-response perspective, massive errors are.

An obvious question now arises: How do we distinguish small errors from massive errors in Scripture? Is there a criterion by which to decide which errors are important and which are trifling? Unfortunately, those who hold to the human-response perspective have yet to furnish such a criterion. Indeed, it is a safe bet that they will never furnish such a criterion. Rather, they will hold that the Holy Spirit, in guiding the community of faith, can be trusted to convey God's revelation through Scripture, preserving the community from massive error and rendering minor errors innocuous. This is of course fideism—faith without reason—and it is very comforting for those who can buy into the system. Rational argumentation goes by the board, and you can go on believing what you've always believed regardless of the challenges that science or historical-critical studies or postmodernity throws your way.

But there is a price to be paid for the comfort of insulating yourself against rational argumentation, and in my view the price is far too high. There is a long list of things I find unacceptable about the human-response perspective: it is parasitic on the divine-inspiration perspective; it hinders us from worshiping God fully with our minds; it revels in the inscrutability of God; it is far too ready to trust historical-critical studies of Scripture and the claims of evolutionary biology; it totalizes proclamation at the expense of persuasion. The list goes on, with each item on the list requiring considerable expansion. Unlike the human-constructivist perspective, a person can do Christian theology properly so-called within the human-response perspective. As far as I am concerned, however, the human-response perspective gives away the store, if not now, then a generation down the line.

Finally, let us turn to the divine-inspiration perspective. Whereas the problem of error did not arise at all for the human-constructivist perspective and arose for the human-response perspective only when confronting the problem of massive error, the divine-inspiration perspective leaves no room for error whatsoever. Indeed, an omnicompetent God intent on communicating truthfully by means of human language is simply not going to err.

Recall, errors are always committed by persons and always signal a lack of competence. Of course, if a person believes in an incompetent deity, then he or she is free to attribute error to Scripture even from a divine-inspiration perspective. But every coherent doctrine of God that I know ascribes a host of perfections to God, and one of those perfections is certainly the competence of God to accomplish his intentions. Thus when God intends to state the truth about some matter, we can rest assured that God will be successful in stating the truth and won't state a falsehood. To reiterate, the divine-inspiration perspective combined with any reasonable doctrine of God is going to yield inerrancy for its revelatory texts.

Well now, that certainly seems to settle matters, doesn't it? The human-constructivist perspective is not even Christian, and the human-response perspective is highly problematic. By default it therefore follows that the divine-inspiration perspective must be correct. Yes? Of course things are not quite that simple. The three perspectives do not exhaust the space of logical possibilities. Moreover, the divine-inspiration perspective may be sufficiently problematic in its own right so that the other two perspectives, despite their faults, may not look so bad on second thought. What I propose to do then in what remains of this essay is show that the divine-inspiration perspective is tenable, that it is capable of withstanding the main criticisms that have been brought against it to date and that it can hold its own against the other two perspectives.

Because the very idea of an inerrant Scripture is so alien to the contemporary theological scene, let's start by removing some misconceptions. First off, let's be clear that error is not a necessary feature of human language use. To err is certainly human but not an essential feature of our humanity. To employ an analogy (and it is only an analogy), Jesus, the incarnate God, was fully human but did not sin. So too Scripture, the divine revelatory text, is a fully human production but without error. We all are capable of making true assertions and of stringing true assertions together. A person can even write a computer program that will generate infinitely many true assertions, none of which will be in error (e.g., $0 < 1$, $0 < 2, 0 < 3 \ldots$) The wide prevalence of error in human practice is an accidental, not an essential, feature of human practice. There is therefore nothing inherently absurd about an inerrant Scripture.

Nor is it absurd to think that God might actually be capable of communicating with humanity in language understandable to humanity. Calvin saw God's revelation in Scripture as an accommodation of the divine majesty to our human frailty. Certainly God's thoughts are higher than our thoughts, and there are many thoughts God has that are not expressible in human language. But God also has thoughts that are accessible to us and that he means to communicate with us, not the least of which is that we are to love him and our neighbor. To deny that God can speak to us in human language is to impose an entirely gratuitous constraint on theology.

God's "wholly otherness" is not destroyed by God communicating with us in human language. Just as a shepherd is not "sheepified" by tending sheep, so God is not anthropomorphized by speaking to us in human language. God is not wholly other because he is inscrutable and can't properly express himself in human language. God is wholly other precisely because as God of the whole universe he condescends to communicate with creatures made of clay. Potentates, tyrants and sages may revel in inaccessibility and inscrutability. But this is not how God is revealed in Christ. The God in Christ is Abba, Father (cf. Romans 8:15). I know of no father who does not speak the language of his children.

But if God is capable of speaking in human language and has actually spoken in the Scriptures of the Old and New Testaments, why is the Scripture riddled with so many inconsistencies, repetitions, scientific bloopers, moral monstrosities and historical glitches? In short, why are there so many errors? Before calling in the results of our earlier examination of error to answer this question, it is best to address an evasion that all too frequently comes up at this point and muddies the waters. Within evangelical circles it is common to distinguish an "inerrancy" view of Scripture from an "infallibility" view, with inerrancy being the stronger view. As far as etymology is concerned, the meaning of inerrancy and infallibility should, of course, be the same. Inerrancy derives from the Latin noun *error*, meaning error or mistake, whereas infallibility derives from the Latin verb *fallor*, meaning to deceive or lead astray. Given these root meanings, it's clear that infallibility and inerrancy should mean substantially the same thing. That they don't derives from some fancy theological footwork.

Within evangelical circles the idea that Scripture does not err in matters of faith and practice but can err in other matters has gained wide currency. It is this view that goes by the name of infallibility. Though perhaps initially appealing, infallibility so defined constitutes an incoherent view of Scripture. The problem is that within Scripture, matters of faith and practice are inextricably tied together with matters of history and science. Presumably the Ten Commandments are the very words of God, but the divine command to exterminate all the Amalekites was not. Infallibilists have no clear criterion for distinguishing the things that Scripture gets right from the things it gets wrong. Thus in practice the infallibilist ends up conflating the divine-inspiration perspective and the human-response perspective, appealing to one or the other as convenience dictates. But these perspectives are fundamentally incompatible. If God is verbally communicating through Scripture, then attributing error to Scripture is incoherent. Alternatively, if Scripture is merely the record of human responses to divine actions, then errors can be imputed just as readily at the level of faith and practice as at the level of science and history.

Well then, what are we to make of all the errors in Scripture? By now it's clear that the worst thing an apologist can do in responding to this question is itemize all the problematic passages in Scripture and then point by point try to argue that these passages are free from error. This strategy cannot succeed. That the Scripture contains problematic passages has been recognized by the church from its inception. Even Scripture itself acknowledges as much, for we read in 2 Peter 2:16 that the apostle Paul wrote "things hard to be understood." Orthodox theologians throughout church history have recognized that Scripture contains problematic passages that remain thoroughly unresolved. Thus when confronted with the charge of error against Scripture, we have a threefold choice: we can admit error, we can resolve the supposed error, or we can admit perplexity. Often a supposed error in Scripture can be resolved, with the charge of error then being decisively refuted (recall, for instance, the charge by biblical scholars last century that the Hittites never existed; once archeologists discovered the capital city of Hattusa, this error evaporated). But if a problematic passage does not yield to our attempts to resolve it, what shall we do? Our choice then becomes twofold: we can either admit error or admit perplexity.

But doesn't admitting perplexity become a cop-out after a while? Isn't it more honest simply to admit that Scripture represents the bumbling efforts of a bunch of Middle Eastern rubes? But turn this line of attack around: Isn't charging the Scripture with error simply a sign of our own self-assertion, elevating our own twentieth-century secular perspectives against the perspective from which God views the world? Yes, God is a rational personal agent who operates from a perspective of his own, what philosophers refer to as a God's-eye point of view. Since academic philosophers these days largely dismiss God, they tend also to dismiss the notion of a God's-eye point of view. But Christian theists ought not to have a problem with a God's-eye point of view. God, as the author of Scripture, operates from an infinite perspective that incorporates all our finite perspectives. Our hermeneutical task then is, as far as is possible with the aid of the Holy Spirit, to enter the divine perspective and thereby understand what God is teaching his church by Scripture. If we take this approach, we won't find any error in Scripture. But if we don't, we can't help but find error in Scripture. The choice then is up to us, which perspective we are going to trust, ours or God's?

5

NATURALISM IN THEOLOGY & BIBLICAL STUDIES

JAY WESLEY RICHARDS

T HROUGH THIS ESSAY I WANT TO HEIGHTEN YOUR AWARENESS OF AN IDEOL-ogy that is frighteningly pervasive, fundamentally anti-Christian and false—namely, naturalism. I hope thereby to "inoculate" you so that you'll recognize naturalism when you encounter it and won't be led astray by its unwitting advocates. I do not mean that all individuals who subscribe to naturalism are hostile to Christian beliefs but rather that once we understand what naturalism is, we see that it contradicts essential Christian beliefs. Unfortunately, there are many Christians who succumb to its assumptions. Such assumptions even permeate the thought of scholars who teach in theological institutions. For this reason it merits close scrutiny.

This essay breaks into three parts. I will first offer a short analysis of naturalism, noting some distinguishing characteristics. This will give us a handle on it. Second, I will mention some helpful arguments against naturalism. Although I think there are many arguments available to indicate that naturalism is likely false or at least lacking any good reason to believe it, my main purpose is to convince you that naturalism just is not compatible with Christian belief, and any scholarship that claims to be Christian cannot be simultaneously laced with naturalistic presuppositions. Third, to supplement the initial abstract analytical treatment I will offer two common examples of the influence of naturalism in one important theological discipline—biblical studies. Of course, biblical studies does not have a corner on the market. And I am not implying that all biblical scholars are closet naturalists (quite the contrary). But I am contending that some are.

I have two underlying goals that form the subtext of the essay: (1) to convince you that naturalistic assumptions find their way into theological disciplines in general and into much of biblical studies in particular, and (2) to urge you to confront and purge such assumptions from your own thinking. Detecting the presence of naturalism in biblical studies can be tricky. A person is unlikely ever to encounter a spirited and consistent defense of naturalism as such in a seminary setting. Its influence is usually more subtle. It often shows up either as unexamined presuppositions or in the guise of theological arguments that on closer inspection reveal ill-conceived efforts at scholarly compromise with naturalism.

Finally, I will recommend some works that I think are essential reading for anyone intent on becoming fully inoculated against the creeping influence of naturalism. By combining the points detailed here with your own critical judgment and discernment, you will be less likely to be buffaloed, hoodwinked or otherwise bamboozled by the siren songs and unwitting advocacy of naturalism that are a part of contemporary seminary education.

A Definition of Naturalism

We may fairly dub naturalism as the "orthodox" metaphysical view of contemporary secular culture. It usually lurks beneath the surface in everyday life and has explicit advocates only among relatively few academics, who hold a disproportionate amount of influence and power.

Metaphysical commitment. Most crucially, naturalism is a metaphysical commitment. Like every broad metaphysical belief, naturalism is concerned with what constitutes ultimate reality, or as C. S. Lewis puts it, the "ultimate Fact."[1] Nature for the naturalist just is the ultimate fact. This belief makes it terribly difficult to get an established definition of the word *nature* to work with in a debate between naturalists and nonnaturalists.

---

[1]C. S. Lewis, *Miracles: A Preliminary Study* (New York: Collier, Macmillan, 1960), p. 7.

The reason is that the naturalist just means everything when he says the word *nature.* C. S. Lewis puts it this way: "Just because the Naturalist thinks that nothing but Nature exists, the word Nature means to him merely 'everything' or 'the whole show' or 'whatever there is.' And if that is what we mean by Nature, then of course nothing else exists."[2] The Christian or other theist will inevitably deny this claim, insisting that there is a greater, self-subsisting Reality, namely God, who himself created and sustains nature. Nature as such is a dependent, and not the ultimate, reality. Of course, the naturalist may tolerate the use of the word *God,* but whatever he means, "God" will always be a part of nature or the cosmos, as a process of becoming, history, the evolutionary process or some such thing. The important point is that nature itself is for the naturalist the ultimate reality. This is a positive and a negative claim. It asserts what exists and what does not exist.

Nothing transcends the regularity of nature. Closely related but subordinate to this fundamental feature of naturalism is the commitment to the ultimate explanatory capacity of natural law. That is, according to the code of naturalism, no reputable scholar is ever to appeal to any category or agency that transcends the regularity of nature. This particular component was easier to apply before the troubling revelations from quantum physicists, who maintain that matter at the subatomic level does not obey deterministic natural laws. Physicists tell us that quantum events are unpredictable, even random. If this is correct then "natural laws" are not inscrutable laws but useful macrogeneralizations ranging over trillions of small quantum events. An analogy would be coin tossing. Any one coin toss is unpredictable, but a billion coin tosses will come out with about 50 percent heads and 50 percent tails. Quantum unpredictability or indeterminacy makes this component of naturalism a little more difficult to maintain on a priori grounds. However, even if the naturalist accepts this interpretation of quantum physics, he or she will still not countenance extra- or supernatural events or *agents* that could have an impact on nature. There may be subatomic randomness. But there most certainly is not any supermaterial agency.

Naturalism contradicts Christian belief. Everyone should be able to agree that naturalism and Christian beliefs are incompatible, whether or not a person is a naturalist. The only people who seem intent on denying

---

[2]Ibid., p. 5.

this obvious truth are certain theologians who want desperately to avoid a conflict with the spirit of the age. But such compromise is not conducive to clarity of thought. Christian belief is a type of "supernaturalism," which connotes at least that nature is *not* the fundamental reality.[3]

Some naturalists warn that supernaturalism leads to a derogation of nature. This is simply not the case. Christian belief in particular does not imply a denigration of nature or a denial of its reality. It requires only that we do not make the physical universe, matter or nature into the fundamental reality that exists *a se*, independently. The Christian doctrine of creation has always provided a robust defense of the reality and importance of nature. Moreover, the belief that the physical universe is created by a rational being is a very stable basis for the assumption that nature has a certain type of regularity (although the Christian supernaturalist will avoid postulating a natural regularity that precludes the possibility of special divine acts in the created order).

Armed with this bare-boned definition of naturalism, we can now consider some popular arguments against this metaphysical monstrosity.

Arguments Against Naturalism

There are so many good arguments against naturalism that it would be redundant and tedious to recount them all here. Instead, I will offer some suggestive and provocative highlights. My purpose is to pique your interest. If these do not convince you, I hope they will encourage you to consult the works in the bibliography at the end of this essay for a fuller treatment of the subject.

Naturalism cannot be established. If we reflect on the epistemic status of naturalism, it becomes clear that it is impossible to establish. This is probably because it is fundamentally a negative claim. If this sounds like an overstatement, try to imagine an experience accessible to a finite mind that could verify it. How could any mind short of an omniscient one claim to have an experience that establishes the truth that there is nothing but physical nature? I do not think there could be any such experience. Of course, someone might insist that it is just unthinkable that there be anything but nature or matter; but that is a confession of that person's psychological condition rather than an argument for naturalism. Now, I am not

---

[3]With this definition I am not addressing the difficult question of how God and nature are related. I am only claiming that for the Christian, nature is not the ultimate reality.

claiming that since naturalism cannot be established, verified or confirmed, it is a meaningless doctrine. On the contrary, I think it is meaningful. I just cannot see how it could ever be confirmed, let alone established.

Of course, it does not follow that an individual cannot believe something unless it is established according to some empirical criteria. We all believe many things that cannot be established "empirically." I doubt I could ever establish that my friends have minds or that there is such a thing as justice. I believe these things nonetheless, and I think I am warranted in so believing. What makes the "unverifiability" of naturalism so destructive to naturalism is that naturalists usually assume their worldview enjoys some sort of scientific pedigree, so that only the uneducated and narrow-minded would dare challenge it. It is this assumption that is untrue. Once we consider the nature of naturalism (namely, a metaphysical commitment), we see that it has no more exceptional epistemic status than the most extravagant commitment of blind faith.

Naturalism is reductionist. While naturalism is often justified as conducive to open-mindedness and clear thinking, in fact it amounts to a ravenous global reductionism. It makes Ockham's razor—which states "do not multiply entities beyond necessity"—into an ultimate metaphysical principle. Now even if we could explain most things without recourse to entities that transcend the physical universe (which is doubtful), does this procedure look like a good idea? If we must choose, surely in matters metaphysical we should prefer prodigality to parsimony, at least when the stakes are so high. Is it rational to subscribe to a belief that, if false, makes it *impossible* to recognize the most fundamental Reality of all? Naturalism, once assumed, proscribes a person from evaluating competing truth claims, such as Christian theism. This alone should heighten our suspicion. If we are going to err, is it not more prudent to allow for the uncritical admission of a few nonexistent fairies and elves, than to rule out the possibility of the God on whom all things depend for their existence?

The naturalist is like the two-dimensional figures in Edwin Abbott's *Flatland,*[4] who cannot conceive of three-dimensional spheres. These two-dimensional figures inevitably interpret their encounters with the three-dimensional spheres that intersect Flatland as mere circles because the figures are confined to a two-dimensional world. From the perspective of Christian theism, naturalists dwell in a two-dimensional worldview.

---

[4]Edwin Abbott, *Flatland* (New York: Dover, 1952).

Naturalism is self-refuting. An intriguing but more difficult argument against naturalism is that it is self-refuting. This argument is found in *Miracles* by C. S. Lewis and more fully in works by Alvin Plantinga. It has inspired several articles in contemporary academic journals such as *Faith and Philosophy.* Simply put, the argument is this: if naturalism were true, a person would have no reason to trust his or her belief that it is. This argument is too complicated to do it full justice here. I recommend chapter eleven of Alvin Plantinga's *Warrant and Proper Function*[5] for anyone interested in a rigorous presentation of it.

The gist of the argument, however, is this. Consider the standard naturalistic explanation for the origin of life, which is that all life evolved *unguided* through natural selection (and some other mechanisms like genetic drift) working on random genetic variation. All the diversity of life is explained in this way. The traits natural selection favors are those that confer on the recipient a survival advantage.[6] So ultimately the origin of our beliefs too must be explained in terms of *survival.*

Natural selection works because some mutations confer on the recipient a *survival* advantage, allowing such individuals to propagate more abundantly than their less well-adapted relatives.[7] While other genetic variations may occur, if they do not affect survival positively or negatively, natural selection cannot work on them. For example, natural selection may provide for sharp horns on water buffalo, but it would not account for a trait such as blue eyes (assuming for argument that blue eyes grant the water buffalo no survival advantage).

Natural selection can also work on inheritable traits that regulate *behavior.* So the water buffalo fortunate enough to inherit a gene that disposes it to run away at the sight of lions will survive to reproduce beyond its unfortunate cousins who see lions as potential mates or furry friends.

Superficially it might seem that this explanation would allow for the production of systems that produce true beliefs, since true beliefs are likely to be conducive to survival. So philosopher Jerry Fodor says, "Darwinian selection guarantees that organisms either know the elements of

---

[5]Alvin Plantinga, *Warrant and Proper Function* (Oxford: Oxford University Press, 1993).

[6]Theorists often note that there are other mechanisms but that natural selection is the most important of these.

[7]For a more complete description of this subject, see Plantinga, *Warrant and Proper Function*, pp. 19-237.

logic or become posthumous."[8] But this inference from Darwinian selection to true beliefs is fallacious because *natural selection works on behavior, not beliefs*. That is, if some behavior bestows on an organism a "survival-enhancing propensity," then natural selection can prefer it. But strictly speaking, natural selection would be blind to beliefs. What the water buffalo *believes* about the lion is irrelevant as long as his behavior enhances his survival. He might believe that when he sees a lion, it's time to migrate quickly to another area in search for food. Or he might believe that the lion is his mommy but believe falsely that the way to get her to love him is for him to run away. Notice that such a false belief will still produce behavior that confers on the water buffalo a survival advantage. The point is that any number of beliefs, most of which are wildly false, is consistent with a survival-enhancing behavior. In fact, almost any belief could be tethered to a certain behavior. As long as the behavior is conducive to survival, it is susceptible to natural selection's invisible hand. Given such a process for the production of belief, how likely is it that any one of our beliefs is true? Ironically, Darwin himself realized this point more poignantly than many of his heirs:

> The horrid doubt always arises whether the convictions of man's mind, which has been developed from the mind of the lower animals, are of any value or at all trustworthy. Would any one trust in the convictions of a monkey's mind, if there are any convictions in such a mind?[9]

While some true beliefs might grant the organism a survival advantage, natural selection cannot pick and choose among beliefs but only among behaviors. Patricia Churchland is a well-known evolutionary theorist, and she understands this well:

> Boiled down to essentials, a nervous system enables the organism to succeed in the four F's: feeding, fleeing, fighting and reproducing. The principle chore of nervous systems is to get the body parts where they should be in order that the organism may survive. . . . Improvements in sensorimotor control confer an evolutionary advantage: a fancier style of representing is advantageous *so long as it is geared to the organism's way of life and enhances the organism's chances of survival.* Truth, whatever that is, definitely takes the hindmost.[10]

---

[8]Jerry Fodor, quoted in Plantinga, *Warrant and Proper Function*, p. 220.

[9]Charles Darwin, quoted in Plantinga, *Warrant and Proper Function*, p. 219.

[10]Patricia Churchland, quoted in Plantinga, *Warrant and Proper Function*, p. 218, emphasis in the original.

So if this naturalistic account is true, there is a remarkably low probability that any of our beliefs is true. Most simply put, *natural selection
working on behavior vastly underdetermines true belief. Since the theory
itself is commended for belief, it has a component that generates skepticism.* And notice that this skepticism gets turned back upon the theory
itself because among those of our beliefs would be naturalism combined
with the Darwinian account. So if they were true, we would have little reason to trust that our belief in them was true. So the theory naturalistically
construed is self-refuting.

Hybrid Forms of Naturalism

If I ended this essay with an analysis of undiluted naturalism, I doubt few
readers would be tempted to adopt it as a life philosophy. Moreover, in the
pure form in which we have considered it here, probably few of us would
deem it compatible with Christian belief. Unless a person is in a discipline
that is explicitly naturalistic, he or she is unlikely to encounter such undiluted naturalism. In seminary particularly, he or she is likely to encounter
a series of halfway covenants, attempts to compromise and reconcile
incompatible ways of viewing the world. Because this leads to multifarious hybrids between two species of beliefs, the variety of such hybrids is
dizzying and vast. So it is impossible for me to give a succinct analysis of
the "nature" of naturalism as you are likely to come across it at, say, Princeton Theological Seminary. If you were in biology at Princeton University
or physics at MIT, you might encounter naturalism in a purer form. But in
seminary, you are more likely to face some hybrid version. So the best I
can do is mention a couple of examples of the influence of naturalism in
biblical studies and hope that this will suffice to help you identify it when
you happen upon it.

Methodological naturalism. If you press the purveyors of such a hybrid,
rather than getting a defense of metaphysical naturalism, what you are
likely to get is a defense of "methodological naturalism." Methodological
naturalists need not contend that metaphysical naturalism is true; they
only insist that all proper scientific explanations of phenomena will
appeal to strictly naturalistic causes. So, for example, they claim that *scientific* biblical scholars will forego any appeal to divine agency and will
seek explanations that are naturalistic. Now why should the Christian
accept such a claim? Why should Christian biblical scholars restrict themselves with such a biased definition of science?

There are several motivations for a Christian to acquiesce to methodological naturalism. One may be that some Christian scholars, as C. S. Lewis puts it, seek to be "honourable to the point of being Quixotic. They are anxious to allow to the enemy every advantage he can with any show of fairness claim. They thus make it part of their method to eliminate the supernatural wherever it is even remotely possible to do so, to strain natural explanation even to the breaking point before they admit the least suggestion of miracle."[11] Another reason is no doubt that many seek to avoid conflict. There are probably other less honorable motives, such as fear of being ridiculed or simply a tendency to succumb to the groupthink to which all humans are susceptible, including academics. This response can have very practical justifications. Scholars who challenge the reigning intellectual orthodoxy are likely to impede their chances for tenure, acclaim and publishing opportunities. Finally, there are some scholars (I have met them myself) who are unaware that they have imbibed from the fountain of naturalism. Of course, pointing out the motivations for accepting a belief does not amount to an argument for the falsity of that belief; so we should not make too much of such motivations.

I think that methodological naturalism is flawed in general, but I will not belabor that point. For even if it were appropriate in some disciplines, it seems clear that additional difficulties accrue to it for any Christian biblical scholar because there are certain biblical events that the Christian affirms that any naturalistic methodology must deny. This does not mean that a Christian scholar will appeal to divine agency at every turn. But surely in biblical history there are some key points at which appeal to divine agency is mandatory for the believer. To require methodological naturalism at those points would be equivalent to denying the faith. Again, as C. S. Lewis puts it, "A naturalistic Christianity leaves out all that is specifically Christian."[12]

So, for example, if some Christian biblical scholar affirms the reality of Christ's resurrection, he or she will deny the truth of any historical reconstruction that does not accommodate it. But if so, then, if the Christian biblical scholar adheres to methodological naturalism, he or she will be committed to a methodology that will inevitably lead him or her into error. This does not seem reasonable. Surely the main reason an individual

---

[11]Lewis, *Miracles*, p. 164.
[12]Ibid., p. 68.

would follow such a methodology would be because he or she thought it was likely to preserve truth. If some naturalistic definition of "science" prevents him or her from pursuing the truth, then the person should resist that definition of science, not engage in theological acrobatics to oblige it. If there are events in biblical history that resist naturalistic explanation, then sticking to a naturalistic methodology unnecessarily restricts the options. Phillip Johnson puts it this way: "Methodological naturalism is a bias in the sense that it constricts the mind, by limiting the possibilities open to serious consideration. Theistic realism opens the mind to additional possibilities, without preventing the acceptance of anything that really is convincingly demonstrated by empirical evidence."[13]

Theological justifications for methodological naturalism. Besides an argument from the definition of science, many biblical scholars offer theological justifications for methodological naturalism. A common strategy among Christians who seek a reconciliation with naturalism is to define God's relation to the physical universe in such a way that God's actions in the universe do not violate any naturalistic scruples. Probably the most relevant and sensitive of these scruples is the claim that the cause-and-effect nexus, the regularity of so-called natural laws, is not to be violated. More specifically, any exceptions to the closed system of nature such as are often purported in miracles are unthinkable. Among theologians and biblical scholars a popular way of avoiding conflict on this front is to conceive of divine action in a way that does not invoke any supposed "exceptions." Since this maneuver is often complicated and obscure, it helps to hide what is really happening.

They may bolster the strategy with the contention that it would really be unmajestic or somehow inappropriate for an omnipotent God to violate natural laws anyway since he is the ultimate source of those laws. Only an imperfect craftsman would set up a series of regular laws only to go back and tinker with them later. Therefore, methodological naturalism serves to protect divine majesty since it prohibits appeals to any Heavenly Tinkerer. Or so the argument goes. Such a strategy essentially claims to deny *A* in our definition of naturalism but concede *B*.

There is a hornets' nest of dangers here, which I can only mention in passing. Perhaps most importantly, we should avoid allowing naturalism

---

[13]Phillip E. Johnson, *Reason in the Balance: The Case Against Naturalism in Science, Law & Education* (Downers Grove, Ill.: InterVarsity Press, 1995), p. 168.

to define the terms of debate. On the one hand, we should not join a pusil-lanimous retreat from the claim that God can and does effect unique events in the physical universe. On the other hand, we do not want to be so mesmerized by the naturalistic portrayal of the regularity of nature that we uncritically define divine action in general or miracles in particular as intrinsically a "violation of natural laws." Unfortunately, steering the course with adequate nuance would require a lengthy discussion of the notion of miracle, which I cannot enter here. Nonetheless, let us be aware of the issues that lurk in the neighborhood of this discussion.

That said, I think we should initially be suspicious of "theological" arguments like this one, since they seem to attract most of their support among those already troubled by naturalism. More pointedly, these arguments look tailor-made to avoid conflict with naturalism and do not seem to issue from obvious theological commitments. After all, it's not as if we have access to some a priori principle of what is and is not appropriate for God to do. If God has revealed himself as Christians claim, then surely it is more appropriate to allow the specifics of that revelation to shape or even override our initial impressions of divine propriety. And is it not an unavoidable part of the Christian and biblical portrayal of God that he can and does act in such ways that are not merely reducible to or synonymous with the regularities we often label "natural law"? Christians claim that God parted the Sea of Reeds, fed Israel manna, conceived a child in the womb of a virgin, became incarnate and raised the dead. Any account of God that gets fidgety when confronted with these claims is going to have to do some masterful maneuvering to maintain the label "Christian."

Examples of Naturalism in Biblical Studies

Such fidgetiness is betrayed frequently in biblical studies. While there are many valiant biblical scholars who successfully integrate their religious beliefs into their academic methodology, there are at least as many who have been sucked into the vortex of naturalism. Let's consider just two examples where naturalism tends to show itself: the dating of the writings of the Synoptic Gospels and scholarly evaluations of the Gospels' portrayals of Jesus.

Dating of the Gospels. There are many factors that go into the determination of the date and authorship of the Synoptic Gospels. For simplicity let's assume the Marcan hypothesis, according to which Matthew and Luke used Mark in compiling their Gospels. If this is correct, then Mark is

the earliest Gospel. Of all the passages in Mark, probably the linchpin for
dating it (and *a fortiori*, the Synoptics) is how a scholar evaluates the status of Jesus' words concerning the destruction of the temple in Jerusalem.
In Mark 13:1-2 the disciples comment on the temple, whereupon Jesus
declares, "Not one stone here will be left on another; every one will be
thrown down." Then, in verse 14 he says, alluding to a phrase from
Daniel, "When you see 'the abomination that causes desolation' standing
where it does not belong . . . then let those who are in Judea flee to the
mountains" (NIV).

These words of Jesus are decidedly vague and therefore susceptible to
various interpretations. Nevertheless, most scholars think that Mark (or
whoever the author is) intended them to be read as a reference to the siege
and fall of Jerusalem led by Titus in A.D. 70. Of course, they could be a reference to Caligula's failed attempt to put a statue of himself in the temple
in A.D. 40. Moreover, the passage's vagueness could be a hint that Jesus'
words connote a more general claim, since even the details it has don't
quite square with the events surrounding the siege in A.D. 70. For, whereas
Jesus warns that the inhabitants of Jerusalem should flee to the hills of
Judea, tradition claims that in A.D. 70 the Christians fled to Pella, "a low-
lying city east of Jordan."[14]

Still, let's set all this aside and assume that Mark intends these words to
be a prediction of a future event by Jesus. If we assume this, which many
scholars do, then we are confronted with a dilemma. For on naturalistic
scruples detailed predictions concerning future events are impossible.
Therefore, assuming (1) this passage purports to be a prediction about the
siege of Jerusalem in A.D. 70, and (2) predictions of future events are
impossible, then we can conclude that Mark, or this portion of it, was
written around or most likely after A.D. 70. If we tie (1) and (2) to (3), the
priority of Mark, then we have a bottom limit for the date of all the Synoptics at about A.D. 70. Succinctly put, the conclusion by scholars of a naturalistic bent is that the words in Mark 13 (and their parallels in Mt 24:15
and Lk 21:20) must be a *vaticinium ex eventu*. That is, they must have
been written after events of which they pretend to be a prediction.

But what if the scholar does not assume (2) (i.e., predictions concerning
future events are impossible)? What if the scholar judges that if Jesus is

---

[14]Donald Guthrie, *New Testament Introduction* (Downers Grove, Ill.: InterVarsity Press,
  1990), p. 87.

who Christians say he is, such a prediction is certainly possible? It does not follow that that scholar will inevitably date the Gospel of Mark earlier than A.D. 70. Even if Mark 13 is a legitimate foretelling of a future event, Mark might still have been written after A.D. 70. There are other considerations that go into date assignment for the document besides this one. Nevertheless, it should be clear that a scholar who does not assume (2), or who positively denies it, will not bring presuppositions to the text that entail that it was written around or after A.D. 70. So a naturalistic presupposition exercises a crucial influence on such technical matters as the dating of a document.

For the nonnaturalist, there are alternatives. To see this more clearly, consider the parallel text in Luke 21, which has slightly more detail than the text in Mark. In Luke, Jesus says Jerusalem will be "surrounded by armies." If a reader assumes the text was written after the destruction of the temple, he or she will count this extra phrase as evidence for that assumption and inevitably date Luke after A.D. 70. But it is quite conceivable, all else being equal, that a nonnaturalist, assuming the literary unity of Luke-Acts, could argue for a date around A.D. 60-61 since Acts ends there abruptly and does not allude to any important events from A.D. 60 to 70. If this reasoning is joined with the Marcan hypothesis, then it would lead to a date for Mark prior to A.D. 61. Whether or not this is correct, it is at least plausible. A rational person could be convinced by such an argument.

My point is not that nonnaturalists will automatically give earlier dates to the Synoptic Gospels and Acts. My point is that naturalistic assumptions are a significant constraint on the matter of dating these texts. And this is the case even among many scholars who, if asked, would positively deny that naturalism governs their thought. In fact, professors often avoid noting in lectures the importance of this single judgment for dating the Synoptics, but the student who is aware of it can easily detect its effect.

Development of beliefs about Jesus. Closely related to the naturalistic prejudice against putative predictions of the future is skepticism concerning the accuracy of exalted portrayals of Jesus in the New Testament. In general, the more lofty a depiction of Jesus is, the more likely that scholars will assign it a late date. Of course, no one doubts that development occurred in the church's understanding about Jesus. Although a person can effectively argue, for instance, that the doctrine of the Trinity is implicit in the New Testament, it is nowhere named or taught explicitly in the canon. This doctrine was not articulated formally until the Council of Nicaea in A.D. 325. And of course, reflection on its meaning and on the nature of the person of Christ continued to develop after that. So there is nothing intrinsically naturalistic in the claim that doctrinal beliefs underwent development after Jesus' life, death and resurrection. However, reconstruction of the nature of that development will look very different depending on whether a person assumes naturalism or its denial. And again, such judgments will go into his or her conclusion regarding the dating and authorship of the New Testament documents.

Biblical scholars affected by naturalism evince embarrassment at texts that imply that Jesus was aware of his divine status or that his followers were quickly convinced of it. The more comfortable picture is one in which the second or later generations after Jesus' death came to think of him as divine. For Jesus or his direct acquaintances to believe that he was divine looks too much like a surd, a discontinuity with the way we expect things to evolve historically. To accept it, we would need to postulate some sort of "breaking in" on the usual course of things, which, as we have noted, is repugnant to the naturalistic spirit. That the village skeptic should display such an attitude is not surprising. What is troubling are biblical scholars who are officially opposed to naturalism but who nevertheless acquire this attitude in their scholarly pursuits.

One question draws out the crucial matter at stake: Did the incarnation and resurrection of Christ create the church, or did the church create the incarnation and resurrection? If we assume the latter, then we will have to postulate a considerable amount of time in order for legends to build up around the person of Jesus, about what he said about himself, and about his birth and resurrection. To make such development plausible, many key players and eyewitnesses will need to have died off. No one could still be around who remembered where Jesus was buried, since an exhumed body would no doubt have refuted the fanciful claims about his resurrection.

I think you get the idea. A person will need to allow space for the growth of legendary accretions. If an individual assumes that an incarnation and resurrection are impossible, he or she will need to permit sufficient time for such fanciful ideas to develop and will likely postulate a *later* date for the writing of the Gospels (and other New Testament documents) than someone who does not assume this (all things being equal). If that date goes past, say, A.D. 95, then he or she is likely to doubt the accuracy of the traditional authorial assignments of the Synoptic Gospels, since Matthew, Mark and Luke would all be dead or at least very forgetful.

In source critical terms, naturalism will affect the same sorts of judgments. Naturalists will inevitably date texts that have an exalted view of Jesus as later "strata." They will usually deny that anything implying, say, Jesus' deity is first strata material. This is all very simplified and generalized, but it should be clear that bringing naturalistic assumptions to biblical scholarship has very far-reaching implications. I could multiply examples, but I will stop here.

Conclusion

Obviously there is no way to detail every form which naturalism might take in a theological setting. I hope I have provided enough to assist you in detecting it on your own. Naturalism permeates virtually our entire intellectual milieu, and unfortunately this includes theological studies as well. But its "degree of saturation" varies from scholar to scholar and from discipline to discipline. If you are discerning and sufficiently critical in your thinking, you will recognize such variation even among the faculty of Princeton Theological Seminary and the texts you read here. Some will be fully aware of the issues we have discussed; others will not. Some will be faithful to the witness of Scripture; some will be less so. Some will make abrupt and inconsistent exceptions to a generally naturalistic methodology for certain central events such as Christ's resurrection. Some will resist naturalism wherever it rears its ugly head. Some will do its bidding without resistance. If I could offer an injection that would inoculate us all against the influence of naturalism, I would. Instead I have only words. However, instead of offering you my words, consider C. S. Lewis' epilogue to *Miracles:*

> When you turn from the New Testament to modern scholars, remember that you go among them as a sheep among wolves. Naturalistic assumptions, beggings of the question . . . will meet you on every side—even from the pens of clergymen. This does not mean . . . that these clergymen are disguised apostates who deliberately exploit the position and the livelihood given them by the Christian Church to undermine Christianity. It comes partly from what we may call a "hangover." We all have Naturalism in our bones and even conversion does not at once work the infection out of our system. Its assumptions rush back upon the mind the moment vigilance is relaxed.

In using the books of such people you must therefore be continually on guard. You must develop a nose like a bloodhound for those steps in the argument which depend not on historical and linguistic knowledge but on the concealed assumption that miracles are impossible, improbable or improper. And this means that you must really reeducate yourself: you must work hard and consistently to eradicate from your mind the whole type of thought in which we have all been brought up.[15]

If you seek a nose like a bloodhound for sniffing out naturalism, I recommend that you read the books in the bibliography below. Exposure to such writings, combined with vigilant prayer and critical judgment, is the only currently available antidote to the infection of naturalism.

Bibliography on Naturalism

Abbott, Edwin. *Flatland*. New York: Dover, 1952. This is not an argument against naturalism per se, but it does illustrate the ways in which a negative belief system like naturalism can prevent a person from seeing the truth.

Guthrie, Donald. *New Testament Introduction*. Downers Grove, Ill.: InterVarsity Press, 1990. Like Harrison's book this is a great resource as a sort of traditionalist "loyal opposition" to the type of New Testament studies that makes its peace with naturalistic methodology. Especially see chapter one and appendix D, "Further Reflections on the Synoptic Problem."

Harrison, Roland Kenneth. *Introduction to the Old Testament*. Grand Rapids, Mich.: Eerdmans, 1988. Parts one through six are excellent for a vigorous response to naturalism in Old Testament studies. The book as a whole is a great resource for any student in the field who seeks exposure to both the prosecution and the defense.

Johnson, Phillip. *Reason in the Balance: The Case Against Naturalism in Science, Law & Education*. Downers Grove, Ill.: InterVarsity Press, 1995. This is another very accessible treatment of naturalism and its pervasiveness in American society, particularly in academia. Chapters two through six and the appendix "Naturalism, Methodological & Otherwise" are particularly helpful. His focus on intelligent design as a legitimate scientific hypothesis highlights another field in which seminarians are likely to encounter residual naturalism: in systematic theology, particularly the treatment of the doctrine of creation. This is another interesting topic, which I do not consider here.

Lewis, C. S. *Miracles: A Preliminary Study*. New York: Macmillan, 1960. This is probably the best and most accessible treatment of miracles and naturalism, especially chapters one through ten.

Plantinga, Alvin. *Warrant and Proper Function*. Oxford: Oxford University Press, 1993. Chapter eleven, "Naturalism Versus Proper Function?" and chapter twelve, "Is Naturalism Irrational?" are especially relevant. Neither of these chapters is easy reading, but they contain perhaps the most precise formulation of the perennial problem of naturalism: If it's true, we do not have any reason to believe that is true. See also Plantinga's revision of this argument in *Warranted Christian Belief* (Oxford: Oxford University Press, 2000).

---

[15]Lewis, *Miracles*, pp. 164-65.

6

OLD PRINCETON & THE DOCTRINE OF SCRIPTURE

RAYMOND CANNATA

O N SEPTEMBER 14, 1889, CHARLES AUGUSTUS BRIGGS, DAVENPORT PRO-
fessor of Hebrew and Cognate Languages at Union Theological Seminary in
New York, caused a major stir in the church and in the academy with the
publication of a new book. Simply titled *Whither?* it was in fact a "wither-
ing" attack on Princeton Seminary and particularly its teaching on the doctrine of Scripture. Briggs was never one to spare anyone's feelings, but he
did recognize the need to explain the seeming severity and brutality of the
tone of his critique.[1] In the preface he makes clear that the stakes are so high
that all means are justified. He believed that the church might be on the
brink of entering into a great religious promised land, where, in Briggs's
words, "the barriers between the Protestant denominations may be removed
and an organic union formed. An Alliance may be made between Protestantism and Romanism and all other branches of Christendom."[2]

---

[1]Lefferts Loetscher, though clearly sympathetic with Briggs's perspective, acknowledges
that in this book Briggs's "tone was so far from objective that many, including some of
Briggs' friends, regretted it" (*The Broadening Church* [Philadelphia: University of Pennsylvania Press, 1964], p. 48).

[2]Charles A. Briggs, *Whither?* (New York: Charles Scribner's Sons, 1889), p. xi.

Briggs felt that there was chiefly one speed bump on the highway leading to utopia, and this was precisely where the road cut through Princeton,
New Jersey. If it had been up to him, he would have built the road to avoid
Princeton, but it was too late for that now. He explains, "The theology of
the elder and younger Hodge that has in fact usurped the place of the
Westminster theology in the minds of a large proportion of the ministry of
the Presbyterian Churches, now stands in the way of progress . . . and
there is no other way of advancing truth except by removing the errors that
obstruct our path."[3] Yes, apparently two men, both deceased, were somehow single-handedly responsible for delaying the coming of the millen-
nial kingdom on Earth through their poisonous influence on their
followers. This being the case, they must be refuted, discredited and
destroyed by whatever means necessary.

Briggs was not bluffing. In the next three hundred pages he goes to such
great pains that he embarrassed even his most sympathetic liberal supporters. Dripping with heavy sarcasm, he attempts to lay bare every conceivable potential weakness in the Princeton doctrine of Scripture. For
starters, he charges that the Princeton doctrine of full divine inspiration of
Scripture leaves no room for the human element in its authorship. Further,
its claim of the errorlessness of the Bible was being rendered progressively
more absurd with each new finding of higher criticism. To evade the plain
truth that our text undeniably contains errors, the Princeton divines had
invented a novel new theory that inspiration was only guaranteed for the
original (forever lost) autographs. This is a cop-out, a calculated dodge,
Briggs charges. It is also ahistorical and at odds with what the saints
through the ages have always taught. Most of all, such a formulation was
utterly foreign to what the Bible teaches about itself. It is doing violence to
the very texts it hoped to validate. Princeton had somehow "narrowed"
the Westminster Confession, Briggs contends, and twisted it into a very
un-Reformed caricature. He labels the Princetonians "muddy scholastics,"
extreme "rationalists," "betrayers" and ultimately "failures." Their doctrine of infallibility had risked the whole authority of Scripture on one
proved error, and their retreat to the nonexistent "original autographs"
renders our English translations of tainted copies utterly unreliable.

James McCosh, Presbyterian divine, world-renowned metaphysician
and president of Princeton College, swiftly penned a firm rebuttal to

---

[3]Ibid., p. x.

Briggs's book *Whither?* which he titled *Whither? O Whither? Tell Me Where.* The seminary did not greatly need his aid at the time. For one thing there was no one in the English-speaking world who could surpass the massive learning, lucid pen and sheer intellectual powers of the seminary's own B. B. Warfield. And the church as a whole, including its Presbyterian variety, seemed to enjoy a fairly clear consensus on the issue. When all sides had had their say, Briggs was refuted by the 1892 General Assembly of the Presbyterian Church, which passed its famous Portland Deliverance requesting that all who denied the inerrancy of Scripture withdraw from the ministry. When Briggs went a step further in a highly inflammatory one-hundred-minute address in 1893, heresy charges were sustained against him, soon resulting in the departure of Union Seminary and him from the Presbyterian Church. The 1892 assembly's pronouncements were reaffirmed each year they were reintroduced, and inerrancy was declared an "essential and necessary" article of faith at the 1910, 1917 and 1923 assemblies.

In a sense, however, Briggs has been vindicated by history. Those in the present-day church who wish to challenge the full inspiration of Scripture generally find it necessary to level basically the same charges Briggs first outlined unsuccessfully one hundred years ago. Presbyterian scholars Donald McKim and Jack Rogers have echoed a very similar line of criticism in their recent book-length works on Scripture, dwelling largely on what they find deficient with Old Princeton.[4] Professor Daniel Migliore contends that the teaching of scriptural infallibility can be attributed directly to a reactionary response to the "rising tide of modernity." He argues that Warfield and Hodge's teachings are a Protestant version of Vatican I-style papal infallibility and became more "defensive" and "strident" over time.[5] Winthrop Hudson charges that "Hodge attempted to keep Presbyterianism in a theological straight-jacket."[6] John Oliver Nelson, formerly a trustee of Princeton Theological Seminary, contended that the Old Princeton doctrine of Scripture leads to a

---

[4]See especially Jack Rogers and Donald McKim, *Authority and Interpretation of the Bible* (New York: Harper & Row, 1979), and Donald McKim, *What Christians Believe About the Bible* (Nashville: Thomas Nelson, 1985).

[5]Daniel Migliore, *Faith Seeking Understanding* (Grand Rapids, Mich.: Eerdmans, 1991), p. 44. Dr. Migliore is Arthur M. Adams Professor of Systematic Theology at Princeton Seminary.

[6]Winthrop Hudson, *Religion in America* (New York: Scribners, 1981), p. 167.

"legalistic" and "impersonal" theology.[7]

Some of the most severe critics have been certain evangelicals who have embraced Princeton's intellectual rigor, Reformed theology, warmhearted piety and academic achievement while rejecting out of hand the doctrine of Scripture that undergirds all these. For example, the evangelical George Marsden, while highly appreciative of nearly all other aspects of Old Princeton, contends that their beliefs on Scripture were "in fact built on a foundation of superficial accommodation to the modern scientific revolution."[8] They were "so committed in principle to a scientifically based culture even while the scientifically based culture of the 20th century was undermining belief in the very truths of the Bible they held most dear. . . . To them, however, it might not have been obvious how hopeless their position was."[9]

You have no doubt heard these mantras before.[10] The next obvious question is: Why in the world are we even bothering to discuss this? Why waste our valuable time on a teaching that everybody would seem to agree is worthless? Frankly, because I think we have been deceived. I unapologetically confess to you that I think that Old Princeton may very well provide some critical clues to help us find our way out of the contemporary epistemological maze.

I have learned two things recently by reading the secondary literature on Old Princeton: (1) all the critics agree that understanding Old Princeton on Scripture is utterly essential, and (2) very few of these critics seem to have actually read much or any of what Old Princeton actually said! I sincerely believe that. Work through contemporary textbooks of history and of theology and practically every one will contain at least a paragraph on Old Princeton's doctrine of Scripture, yet few will contain more than a page. Moreover, these textbooks all seem to quote the exact same sound

---

[7]John Oliver Nelson, "Charles Hodge: Nestor of Orthodoxy," in *The Lives of Eighteen from Princeton*, ed. Willard Thorp (Princeton: Princeton University Press, 1946), p. 209.

[8]George Marsden, "Collapse of American Evangelical Academia," in *Faith and Patriarchy*, ed. Alvin Plantinga and Nicholas Wolterstorff (Notre Dame: Notre Dame Press, 1983), p. 241.

[9]George Marsden, "Evangelicals and the Scientific Culture," in *Religion and Twentieth Century American Intellectual Life*, ed. By Michael Lacey (Cambridge: Cambridge University Press, 1989), p. 26.

[10]See also James Barr, *Fundamentalism* (London: SCM Press, 1977), or Loetscher, *Broadening Church*.

bites from Warfield and Hodge. Warfield alone penned at least two full bookshelves worth of material, and yet it would appear from what his critics quote that all he had to say on Scripture was contained in a few sentences. A reader quickly gets the strong sense that the modern historians and theologians are not reading the Old Princetonians—they are reading what *each other* says about the Princetonians.

Nonetheless, a small but elite army of very able and gifted scholars has stepped forward in the last few years to forcefully argue that the Princeton formulations are about the most thoughtful, faithful and relevant yet articulated by the church.[11] In fact, this essay is largely a presentation of the fine insights shared by these scholars. But one point in which virtually all theological camps currently seem to agree on is the *significance* of Old Princeton. So let's take a closer look and judge for ourselves.

Old Princeton's Understanding of Scripture

We will start by carefully examining the following statement by a prominent late-nineteenth-century biblical critic:

> It is not merely in the matter of verbal expression or literary composition that the personal idiosyncrasies of each [biblical] author are freely manifested, . . . but the very substance of what they write is evidently for the most part the product of their own mental and spiritual activities. . . . [Each author of Scripture] gave evidence of his own special limitations of knowledge and mental power, and of his defects.[12]

Now listen very carefully to another:

> [The Scriptures] are written in human languages, whose words, inflections, constructions and idioms bear everywhere indelible traces of error. The record itself furnishes evidence that the writers were in large measure dependent for their knowledge upon sources and methods in themselves fallible,

---

[11]Geoffrey Bromiley, D. A. Carson, W. Robert Godfrey, Roger Nicole, Moisés Silva, James I. Packer, Wayne Grudem, John Woodbridge, John Gerstner, David Calhoun, Walter Kaiser, Carl F. H. Henry, John Stott, R. C. Sproul, James M. Boice, Andrew Hoffecker, Mark Noll and David Wells (to identify just a few) are among those who have endorsed the Old Princeton view of Scripture. The International Conference on Biblical Inerrancy (ICBI) called together three hundred scholars and pastors to Chicago in October of 1978. Their nineteen-article "Chicago Statement" is basically a modern reaffirmation of the Old Princeton view.

[12]I've borrowed this quote and several of those which will follow from Moisés Silva's excellent essay titled "Old Princeton, Westminster, and Inerrancy," in *Inerrancy and Hermeneutic*, ed. Harvie M. Conn (Grand Rapids, Mich.: Baker, 1988), pp. 67-80.

and that their personal knowledge and judgments were in many matters hesitating and defective, or even wrong.

Who do you think wrote those words? Maybe Charles Briggs? Some other nineteenth-century progressive like David Swing? No, these two passages come from the famous 1881 article titled "Inspiration" by none other than Princeton's own B. B. Warfield and A. A. Hodge.[13]

This brings us to our first major point about Old Princeton's doctrine of biblical inspiration: this view contains several subtle but very important qualifications. The passages above illustrate the first one: the Old Princetonians taught that somehow taking full account of the human qualities of Scripture does not diminish its authority as divinely inspired and free of falsehood.[14]

So what does it mean for the Princetonians to take the human qualities of the text seriously? It means that a reader needs to distinguish between the official teachings of Scripture and the personal opinions of its writers. Warfield states:

> Paul shared the ordinary opinions of his day in certain matters laying outside the scope of his teachings, as, for example, with reference to the form of the earth, or its relation to the sun; and it is not inconceivable that the form of his language, when incidentally adverting to such matters, might occasionally play into the hands of such a presumption.[15]

The reader should expect inspired biblical passages to contain expressions that reflect the commonly held historical and scientific conceptions of the culture in which they were written. As Professor Silva of Westminster Seminary reminds us, "Inspiration does not convey omniscience."[16] But while a passage will reflect culturally bound errors, no doubt incidentally believed by its author, the Holy Spirit has

---

[13]"Inspiration," *Presbyterian Review* 2 (April 1881): 225-60. The largest collection of Old Princeton work on the doctrine of biblical inspiration can be found in the anthology of Warfield essays titled *The Inspiration and Authority of the Bible* (Phillipsburg, N.J.: Presbyterian and Reformed, 1948), which currently remains in print.

[14]A quick aside about the qualifications that follow. I hope that we can avoid two approaches to the qualifications: one is to dismiss them as cop-outs, escape clauses that water down the teaching in order to avoid vulnerabilities; the other is to so focus on the qualifications that we neglect the central thesis that is being qualified.

[15]Warfield, *Inspiration and Authority*, pp. 196-97. Originally from an article titled "The Real Problem of Inspiration," *Presbyterian and Reformed Review* 4 (1893): 177-221.

[16]Silva, "Old Princeton, Westminster, and Inerrancy," p. 71.

prevented it from teaching the falsehood or error, yet without overriding the personal traits of the author. Warfield makes the critical distinction between the "official teaching" of Paul and those "matters lying outside the scope of his teachings." The issue raised is of authorial intent or purpose. This is where careful, faithful exegesis comes in. Not everything found in Scripture is affirmed or taught by its authors (e.g., "There is no God," Ps 14:1). Each text must be studied for what it is actually teaching.

So, for example, if the biblical author incidentally states that in the midst of a course of events the sun was "rising over the horizon," he may have believed, falsely, that the earth was flat and that the sun was literally moving across the crystal dome that covered the Earth. His figure of speech may reflect that falsehood, yet it is not taught by the text. In reporting this he is speaking phenomenologically (as our modern TV weather forecasters do), expressing the time of day, not the astronomy. And as one commentator states, "What Moses or the prophets . . . understood by the words they wrote down under inspiration is quite secondary to the question of what God Himself meant by those words."[17]

Likewise, when we read Paul's mention in 1 Corinthians 10:8 of the twenty-three thousand Israelites who died because of their immorality, which is in tension with Numbers 25:9, where the figure is reported as twenty-four thousand, the doctrine of inspiration is not challenged. As Calvin says, "It is not unheard of, when there is no intention of making an exact count of individuals, to give an approximate number. . . . Moses gives the upper limits, Paul the lower."[18] Obviously neither writer ever intended to state the exact number. If they had, the numbers would not have been rounded off.

This is not too difficult to see, but this principle can be strained when we confront a truly thorny passage such as, for example, Genesis 1—3. All the Princeton theologians believed in a literal, historic Adam and Eve. We might assume then that their belief in the inspiration of Scripture demanded such a belief in itself, but it did not. Their doctrine of full

---

[17]Gleason Archer, "Alleged Errors," in *Inerrancy*, ed. Norman L. Geisler (Grand Rapids, Mich.: Zondervan, 1980), p. 67.

[18]John Calvin, *The First Epistle of Paul the Apostle to the Corinthians* (Grand Rapids, Mich.: Eerdmans, 1961), pp. 208-9.

biblical inspiration does not necessarily require that a given narrative be read literally. That decision must be arrived at by exegetical evidence, understandings of genre distinctions, the context and so forth. Yes, a reasonable exegete would have to agree that the author intended for Genesis 1—3 to be read literally. When we turn to Paul's inspired interpretations of Genesis 1—3 in 1 Corinthians 15 and Romans 5, it seems nearly certain that the sacred authors intended for the readers to take the historical claims of the passage literally. Even though the historicity of Adam may not be the most important point of the text, it does seem clearly to be taught by the author.

Such an interpretation, however, is independent of any commitment to inerrancy. These are two separate issues. There are other narratives that Princeton and their followers would clearly not read as historical, such as the events described in Jesus' parables, for example. A person could safely argue that Jesus was not teaching in the twelfth chapter of Mark's Gospel about an actual vineyard owner who rented his land to wicked tenants. Likewise, someone else could theoretically argue (though I believe it would be virtually impossible) that Genesis 1—3 does not intend to teach that its events actually happened historically. This is a matter of exegesis, however, quite separate from the doctrine of inspiration. A commitment to this understanding of biblical inspiration does not necessarily tie a reader to any particular interpretations at all.

Likewise, on the issue of authorship, the Princetonians generally arrived at traditional postures, but this was not always necessary to their doctrine of inspiration. If a book of the Bible clearly claims to be written by Paul, then their view of divine inspiration holds that it must be. Clearly anyone subscribing to this view of Scripture would seem compelled to insist on Paul's authorship of all thirteen epistles that bear his name. But this is a decision of exegesis. So in theory a Princetonian could conceivably hold that David did not write some of the psalms that bear his name, if it could be shown somehow that such designations in the psalms genre were not intended to teach that he did.

Another qualification, or nuance, of the Princeton teaching that must be noted is that the Holy Spirit's unfailing guidance applies only to the creation of the *original autographs* of the biblical texts. Just as our current interpretation of the Bible is not guaranteed, neither is the honesty or the workmanship of those who over time copied its texts. Thus our current

Bible is not, strictly speaking, completely free of error.[19]

Another point sometimes missed by critics is that the Princetonians did not conceive of divine inspiration as a form of dictation, as had some of the medieval paintings, depicting the Holy Spirit whispering in Moses' ear. The Princeton divines taught that divine inspiration came by a variety of modes, some supernatural and some quite mundane. Sometimes the biblical writers, such as Matthew or John, simply reported what they remembered under the subtle but invisible guidance of the Holy Spirit. Other writers, such as the prophets, received visions or angelic visits. In either case the result, by God's will, was the same, again without doing violence to the styles, cultural contexts or personalities of the individual authors.

Still another often forgotten but critically important element of the Princeton conception of Scripture was the central role of the Holy Spirit in confirming its authority in our hearts. Ernest Sandeen expresses the misguided sentiment of many of the critics when he charges:

> The witness of the Spirit, though not overlooked, cannot be said to play any important role in the Princeton thought. It is with the external not the internal, the objective not the subjective, that they deal.[20]

This is a favorite charge of many Barthians[21] and some of the Kuyperian[22] critics, who have been alarmed by the supposed rationalistic foundations of the Princeton epistemology.

Because the Princetonians, classic Common Sense Realists, held to certain universal features of rationality shared by all humans, regenerate or not, they believed that evidences were a useful and legitimate preparation for the special grace of the gift of faith. But they were also solid "high" Calvinists, so for them this never meant that a person could *rationally compel* anyone to faith or *prove* that the Bible is the

---

[19]See B. B. Warfield, "The Inerrancy of the Original Autographs," in *Selected Shorter Writings of Benjamin B. Warfield*, ed. John E. Meeter (Nutley, N.J.: Presbyterian and Reformed, 1973), 2:585.

[20]Ernest R. Sandeen, *Roots of Fundamentalism* (Chicago: University of Chicago Press, 1970), p. 118.

[21]Swiss theologian Karl Barth (1886-1968) was perhaps the greatest of the neo-Reformed (some label "neo-orthodox") dialectical thinkers who emerged following World War I.

[22]Abraham Kuyper (1837-1920) taught for many years at the Free University of Amsterdam (Netherlands). His brand of Reformed theology remains influential in many orthodox and evangelical circles.

Word of God. But they did believe that evidences could and should be mustered as secondary causes, under God's sovereign supervision, to illustrate that the Bible is trustworthy and thus prepare the way for the gracious miracle of saving faith. Despite misunderstandings of Old Princeton, they were not un-Reformed or bare rationalists in this area. They always emphasized that ultimately commitment to biblical authority came only by the special work of the sovereign Holy Spirit. Evidence can show that the Bible is trustworthy, but evidence alone can never be sufficient to bring conviction to our souls that it is the Word of God or bring submission to its authority. Only the testimony of the Holy Spirit can accomplish this.[23]

The Historical Basis of Old Princeton's Understanding of Scripture

We have sketched a very basic outline of what the Princeton doctrine of biblical inspiration taught and did not teach. Nonetheless, a whole other line of criticism remains to be addressed: the charge that this Princeton enterprise is really a novelty, outside of the mainstream of historic Christianity. These critics tell us that this formula for scriptural interpretation was the result of a reaction to late nineteenth-century modernist theological and biblical-critical threats. Not until the late 1870s did the Princetonians abstract and exaggerate the tendencies of the narrow school of seventeenth-century Reformed "scholastics" (i.e., Francis Turretin)[24] to come up with a creative but unwarranted invention. While these critics acknowledge that the church has always taught the authority of the Word of God mediated through the biblical text, they hold that inerrancy was not self-consciously attributed to every statement of the Bible, such as its natural or historical claims. Likewise, it is contended, the church has never conceived of the notion of inspiration residing in the original autographs. It is argued that whatever the church has believed about Scripture was never systematized or placed in a neat, rationalistic formula like Prince-

---

[23]See Andrew Hoffecker's excellent *Piety and the Princeton Theologians* (Phililpsburg, N.J.: Presbyterian and Reformed, 1981).

[24]Francis Turretin (or Turretini), seventeenth-century Genevan theologian, authored a two-thousand-page Latin work, *The Institutes of Elenctic Theology*, which was the basic systematics text at Princeton Seminary for nearly fifty years. An English translation made by Princeton College professor George Musgrave Giger in the mid-nineteenth century has been published in three volumes (Phillipsburg, N.J.: Presbyterian and Reformed, 1992).

ton's. To do so would allegedly have signaled a disregard for the living character of the Word of God.[25]

This is a serious charge. To answer it comprehensively, however, would require broadening the scope of this talk from about one hundred twenty years to almost two thousand years. We will only have time to touch on this a little. However, I hope to illustrate that views very similar to those of Old Princeton were voiced by many of the greatest Christian saints, Reformed and otherwise, since the earliest days of the church.[26]

Geoffrey Bromiley, best known for being the key English language translator of Barth's *Church Dogmatics*, has written an essay titled "The Church Fathers and Holy Scripture" in which he convincingly demonstrates that all the major elements of the view of biblical inspiration that I have discussed were present in varying combinations in such luminaries as Tertullian, Gregory of Nyssa, Cyril of Jerusalem, John Cassian and others.[27] Augustine's views are particularly noteworthy: "The evangelists are free from all falsehood, both from that which proceeds from deliberate deceit, and that which is the result of forgetfulness." And, "If any, even the smallest, lie be admitted in the Scriptures, the whole authority of Scripture is presently invalidated and destroyed."[28] Further, when discussing his approach to seeming errors in Scripture, Augustine makes clear his conception of the distinction between the autographa and the copies of text: "I decide that either the text is corrupt, or the translator did not follow what was really said, or that I failed to understand it."[29]

---

[25]See Sandeen, *Roots of Fundamentalism*, p. 106.

[26]Several of the examples that follow can be found in D. A. Carson and John D. Woodbridge, *Scripture and Truth* (Grand Rapids, Mich.: Zondervan, 1983), especially Woodbridge and Randall Balmer's essay "The Princetonians and Biblical Authority: An Assessment of the Ernest Sandeen Proposal," pp. 245-79.

[27]Geoffrey Bromiley, "The Church Fathers and Holy Scripture," in *Scripture and Truth* (Grand Rapids, Mich.: Zondervan, 1983), pp. 195-220. See also the essay in defense of the Old Princeton position written by Robert D. Preus, president of Concordia Seminary (Lutheran), "The View of the Bible Held by the Church: The Early Church Through Luther," in *Inerrancy*, ed. Norman L. Geisler (Grand Rapids, Mich.: Zondervan, 1980), pp. 355-82.

[28]Augustine *De Consensu Evangelistarum Libri* 2.12. See also A. D. R. Polman, *Word of God According to St. Augustine* (Grand Rapids, Mich.: Eerdmans, 1961), pp. 56, 66; B. B. Warfield, *Calvin and Augustine* (Phillipsburg, N.J.: Presbyterian and Reformed, 1990), pp. 461-62.

[29]Augustine's Letter 82 to Jerome, as cited in Bahnsen in *Inerrancy*, ed. Norman L. Geisler (Grand Rapids, Mich.: Zondervan, 1980), p. 156.

Likewise, as many Reformation scholars have pointed out, Luther explicitly contends for an errorless Scripture. It is difficult to believe otherwise in the face of Luther's central teachings: "But everyone, indeed, knows that at times the Church Fathers have erred as men will; therefore, I am ready to trust them only when they prove their opinions from Scripture, which has never erred."[30] Elsewhere he states that Scripture is "perfect: it is precious and pure: it is truth itself. There is no falsehood in it."[31] And again, "Not only the *words* but also the *expressions* used by the Holy Spirit and Scripture are divine."[32] Luther contends, "One letter, even a single tittle of Scripture means more to us than heaven and earth. Therefore we cannot permit even the most minute change."[33]

Donald McKim and Jack Rogers have gone to great pains to argue that Calvin taught that the Bible was only "partially inspired" and written in "imperfect language," citing as examples his commentaries, which indicate that certain passages were not written in an "exalted style." A closer examination does not sustain this conclusion, which is based on an unfortunate misunderstanding of the characteristics of inspiration. As Robert Godfrey has illustrated so well in his essay in *Scripture and Truth*, Calvin, like the Princetonians, understood that full divine inspiration did not controvert the humanity and limitations of the biblical authors. As the Word of God incarnate could be fully human, with all the limitations that this entailed, and yet be totally free of sin and error, so the written Word of God could be fully human and yet free of sin and error.[34]

Additionally, in his commentary on Acts 7:14, John Calvin shows an understanding of the difficulties involved in transmitting the text. He comments that when the copyists' human errors are found to have corrupted the original text, they are to be corrected. This is completely harmonious with what became the great Old Princeton textual criticism project, in

---

[30]*Luther's Works* [hereafter *LW*], ed. J. Pelikan and H. T. Lehmann (Philadelphia: Fortress; and St. Louis: Concordia, 1955), 32:11. Each of the Luther quotes that follow can be found in W. Robert Godfrey, "Biblical Authority in the Sixteenth and Seventeenth Centuries: A Question of Transition," in *Scripture and Truth* (Grand Rapids, Mich.: Zondervan, 1983), p. 227.

[31]*LW*, 23:236.

[32]Cited by A. Sevington Wood, *Captive to the Word* (Grand Rapids, Mich.: Eerdmans, 1969), p. 143.

[33]Cited by Wood, *Captive to the Word*, p. 145.

[34]This is also argued in J. I. Packer's *"Fundamentalism" and the Word of God* (Grand Rapids, Mich.: Eerdmans, 1958).

search of arriving ever closer to the original, uncorrupted autographs.

Calvin held to a Bible that in its original form was inspired and error-less not only in matters pertaining to salvation but in all areas to which it intended to speak. Calvin contended that this is the sane conclusion from a close reading of the text, but that a person will only become convicted of this truth and committed to it by the special gracious work of the Holy Spirit; an emphasis again shared with Old Princeton.[35] Both Barth and Brunner contended that Calvin held to an errorless Scripture, though they both differed with Calvin on this point.[36]

William Ames, philosophical Ramist, covenant theologian and un-doubtedly not a so-called "seventeenth-century Reformed scholastic" can serve as our representative Puritan on Scripture. In his most famous work, *The Marrow of Sacred Divinity*, he provides his principles for understanding Scripture. Among these we read:

> In all those things made known by supernatural inspiration, whether matters of right or fact, God inspired not only the subjects to be written about, but suggested the very words in which they should be set forth. But this was done with a subtle tempering so that every writer might use the manner of speaking which most suited his person and condition.

Again the essential elements to our discussion are plainly present. Further, he includes an appeal to inspiration applying to the original autographs only: "Hence no versions are fully authentic except as they express the sources, by which they are also to be weighed."[37]

The normative Presbyterian creed, the Westminster Confession of Faith

---

[35]See Godfrey, "Biblical Authority in the Sixteenth and Seventeenth Centuries," pp. 225-34; J. I. Packer, "Calvin's View of Scripture," in *God's Inerrant Word*, ed. J. W. Montgomery (Minneapolis: Bethany House, 1974), pp. 95-114; John Murray, *Calvin on Scripture and Divine Sovereignty* (Grand Rapids, Mich.: Baker, 1960); Kenneth Kantzer, "Calvin and the Holy Scriptures," in *Inspiration and Interpretation*, ed. John F. Walvoord (Grand Rapids, Mich.: Eerdmans, 1957); John H. Gerstner, "The View of the Bible: Calvin and the Westminster Divines," in *Inerrancy*, ed. Norman L. Geisler (Grand Rapids, Mich.: Zondervan, 1980), pp. 383-410.

[36]That Barth believed that Calvin (and Luther) had (incorrectly, in Barth's opinion) adopted the medieval view of the full inspiration and inerrancy of Scripture, see Barth's *Church Dogmatics: Doctrine of the Word of God*, part 2 (Edinburgh: T & T Clark, 1975), pp. 520f. Similar sentiment is found in Emil Brunner, *The Christian Doctrine of God*, trans. Olive Wyon (Philadelphia: Westminster Press, 1959), p. 111.

[37]William Ames, *Marrow of Sacred Divinity*, ed. John Eusden (Boston: Pilgrim, 1968), pp. 185-86, 188-89, cited in Woodbridge and Balmer, "Princetonians and Biblical Authority," p. 257.

(1646), of course teaches the view of scriptural inspiration that the Princetonians articulated.[38] Warfield liberally quotes long passages from the writings of Richard Baxter, John Lightfoot, Bishop Ussher and other standard Reformed figures to support his position.

I could dwell on figures from church history at length and still do an inadequate job. But as even a cursory glance illustrates, what we call the Princeton view of Scripture was in the very least a viable, well-represented Christian position long before the first brick of Alexander Hall was laid down.

Let's move on, then, to the immediate nineteenth-century context. You will recall that Sandeen, McKim and Rogers, among others, charge that what has become known as the "Princeton position on Scripture" was a reaction to higher critical attacks on Scripture beginning in the 1870s. It allegedly did not crystallize until the 1881 article by A. A. Hodge and B. B. Warfield. Prior to that, some of these notions were assumed by the church because there existed no challenges to Scripture's truthfulness, but these thoughts were not yet ordered into their supposedly rigid, scholastic system. This Rogers and McKim thesis has been adopted uncritically in many circles, despite the overwhelming evidence against it. It is just so handy for those who do not like Princeton's theology—it even allows a critic to lay the blame for fundamentalism at their door.

Some of the problems with this account are obvious. First, the notion that there were no challenges to Scripture's trustworthiness prior to Wellhausen and Robertson Smith is absurd. From the beginning of the Enlightenment, at least, doubts about the Scripture's accuracy were lodged openly and often. Many an eighteenth-century rationalist enchanted large audiences with charges that the biblical narratives were myths rather than history. Doubts about the authenticity of the miracle accounts, including the resurrection, were common if unpopular. Before Darwin or Wellhausen, Voltaire was a household name. Thomas Paine, who sold 1.5 million copies of his 1791 work the *Rights of Men*, boasted in his even more popular *Age of Reason*, "I have gone through the Bible as a man would go through a wood with an ax and felled trees. Here they lie and the priest may replant them, but they will never grow."[39] To act as if there were no challenges to biblical trustworthiness prior to the rise of

---

[38]See especially its first chapter.

[39]See Iain Murray, *Revival and Revivalism* (Carlisle, Penn.: Banner of Truth, 1994), p. 113.

modern German higher criticism is frankly ridiculous.

These critics further contend that the elder Hodge (Charles) and Archibald Alexander would not have recognized the younger Hodge (A. A.) and Warfield's formulation of scriptural inspiration. As evidence they repeatedly cite a *single* illustration Charles Hodge once made in reference to difficult passages of Scripture:

> The errors in matter of fact which skeptics search out bear no proportion to the whole. No sane man would deny that the Parthenon was built of marble, even if here and there a speck of sandstone should be detected in its structure. Not less unreasonable is it to deny the inspiration of such a book as the Bible, because one sacred writer says that on a given occasion 24,000, and another says 23,000, men were slain. Surely a Christian may be allowed to tread such objections under his feet.[40]

Unfortunately these critics rarely cite Hodge's *very next* lines:

> Admitting that the Scriptures do contain, in a few instances, discrepancies which with our present means of knowledge, we are unable satisfactorily to explain, they furnish no rational ground for denying their infallibility.[41]

A few pages later in the same work Hodge states, "The whole Bible was written under such an influence as preserved its human authors from *all* error, and makes it for the Church the infallible rule of faith and practice."[42]

The case is equally as plain and obvious for Archibald Alexander. The seminary's founder wrote a book entitled *Evidences of the Authenticity, Inspiration, and Canonical Authority of the Holy Scriptures* in 1836 in which he defined inspiration as

> SUCH A DIVINE INFLUENCE UPON THE MINDS OF THE SACRED WRITERS AS RENDERED THEM EXEMPT FROM ERROR, BOTH IN REGARD TO THE IDEAS AND WORDS. This is properly called PLENARY inspiration. Nothing can be conceived more satisfactory. Certainly, infallible certainty, is the utmost that can be desired in any narrative; and if we have this in the sacred Scriptures, there is nothing more to be wished in regard to this matter.[43]

---

[40]Charles Hodge, *Systematic Theology* (Grand Rapids: Eerdmans, 1990), 1:170.

[41]Ibid.

[42]Ibid., 1:180.

[43]Archibald Alexander, *Evidences of the Authenticity, Inspiration, and Canonical Authority of the Holy Scriptures* (Philadelphia: Presbyterian Board of Publications, 1836), p. 230; cf. Woodbridge and Balmer, "The Princetonians and Biblical Authority," p. 265.

In regard to perceived errors in the Bible, Alexander notes that "some slight inaccuracies have crept into the copies of the New Testament through the carelessness of transcribers,"[44] again anticipating the thoughts of the 1881 "Inspiration" article.

As numerous historians have demonstrated, this was the general, though not unanimous, consensus of orthodox Christians of that time. There were disputes about the mode of inspiration, but most agreed on its effects: the Bible was free of error.[45] Warfield and Hodge clearly did not perceive that their article was in any way revolutionary or novel, nor, if one reads reviews of it, did their contemporaries. You will recall that Charles Briggs blamed the older Charles Hodge for the Princeton view of inspiration as much as he did the elder's son, A. A. Hodge.

Certainly a person could charge that the church was wrong about scriptural inspiration during its first nineteen hundred years, but no one can reasonably argue that the Princeton view is not historical or catholic. The uniqueness of the Princeton view is not found in what it said but in the clarity and quality with which it was articulated. It is a model for this view of inspiration because of the influence of its voice and the unmatched achievements of its proponents. It has become a target these days largely because of its immense success.

Conclusion

We now have a sketch of the way the Old Princeton divines understood Scripture. The obvious question that follows is: So what? What can be learned from all this, besides the fact that some long-departed scholars have been badly misunderstood? My intention is not to raise up a pantheon of our Princeton "household gods"—this should not be about ancestor worship. This is not intended to be merely an exercise in antiquarianism or nostalgia. I think that the Princeton experience has some profound words to speak to us today, things that need to be heard even more now than in the time that they were first spoken.

First of all, if nothing else, I believe that the Princetonians can teach us about the proper approach to reasoned theological discourse. As Balmer

---

[44]Alexander, *Evidences of the Authenticity*, p. 112.

[45]See, for example, the American Sunday School Union's *Union Bible Dictionary* (1839), the most popular book of its kind, for its article "Inspiration," as cited in Woodbridge and Balmer, "The Princetonians and Biblical Authority," p. 264.

and Woodbridge point out, there are two tempting approaches, very unhealthy but all too common, which the Princetonians never succumbed to in the midst of difficult debate. The first wrong-headed approach is one of combative dogmatism. In an individual's enthusiasm to defend the truth as he or she understands it, the person never comes to fully appreciate his or her opponents' positions. Facts become unimportant, while clever rhetorical devices are implemented. An equally wrong-headed approach is found on the other extreme. Here an individual becomes less interested in truth itself than in its pursuit. In an attempt to keep all opinions in perfect balance, he or she becomes disdainful of anyone who claims that one opinion is better or worse than another. De facto relativism sets in. Fortunately, the Old Princetonians never fell into either of these traps. Instead they eagerly engaged in lively, vigorous debate, without resorting to cheap tactics. Their Common Sense Realism approach made this possible. Unlike extreme Barthianism or certain individualistic existentialisms, Old Princeton theology was, and is, able to engage in open dialogue on Scripture because of its commitment to certain universal rational principles present in all debate partners. Further, their understanding of natural theology made them open to gaining truthful insights from even the most strident atheists.

So, if a critic finds none of the elements of the Princeton doctrine of Scripture convincing, at the very least he or she can profit from observing the Princeton model for rational discourse. Of course, the Princeton divines had much more to offer than that. All orthodox Christians over the centuries have believed that the Word of God written was central to a living, faithful relationship to our Lord. Understanding the nature of God's self-disclosure to his people can seem like a greased pig, especially to the modern believer set amidst a swirling galaxy of contradictory theories about the Bible. If we are indeed called to submit ourselves to the authority of this book, there are immensely complicated issues that must be resolved. Few, if any, of these difficulties were not engaged in an extremely sophisticated and thoughtful, yet warm-hearted, manner by the Princeton divines. Their work offers an excellent place to discover clues for escaping the modern epistemological maze. If nothing else, a person who has engaged the Old Princetonians will find that his or her focus is continually on the God of grace, whose precious Word will never pass away.

PART 3

CHRISTOLOGY

7

IS THE DOCTRINE OF THE INCARNATION COHERENT?

JAY WESLEY RICHARDS

Christ is a merciful and faithful high-priest. He is just the Savior we need.
God as God, the eternal Logos, could neither be nor do what our necessities demand.
Much less could any mere man, however wise, holy, or benevolent,
meet the wants of our souls. It is only a Savior who is both God and man
in two distinct natures and one person forever,
who is all we need and all we can desire. As God He is ever present,
almighty and infinite in all his resources to save and bless;
and as man, or being also a man, He can be touched with a sense of our infirmities,
was tempted as we are, was subject to the law which we violated,
and endured the penalty which we had incurred.
In Him dwells all the fullness of the Godhead, in a bodily form,
in fashion as a man, so as to be accessible to us,
and so that from his fullness we can all partake.
We are therefore complete in Him, wanting nothing.

CHARLES HODGE, *SYSTEMATIC THEOLOGY*

THE AUTHORS OF THE CONTROVERSIAL *MYTH OF GOD INCARNATE* SEEK TO identify numerous errors in the traditional incarnational formula articulated at the council of Chalcedon (A.D. 451). Most of their criticisms need not be particularly troubling to Christians committed to biblical authority and a supernatural God. However, one claim may invoke pangs of doubt for such a Christian: the charge of *incoherence*. This charge is not new to twentieth-century theology. But if it proved true, the Christian who confesses the Chalcedonian understanding of Jesus as "truly God and truly human" would be guilty of affirming not just a falsehood but sheer nonsense.

Most of their charges are easily refuted by exposing their philosophical and theological commitments. For example, they clearly share Friedrich Schleiermacher's understanding of religious language as essentially experiential and derivative. They evince embarrassment at the metaphysical and ontological realism of the Chalcedonian formulation and its resultant soteriological exclusivism. They are acutely aware of the need for modern Christianity to adapt itself to "something which can be believed by honest and thoughtful people who are deeply attracted by the figure of Jesus and by the light which his teaching throws upon the meaning of human life."[1] And in attempting to contrast the biblical witness of Jesus and the Chalcedonian creed, they frequently contrast not the actual biblical text (particularly the Gospel of John) but their own naturalistic reconstruction of Jesus as he "really was." However, because the claim of incoherence of the traditional doctrine of the incarnation is the strongest accusation made by the authors, it is to this claim that we should attend.

Although this indictment takes various forms, John Hick puts it clearly and starkly:

> Orthodoxy insisted upon the two natures, human and divine, cohering in the one historical Jesus Christ. But orthodoxy has never been able to give this idea any content. It remains a form of words without assignable meaning. For to say, without explanation, that the historical Jesus of Nazareth was also God is as devoid of meaning as to say that this circle drawn with a pencil on paper is also a square.[2]

Since incoherence entails impossibility, Hick insists that Chalcedonian incarnationalism should be relegated to the category of *myth*, an idea or image that, while not "literally true," is "applied to someone or something ... which invites a particular attitude in its hearers. Thus the truth of a

---

[1]John Hick, ed., *The Myth of God Incarnate* (Philadelphia: Westminster Press, 1977), p. ix. Tellingly, the 1993 reprint does not earnestly address the criticisms considered here.
[2]Ibid., p. 178.

myth is a kind of practical truth consisting in the appropriateness of the attitude to its object."[3]

Hick is clear: the traditional incarnation doctrine does not convey metaphysical truth or a christological, ontological proposition but expresses the feelings and religious experiences of its adherents. Whether or not Hick is correct, there should be no doubt that this was *not* the intention of the five hundred bishops and representatives who met at Chalcedon in A.D. 451. An affirmation of incoherence does not appropriately express the attitude of the bishops at Chalcedon, and it is not the intention of the vast majority of Christians who claim to believe it as objectively true. The average Christian believes he or she is affirming a truth prior to and separate from his or her belief in it. If millions of Christians over a fifteen-hundred-year span have believed something actually incoherent, transferring the belief to the realm of myth will not solve the problem.

From the square circle analogy, we can infer that Hick assumes that the concept of *humanity* and the concept of *divinity* contain essential properties that are logical complements of each other (i.e., they are mutually exclusive). Therefore, such properties cannot be predicated of one and the same individual, in this case, Jesus of Nazareth. If such an assumption were true, the claim of incoherence would prevail. But is it clear that humanity and divinity stand in such logically complementary positions to each other? I think not, but before considering a potential refutation we should grant that the incoherence charge has a certain prima facie plausibility. After all, Christians insist, as Scripture clearly teaches, that there is an immense ontological difference between God the Creator and human creatures[4]—infinite versus finite, omniscient versus nescient, uncreated versus created. Just how is it that both humanity and divinity can be predicated of Jesus? Every Christian theologian has struggled over this question, from the first century to the twentieth. Before we glibly offer an answer to the dilemma, we should admit honestly the difficulty of what we declare to be the truth of the incarnation.

Nevertheless, in the end I think Hick is wrong and can be shown to be so with the help of proper distinctions and philosophical categories. To be vindicated from the accusation of incoherence, the defender of the incarnation need only show that there is a *possible* formulation of it that does

---

[3]Ibid.
[4]Ibid., p. 18.

not violate the logical requirement of the indiscernibility of identicals. That is, for a person to claim that the man Jesus is the same individual as God the Son, the former must share "all and only the properties" of the latter.[5]

But before we note how the doctrine of the incarnation can be pulled free from this contest, we should consider the other (I think legitimate) option available to us, particularly as believers in divine revelation: mystery or paradox. Paradox has always been a part of the Christian tradition and enjoys a fairly prominent role in traditions such as Lutheranism. Paul glories in the fact that God should choose such a lowly means as the cross to display his power and confound the wisdom of the Greeks (1 Cor 1:18-31). In fact, the very transcendence of God should lead us to suspect that some of his truth can only be affirmed in human categories by means of paradox, an *apparent* self-contradiction. At the very least, it should make us suspicious of detractors such as Hick who imply that the attributes of divinity relative to humanity are as distinct as those of a square to a circle. If we truly believe in such a God, we should not be dismayed by our relative inability to understand or define his revelation to us.

Christians loyal to Chalcedon are not the only ones to appeal to paradox. Frances Young, another contributor to *The Myth of God Incarnate*, after rejecting the traditional view of incarnation as nonsense, resorts to paradox to explain her experience as a Christian: "The Christian believer lives in more than one dimension."[6] She even marshals the support of the scientific analogy of the seemingly contrary views of light as both particle and wave, depending on the context.[7] If even science is allowed the use of paradox every so often, why isn't she? We may think her point valid, although we may be baffled at her willingness to reject a traditional christological paradox only to make up her own existential one!

An individual might legitimately conclude that the Chalcedonian theologians felt compelled to settle for paradox in their creed.[8] After all,

---

[5]Morris describes this briefly in *The Logic of God Incarnate* (Ithaca, N.Y.: Cornell University Press, 1986), pp. 17-18.

[6]Frances Young, "Two Roots or a Tangled Mess?" in *The Myth of God Incarnate*, ed. John Hick (Philadelphia: Westminster Press, 1977), p. 33.

[7]Ibid.

[8]For a sophisticated—and difficult—treatment of Chalcedon which appropriates and partially transcends this spirit of paradox, see James E. Loder and W. Jim Neidhardt, *The Knight's Move* (Colorado Springs, Colo.: Helmers & Howard, 1992).

every christological heresy that the church had had to combat had assumed that "humanity and divinity are not compossibly exemplifiable by one and the same bearer of properties."[9] For the sake of consistency the Arians, Nestorians and Eutychians had all abandoned one horn of the dilemma, only to be impaled on the other. The formulators at Chalcedon sought to affirm what was clear from the biblical data but exclude the possibility of the errors that had arisen since Nicaea.[10] The creed might have been more a set of boundaries beyond which the faithful must not go, rather than an explication of the intricacies of the incarnation. While this may have been the beginning of centuries of frustration for Christian theologians, it nevertheless served to preserve the tension and the mystery of the incarnation. It also signals the importance of biblical authority for the framers of the creed.[11] If they were primarily concerned with Hellenizing the biblical Jesus, as the authors of *The Myth of God Incarnate* imply, they could have made it much more congenial to logic.

Having said this, we might agree that an appeal to paradox could "protect" us from the skeptic's charge but still feel some unease because the difference between paradox and self-contradiction is very difficult to determine. How can we know we are not merely shrouding nonsense? The orthodox will eschew any Hegelian funky fusion of the natures into a heterodox synthesis, but I would like to demonstrate that the charge of inevitable incoherence is false. Moreover, any appeal to mystery and paradox may unwittingly play into the hand of trendy agnosticism. Fortunately, we are not left in such a frustrating quandary. We may have to conclude that Chalcedon was left with paradox because of the philosophical categories available to its framers; nevertheless, we may be in a position to resolve it (at least partially). Some paradoxes may be irreconcilable in a certain conceptual framework, such as the wave-corpuscular views of light. But others can be resolved by further developments.

In 1890 the scientist Ludwig Boltzmann was forced to postulate a series of paradoxes within the paradigm of classical mechanics in order to account for known facts about thermal energy. Later these paradoxes were

---

[9]Morris, *Logic of God Incarnate*, p. 20.

[10]Craig A. Blaising, "Chalcedon and Christology: A 1530th Anniversary," *Bibliotheca Sacra* 138 (October-December 1981): 326-27.

[11]Ibid., pp. 330-34.

resolved by Niels Bohr's account of the structure of the atom.[12] Similarly, elements of Greek philosophy may have hindered the council at Chalcedon from moving beyond paradox. But a biblically loyal contemporary articulation might not be so hindered.

Since the apparent contradictions in the doctrine of the incarnation involve what are taken to be essential and logically incompatible properties of human nature and divine nature, any nuance or correction will most likely occur at this level. We may begin by asking: Is it really so obvious that God and human beings occupy such mutually exclusive logical territories?[13] In addition, we must answer the question: What are our primary commitments? If the incarnation is one such commitment, we should be willing to formulate our understanding of human and divine nature in light of it. This does not mean we must reject all a priori intuitions on these matters but only that such intuitions should be subject to correction by the reality of the incarnation. Alongside allergic reactions to all things supernatural and metaphysical, this seems to be a central problem for the authors of *The Myth of God Incarnate*. They evince a complete refusal to allow the incarnation to function as a "control belief." *Their definitions of humanity and divinity are decided prior to any consideration of the incarnation, and these definitions automatically defeat the doctrine.* So Frances Young tellingly asserts:

> Jesus cannot be a *real* man and also unique in a sense different from that in which each one of us is a unique individual. A literal incarnation doctrine, expressed in however a sophisticated a form, cannot avoid some element of docetism, and involves the believer in claims for uniqueness which seem straightforwardly incredible to the majority of our contemporaries.[14]

In other words, any element of real divinity in Jesus—which is the very *point* of the incarnation—is ruled out of bounds from the beginning. And of course, if Young rules out all elements of incarnation by definition, we should not be surprised that she rejects it. She insists on a definition of "real manness" that excludes the incarnation's very possibility. The uncharitable call this *stacking the deck.*

The incarnationist, on the other hand, will *begin* with the truth of Jesus

---

[12]Alasdair MacIntyre, *Whose Justice? Which Rationality?* (South Bend, Ind.: University of Notre Dame Press, 1988), p. 363.

[13]Herbert McCabe, *God Matters* (London: Geoffrey Chapman, 1987), p. 57.

[14]Young, "Two Roots or a Tangled Mess," p. 32.

as one person with two natures, truly God and truly human, and define essential human (and divine) properties in order to accommodate this claim. To succeed the incarnationist must insist that some attributes normally assumed to be kind-essential to a human being, while they may be nearly universal, are not in fact essential properties for the particular kind *human.* So, for instance, *createdness* may be a property assumed to be essential to the human being, but its universality does not prove its essentiality.[15] *Conception-in-the-womb-of-one's-mother* may earlier have been mistakenly categorized as an essential property of human beings because of its apparent universality. But the birth of the first test-tube baby disproved this intuition. Therefore we need to be very careful about which properties we assign as essential for the kind "human."

It might be the case that all human beings happen to have the property of createdness without this createdness being a necessary, that is, an *essential* property. And so someone (say Jesus) might have the property of eternality in some sense, while still being fully human. All other human beings, also fully human, would thus be *merely* human.[16] Jesus, while fully human, is not *merely* human. He possesses a "higher" set of properties that also makes him fully divine. A similar strategy may then be pursued until the other properties of the human being assumed to be essential by virtue of their apparent universality are "adjusted" or properly nuanced to make room for the possibility of an incarnation.

We need not be swayed by any overly restrictive definition, such as Frances Young's, of a "real man." Nor need we be intimidated by "the present climate" which is "alien to the whole Christian position as traditionally conceived."[17] *While we may hope that we are accepted by our peers outside the church (and even inside), our primary source of authority is not the Zeitgeist* but the revelation of God given to us in Scripture. Insofar as the Chalcedonian creed is a true articulation of that revelation, we are committed to it. The incarnation of God the Son will therefore be the organizing principle of our understanding of the essential properties of the human being and not vice versa. As we will see, this strategy can be

---

[15]Thomas V. Morris, "The Metaphysics of God Incarnate," in *Trinity, Incarnation, and Atonement,* ed. R. Feenstra and C. Plantinga (South Bend, Ind.: University of Notre Dame Press, 1989), p. 116.

[16]Ibid., 117.

[17]Young, "Two Roots or a Tangled Mess?" p. 32.

employed successfully in different ways. Still they all serve to vindicate the doctrine of the incarnation from the charge of its incoherence.

As in so many theological controversies, much seems to revolve around the issue of *authority*. The authors of *The Myth of God Incarnate* assume the traditional view of the incarnation must be judged in the light of inhospitable, even hostile, a priori definitions of humanity and divinity, plus whatever they deem is "intelligible" to a contemporary audience. The cult of the *current* is their authority. Not surprisingly, they judge the doctrine to be incoherent. But for those who trust the authority of Scripture and, derivatively, the Chalcedonian creed, such historical myopia may be rejected. At the very least we are warranted in judging Chalcedon and orthodox christology innocent of the charges leveled against them, unless and until *proven* guilty. We should seek to conform our ideas about God and humanity in the light of the incarnation, since this, not the contempt of our skeptical peers, is our primary authority for considering such matters.

How then to defend the traditional doctrine of the incarnation against the charge of incoherence? If a model can be found that is merely *possible*, the incoherence claim fails. As noted earlier the believer who is committed to the truth of the incarnation will allow that belief to "adjust" his or her definitions of divinity and humanity. This does not mean that a priori intuitions (including the *via negativa* and *via eminentiae*) are all rejected; rather, they are liable to "correction" in light of the incarnation if such correction is deemed necessary to accommodate the reality of the incarnation. Some properties initially thought to be kind-essential to humanity or divinity may have to be ruled *accidental* or common but not *essential* properties. At the least such essential properties may have to be carefully qualified, particularly in the kenotic model. Although numerous formulations are possible, we will look at two fairly plausible ones: the two-minds view, proposed by Thomas Morris, and the careful kenotic view of Ronald Feenstra. Both affirm the Chalcedonian conviction of Jesus as "truly human" and "truly God," and both are coherent. They do not disagree over the reality of the incarnation, which is not itself a model[18] but rather the specific ontological manner of incarnation. Both proposals take seriously the relevant biblical witness, seeking to maintain integrity to the

---

[18]Brian Hebblethwaite, *The Incarnation* (Cambridge: Cambridge University Press, 1987), p. 9.

bases of Christian authority while explicating the doctrine in an intelligible fashion.

Morris wishes to maintain Anselmian intuitions of the divine attributes, in which "God is thought of as exemplifying necessarily a maximally perfect set of compossible great-making properties."[19] Such a commitment may initially appear to make his task more difficult, but if successful he could not be accused of diminishing fairly agreed upon divine attributes in order to "rescue" incarnational doctrine from its detractors. Given Anselmian commitments Morris grants prima facie validity to a number of divine attributes such as omniscience and omnipotence, which are thought to be *necessary* attributes of God. Therefore God could not maintain his divinity if he failed to exemplify such attributes. This strategy seems a good one, for as he argues: "If such an exalted conception of divinity can be squared with the doctrine of the Incarnation, then presumably more modest conceptions can be as well."[20] Undoubtedly, the "more modest conceptions" he has in mind are the kenotic theories.

Granting the Anselmian properties, which Morris takes as comprising a divine kind essence,[21] he makes a few important distinctions. The first is between *kind* essence, "that cluster of properties without which . . . an individual would not belong to the particular natural kind it distinctively exemplifies," and an *individual* essence, "a cluster of properties essential for an individual's being the particular entity it is . . . without which it would not exist."[22] By definition an individual can possess only one individual essence, but there is no logical necessity barring the possibility that some individual, say Jesus, possesses more than one kind essence.

The second distinction is between common or *universal* properties and *essential* properties. Universal properties do not imply necessity. All humans may have been born on earth. But a future person who is born aboard a space station would not be excluded from the human race because birth-on-earth is not a property essential for being human. Similarly, properties like finitude, nescience and nonomnipresence may be

---

[19]Thomas V. Morris, *The Logic of God Incarnate* (Ithaca, N.Y.: Cornell University Press, 1986), p. 76.

[20]Morris, "Metaphysics of God," p. 114.

[21]Ibid.

[22]Ibid., p. 115.

universal for human beings without being necessary.[23]

This leads to the third distinction between being *fully* human and being *merely* human. We are all fully human in that we possess whatever kind-essential properties that are required to make us human. But we are merely human as well; we have only the kind essence of humanity. So Jesus may be fully human without being merely human.[24]

With these distinctions Morris is logically free to predicate certain "divine" properties of Jesus, who possesses two kind essences. Still, he is committed to squaring his theory with the biblical portrayal of Jesus, a person who lacked omniscience, became physically tired and generally exhibited the limiting capacity of a human body and mind. How can a person predicate omniscience and omnipotence to such an individual? Morris seeks to do this by proposing the *two-minds* view, whereby the incarnation

> involved not just a duality of abstract natures, but a duality of consciousness or mentality which was thus introduced into the divine life of God the Son. The two minds of Christ should be thought of as standing in something like an asymmetric accessing relation: the human mind was contained by but did not itself contain the divine mind, or, to portray it from the other side, the divine mind contained, but was not contained by, the human mind.[25]

Although the divine mind of the Son had perfect access to the human mind of Jesus, his human mind had the restraints of a "normal" human mind. Jesus as a mere human individual does not exist. Rather Jesus exists only as ontologically unified with the divine person and mind of God the Son. So this union is *not* analogous to the access God has to other human minds, who are separate individuals. Nor does it amount to saying that in Jesus Christ we have two persons (which would surely be heresy).

While this proposal may at first appear difficult to imagine, it has much in common with some contemporary psychology, neurology and philosophy of mind. As an analogy we might imagine the dual aspect of a dream in which a person is participating in the dream while simultaneously being aware that he or she is dreaming.[26] Many theorists imagine the

---

[23]Ibid., p. 116.
[24]Ibid., p. 117.
[25]Ibid., pp. 121-22.
[26]Ibid., p. 122.

human mind not as a system but as a "system of systems of mentality."[27] These examples may be somewhat esoteric, but anyone can imagine the existence of opposed wills within his or her own mind. So while we may have only partial analogies to the two-minds view, I judge it both intelligible and coherent.

A second possible model appropriates the notion of *kenosis*, whereby God the Son "emptied" himself of whatever attributes (or aspects of attributes) would conflict with him being "fully human" in the person Jesus. Some earlier formulations of kenotic christology are guilty of abandoning the divine attributes as essential, in conflict with the majority of traditional Christian theology. As such they are vulnerable to the charge made by *The Myth of God Incarnate* authors that they resolve the tension by giving up one half of the dilemma. So even a modern kenotic partisan is willing to conclude: "The fact that I believe both that Jesus Christ was God and that Jesus Christ was non-omniscient leads me to deny that omniscience is essential to God."[28] Since by definition an essential property cannot be removed from an individual without altering the identity of that individual, we can only ascribe divinity to the nonomniscient Jesus by denying the attribute of omniscience as kind essential to divinity. While such a strategy is capable of resolving logical difficulties, I think it does too much violence to both the tradition and Anselmian intuitions.

However, Feenstra does not seek to *deny* divine properties such as omniscience as essential to God but to *define* them carefully. So, to make room for incarnation—or, in light of the incarnation—we may say that omniscience in just any sense is not an essential property for God to be God but rather "omniscience-unless-freely-and-temporarily-choosing-to-be-otherwise."[29] If this is what we mean by divine omniscience, then it could consistently be predicated of God in general and of Jesus in particular. Other attributes such as omnipotence and omnipresence, if understood broadly as potential *access* to ultimate power, could be ascribed to Jesus because he may have possessed such power (e.g., in the Gospel temptation narratives) but freely chosen to give it up temporarily. God the

---

[27]Ibid., p. 123.

[28]Stephen T. Davis, *Logic and the Nature of God* (Grand Rapids, Mich.: Eerdmans, 1983), p. 124.

[29]Ronald Feenstra, "Reconsidering Kenotic Christology," in *Trinity, Incarnation, and Atonement,* ed. R. Feenstra and C. Plantinga (South Bend, Ind.: University of Notre Dame Press, 1989), p. 140.

Son, in preexistence and exaltation, would enjoy this full exercise of these attributes but would temporarily suspend them while incarnate on earth for the purpose of redemption—a capacity built in to the *definitions* of the divine attributes.

While Feenstra makes some other distinctions to avoid the accusation that the kenotic Jesus loses his humanity once exalted, this cursory description should suffice to make the two models clear. As I see it, the two proposals could be generally distinguished by what they "alter" in light of the truth of the incarnation. Both agree that the incarnation is a controlling factor and that a priori definitions of either divinity or human-ity should not be allowed to defeat the Christian affirmation of God the Son's actual incarnation in the man Jesus. For the two-minds view, prior-ity is given to the Anselmian attributes of divinity, and so Morris alters the kind-essential properties of "humanness" to resolve the dilemma. Feen-stra, on the other hand, qualifies these divine attributes to make room for the biblical witness to Jesus' "limitedness." So the locus of qualification for the two-minds view seems to be "humanity," and for the kenotic view, "divinity." Both seek to be faithful to Scripture and Chalcedon, but the kenotic view gives less authority to Anselmian intuitions. Both appear to be coherent. If all this is true, how shall we decide which one is prefera-ble?

Although Morris's loyalty to an Anselmian view of God as a maximally perfect being is obvious, I do not think Feenstra would reject the definition of God as a maximally perfect being. What we seem to have is a disagree-ment about *which* properties are the most perfect. Simply put, we have a clash of intuitions.[30] Feenstra would surely object to the accusation that he presents divine attributes that are less than superlative. He could simply argue that a definition of, for example, omniscience that includes the abil-ity to suspend such a capacity is greater than a definition that lacks that capacity. Morris could counter that the ability to suspend omniscience is no more an improvement of necessary omniscience than the ability to sin is an improvement of necessary goodness. It is rather a diminution of the divine property of omniscience. And around we could go with every other attribute, agreeing that God possesses a perfect cluster of attributes but dis-agreeing on what those attributes are.

---

[30]Thomas V. Morris, ed., *The Concept of God* (New York: Oxford University Press, 1987), p. 7.

If the disagreement does in fact exist at the level of intuition, then neither exegetical arguments nor logical arguments will settle the matter (except, perhaps for Philippians 2, which the kenoticist has as a small hook for his theory). One criticism can be given against the kenotic model that is not true of the two-minds view: It seems to depart from the majority of intuitions of the theologians in the historical church. In fact, the passages quoted by Morris from Pope Leo and Athanasius seem to run directly counter to the kenotic strategy.[31] The two-minds model on the other hand seems to be directly in line with the commitments of Leo and Athanasius. So while lesser criticisms about general neatness, satisfaction and plausibility could be raised against the two models, Morris's commitment to the historical Anselmian divine attributes gives the two-minds view a very slight edge over the kenotic one in my opinion. I still think that the kenotic view gives up too much in order to formulate a coherent picture of the incarnation. But I must admit that my conclusion rests on no point of exegesis or logic but rather on intuition.

However, there is a more basic point that we may have forgotten. If we must appeal to intuition to criticize one or the other of these two models, then they *both* appear to be successful in what we might suspect is their primary goal: to articulate a coherent model of the incarnation that is faithful to both Scripture and Chalcedon. To succeed, they need not even assert that their proposal is true but only that it is possible and thus coherent. Insofar as the two-minds view and kenotic model we have considered are able to do this, the charge of incoherence in books like *The Myth of God Incarnate* misses the mark and falls to the ground. Without this formidable accusation, theologians committed to the Christian tradition are free to reflect on and to affirm without undue worry the truth of God incarnate.

---

[31]Morris, "Metaphysics of God Incarnate," p. 120.

8

CHRISTOLOGY & THE "Y" CHROMOSOME

MICHAEL D. BUSH

T HE STATEMENT IN THE APOSTLES' CREED THAT JESUS CHRIST "WAS CON-
ceived by the Holy Ghost and born of the Virgin Mary" does not require
any special explanation. In the biblical narratives of the birth of Jesus this
episode appears in the sequence of events leading to his passion and resurrection. After its appearance in Matthew and Luke nothing special is
made of it. Compared with Hesiod's tale about the emergence of the full-
grown and fully armed Athena from Zeus's head, the story of Jesus' birth is
treated with distinctive modesty and chasteness as one fact among others
that are given about him. In the Bible the unique origin of Jesus Christ is
stated without histrionics, with the same simplicity that is equally striking
in the Easter narratives. Our Lord's mortal life is bracketed by events that
point to his utter uniqueness: he enters the stream of human existence
from outside, in a way that can only look improbable from within, and
rises up out of that stream on the other side, having crossed it diagonally
in the downstream direction; and again the departure—his resurrection
from death to perfected life—can only be surprising and perhaps even
incredible from our point of view from within the stream. Yet the Bible
tells us about them with simple, disciplined language.

The New Testament treats its testimony to Jesus' unique origin as straightforward reporting. Jesus' conception as a human fetus within his mother, without the involvement of a human father, is simply given to us as the original fact about the human life of Jesus. After the passion the tomb is just empty. The New Testament simply records "he is not here" until he appears again the same and yet even more himself. All this is given to us in an unpresumptuous, nonanxious narrative, apparently assuming that the divine power of the reality it depicts is able to create its own credibility with those who have ears to hear.

The Problem of the Y Chromosome

Arthur Peacocke is an articulate spokesman for the case against virgin conception as a meaningful and intelligible doctrine. His basic objection is scientific, and from this he concludes to a further theological objection. The basic problem, according to him, centers on the Y chromosome: "For Mary to have been pregnant with the foetus that became Jesus without the involvement of a human father—that is, without a Y chromosome from (say) Joseph—there are, biologically, only two possibilities. Either (1) Mary provided the ovum which was then transformed by an act of God (impregnation by the Holy Spirit?) into a viable, reproducing cell, as if a sperm had entered the ovum; or (2) there was created such an impregnated ovum within her uterus with no contribution from Mary's own genetic heritage at all."[1] Peacocke concludes that either part (in case 1) or all (in case 2) of Jesus' genetic constitution would have had to be created *de novo* by God at the time of Jesus' conception.

This conclusion is unacceptable to Peacocke for at least three reasons. First, he thinks any such scenario is simply improbable on scientific grounds. The second objection is theological, in that he is concerned that these possibilities are not consistent with the doctrines of God and of creation he has suggested and elaborated earlier in his book in which he says, "It is possible today to believe."[2] The third objection he raises is that, in either case, "it is impossible to see how Jesus could be said to share our human nature" if he were not fully located in the stream of human evolution.[3] His objections then are that to affirm a virginal conception of Jesus is

---

[1]Arthur Peacocke, *Theology for a Scientific Age: Being and Becoming—Natural, Divine, and Human* (Minneapolis: Fortress, 1993), p. 276.

[2]Ibid., p. 277.

[3]Ibid.

to posit an event that is known on scientific grounds never otherwise to occur, to contradict his understanding of who God is and how God acts, and to posit a form of Docetism.

I take it as axiomatic that the reasons for accepting or denying a theory in any field of inquiry must in the final analysis be internal to the field, even if the original insight that leads to the decision comes in from somewhere else. This means that in theology a person looks for genuinely theological reasons for revising or affirming a doctrine or theory or model, even when the motivating insight has come in from somewhere else.

If this is true, then on the face of it Peacocke's assertion that the virginal conception of Jesus should be denied because it places at risk the genuine humanity of Jesus Christ would seem to have real force. The point is internal to theology, and in my opinion Peacocke has given the two conflicting issues (the true humanity of Christ and the virginity of Mary) the correct weight; that is, the humanity of Christ is the more important to preserve and therefore "trumps" the virginity of Mary, if there is a genuine conflict between the two. However, I do not believe that Peacocke has made the case that such a conflict exists.

First of all there is the historical point of which Peacocke is aware, that precisely the *denial* of the doctrine and not its affirmation has been associated with Docetism in the history of Christian thought. Those who wish to deny the true embodiment of God in the human life of Jesus of Nazareth have also, indeed *therefore*, denied the virginity of Mary. Peacocke argues that in light of what we now know about conception, the point now cuts in the opposite direction. We will have to talk about the status of the Y chromosome below and how Jesus might have gotten one, but on this historical point it is enough to observe that whatever may be the case in theory, the denial of virgin conception has historically been associated with a whole range of heterodox Christologies including the Docetic.

The kerygmatic doctrine of virgin conception, once made an article of the creed, was related to the concept of incarnation by affirming that in Mary's womb the Word of God, in an utterly unique event, has become truly human in the way that we are human. It was a statement that Docetists could not affirm. The point was that Jesus developed *in utero* in the normal human way and had a normal human birth, even though he was the Son of God and not of a human father. Something along these lines simply follows from what J. N. D. Kelly calls "the double premise of apostolic Christology, viz. that Christ as a Person was indivisibly one, and that

He was simultaneously fully divine and fully human."[4] It is worthwhile to note this historical point because one of the guiding ideas in what we might call theological "theory choice," as with theory choice in the sciences, is continuity with what we already know. But the historical point does not cut to the heart of Peacocke's claim that the doctrine of virgin conception entails a kind of Docetism. The crux of the matter is the Y chromosome.

Peacocke's charge of Docetism against this doctrine arises from the problem of a Y chromosome in Jesus' genetic makeup, which he had to have had since he was male. With this basic biological fact, we can gladly agree. It does seem to be an "assured result of science," which is no more likely to be disproved than is the roundness of the earth, that genetically normal males have a chromosome that is designated "Y," which carries the genetic material that makes for maleness. Peacocke is obviously right that if Jesus did not have a Y chromosome, he was not, as we believe, truly human, because all men have such a chromosome. The only question is how he got it, and for an answer there are two proposals on the table: either he got it directly from a man, presumably Joseph, who impregnated Jesus' mother in the normal, sexual way, or God provided it in a unique, providential act. Thus far Peacocke and the ecumenical tradition are of one mind.

However, a claim that, if we affirm the virgin conception of Jesus, God would have had to provide a Y chromosome in some way, would not entail that Jesus was not truly human. This is because, assuming (as everyone presumably does) that Jesus had a Y chromosome, the mere fact that he did not receive it from within the stream of human generation does not call his biological humanity into question. If we suppose that Jesus was in the basic biological, chromosomal sense, human, then that is all we need to know. If a modern scientist, say a paleontologist, were able to evaluate Jesus' body, including his chromosomal material, to answer the question whether he was truly human, he or she would, everyone supposes, find that he was. The question is how he came by that body with those chromosomes—through the evolutionary process or in some other way would not come up within the terms of the examination and therefore would not be used to answer the question of his true humanity.

---

[4]J. N. D. Kelly, *Early Christian Doctrines* (San Francisco: Harper & Row, 1978), p. 139. See also J. N. D. Kelly, *Early Christian Creeds* (New York: Longman, 1972).

There are at least two other problems with Peacocke's requirement that for Jesus to be human all his genetic material had to come to him through the normal process. First, it implies a materialist anthropology, and one that turns out not to do at least one thing any anthropology that claims to have theological significance should do, namely give a plausible answer to the question, What is a human being, in distinction from other animals? Peacocke implies that one sine qua non of human beings is full participation in the general evolutionary stream of generation. Yet it is not simply human life but all life as we know it that participates in this biological process. Obviously then such participation cannot be the distinctive characteristic of humanity. Second, this requirement begs the question of the uniqueness of the incarnation, which, as I shall argue later, is virtually the whole content of the doctrine of the virgin conception.

I believe that to suppose that God provided (in some way we cannot know) a Y chromosome in Jesus' cellular makeup does not entail a denial of his genuine humanity. The only question is whether a genetically human Y chromosome was present. Everything we know speaks for and nothing against the supposition that it was. With this bit of reckoning any question of our Lord's true humanity, and therefore of Docetism implicit in the doctrine of virgin conception, is at an end. Peacocke's question about what might be supposed to be encoded on Jesus' Y chromosome is a red herring. At the most mundane, practical level it is irrelevant since we have no reason for thinking Jesus had any children; thus there are no consequences for the evolutionary process, the integrity of which Peacocke is so anxious to defend. More importantly, though, the question is speculative almost to the point of making the Y chromosome a piece of metaphysics.

Consistency with the Concept of God

Peacocke argues throughout his book that the concept of God "in which it is possible to believe" in a scientific age is one that describes a God who does not make exceptions in any sense to the laws of the created order, to which God has in a self-limiting way also agreed to subject the divine purposes and intentions. In a way reminiscent of but not fully continuous with process thought, he speaks of "divine being and becoming."[5] He

---

[5]Sections of *Theology for a Scientific Age* have titles such as "Divine Being and Becoming," "Human Being and Becoming" and "Divine Being Becoming Human."

believes that genuinely random chance functions in the world as a part of the creative process, so that there are occurrences in the world that God does not know before they occur, which are therefore outside God's providence.

It is fully consistent with Peacocke's idea of God that a virgin conception, whether of Jesus or of any living creature, is to be rejected. For such a thing to happen, the only possibility imaginable is that "God must suddenly have brought into existence either (1) a complete spermatozoon, which then entered an ovum of Mary or (2) a completely fertilized ovum. Each of these biological entities, especially the second, is an enormously complex system of actual molecules, some very large such as DNA, engaged in dynamic biological activity in an organization as, or rather more, complex than that of a modern factory!"[6]

The implication apparently is that such a thing would be hard, impossibly hard, for God to do! This claim does not even rise to the level of classical paganism in its conception of God. At least old pagans regarded the gods as the most powerful beings in the universe. It seems that in Peacocke's view, God stands on the scale of cleverness and ability somewhere below a good engineer. Moreover, as Peacocke sees it, to provide a sperm or fully fertilized egg is something that God simply would not do even if he could: "All the evidence is that is *not* how God has created and is creating, as explained in Part I—certainly not the God whose mode of being and becoming we have here been discerning as one in whom it is possible today to believe."[7]

As I intimated above, there is very little common ground between someone whose faith in God falls along such lines and someone else who begins rather with a privileging of the biblical witness on which we could stand to hold a productive conversation. This is very near our theological axioms, the theses that we take to be beyond either the possibility or the necessity of proof. Another way to put it is that Peacocke is operating out of the matrix of English natural theology in which there is a minimization of the role of the Christian Bible as a source of knowledge, and a privileging of the theoretical and practical insights of experimental reason. Another perspective, which I at least would advocate, joins a higher regard for the testimony of the apostles and prophets with a conviction

---

[6]Peacocke, *Theology for a Scientific Age*, p. 277.
[7]Ibid.

that human experience is too corrupted by self-interest to be of much use for theology.

Scientific Implausibility

Peacocke has another objection with which we must contend more vigorously, namely, that given the well-established biological reality of this world, the idea of virgin conception is simply implausible and to be rejected out of hand for the general reason that this is not how babies are made. Peacocke argues, in chorus with every skeptic:

> The relevant facts, determined by the biology of the last one hundred and fifty years, are as follows. Any complete human being begins life by the union of an ovum from a female human being and a spermatozoon from a male one. . . . In the formation of ova and spermatozoa ordinary, somatic cells split so that the members of the various pairs of chromosomes separate out into new "half–cells" (an ovum and a sperm cell) containing one union of two such "half–cells" one from each parent. The mother *always* contributes an X-type chromosome to this new line of cells while the father contributes *either* an X *or* a Y; . . . This is how all human beings begin.[8]

Peacocke is implying, and rightly so if the data that fall under the analysis of "the biology of the last one hundred and fifty years" explain the case of every human life utterly without remainder, that there has never been a human life of whom this process did not obtain in the same way that it obtains for every other. If this is the case, and Jesus is assumed to be truly human, the impossibility on simple biological grounds of his being conceived "without the involvement of a human father"[9] simply follows. Under an empty sky or even in a universe inhabited by the kind of "divine being and becoming" that Peacocke postulates, there is no alternative.

If we can imagine no more powerful meaning of the doctrine of virgin conception than that it is "a wonderworking magical kind of act,"[10] *still more if we suppose it to be nothing more than a legendary story, then we are defeated by the weight of the evidence of biology and experience.*

It turns out though that certainly as early as the end of the second century and (if Raymond Brown is correct) already in the New Testament, it was precisely the natural implausibility of virgin conception that gave

---

[8]Ibid., p. 275.
[9]Ibid.
[10]Ibid., p. 277.

both rise and meaning to the Christian affirmation of it in Jesus' case. A correspondence between those who denied the virgin conception and those who denied in one way or another the reality of the incarnation had emerged by the end of the second century. Among these both the Ebionites, who were a Judaizing sect, and certain adoptionists such as Paul of Samosata, expressly denied the virgin birth (as it was put), because it implied the divinity of Christ and the uniqueness of God's embodiment in him.[11] On the other hand, Docetists denied the virgin conception because they would have nothing to do with the Word of God being in contact with real, worldly and therefore evil, flesh. Even before those variant movements arose, though, this idea had power for Christians: Raymond Brown points out that the meaning of the infancy narratives in Matthew and Luke is that "Jesus is God's Son in a unique manner, for Mary conceived her child through the Holy Spirit without a male partner."[12]

To deny in principle the possibility of virgin conception in the case of Jesus on the ground that, if it were true, it would be unique or (to put it less constructively) an anomaly in human history is to beg the question then. It is and always has been the meaning of the biblical and credal affirmation that the incarnation of God in Jesus Christ is a unique event, utterly without analogy in human history.

I would go further and say that I at least do not know of any theologian who denied this doctrine who did not also either deny the uniqueness of the incarnation or resort to some kind of conceptual funny business to bring off a coherent christology. (Emil Brunner's attempt to deny the virgin conception while hanging on to an anhypostatic-enhypostatic doctrine of the person of Christ comes to mind here.) I am open to correction on this point, but I know of no denial of this doctrine that is *innocent* in the sense that the denial is just a phenomenon in the presentation that has no explicit or implicit consequences.

The Importance of the Virgin Conception

The importance of the doctrine can be sorted into distinct issues.

First, it implies the Christian doctrine of the person of Christ: he is God

---

[11]Kelly, *Early Christian Doctrines*, pp. 139-40.

[12]Raymond E. Brown, *An Introduction to New Testament Christology* (New York: Paulist, 1994), p. 83.

in whatever way the Father is God, except that he is not the Father, and he is human in whatever way we are human, except that he is not alienated from God by sin. The Creed itself sorts this issue into its two sides, by speaking in separate phrases of his conception by the Holy Spirit and birth to the virgin Mary. In light of contemporary criticisms of this teaching, it turns out to be important that the second phrase indicates Christ's *humanity,* and its denial has historically been associated with the denial that Jesus was truly human.

Second, it implies the uniqueness and finality of God's self-revelation in Jesus Christ. Christians believe that Jesus Christ is not one in a series of incarnations of God but is the one unique and final incarnation of God in human life. For this reason this doctrine is scandalous and embarrassing to a religiously pluralistic culture whose axiom is that there must be many expressions of the divine in history. Religious pluralism assumes with Schleiermacher that in particular circumstances anyone might be the incarnation of God. Over against this faith the ecumenical Christian tradition, without meaning to give offense or be quarrelsome, very modestly states this conviction that has grasped us, that in Jesus Christ the God of Abraham, Isaac and Jacob has lived a human life, and we understand this incarnation to be the final and unsurpassable revelation of God's character and identity.

Third, the manner of Christ's conception indicates his holiness. For many classical theologians this point was made through the asexual character of his origin. Today we associate this view with Augustine, but it is by no means unique to him. This link between sex and sin, and the absence of sex with holiness, is debatable and has been vigorously contested in the last fifty years. However, regardless of whether this link is cogent, there is at least one other significant way of understanding the link between virgin conception and holiness that predates Augustine in the history of Christian thought. Such early theologians as Athanasius of Alexandria often spoke of the Logos preparing himself a fleshly temple in the body of the virgin.

One matter that is not significantly at issue in this article of the Creed is any special rank or distinction among the followers of Jesus Christ for his mother. Our Lord himself put to rest all special doctrines of Mary during his own lifetime: "A woman in the crowd called out, 'Blessed is the mother who gave you birth and nursed you.' He replied, "Blessed rather are those who hear the word of God and obey it" (Lk 11:27-28 NIV). The virgin conception of Jesus is a christological doctrine: it is important not for what it tells us about Mary but for what it tells us about Jesus. Of course, it would be too much to claim that it does not tell us anything at all about Mary, but the physiological fact that it indicates is not self-explanatory.

There is no logical connection between virgin conception as such and incarnation as such. The particular virginal conception of Jesus of Nazareth is a witness to the fact that he is the Lord God living a human life, but there is no possibility of a general theory of how virgin conceptions are related to incarnations of God. As John Leith has pointed out in his book *Crisis in the Church,*[13] there could be a million virgin births without an incarnation of God. The reality to which this particular physiological fact points is therefore not the distinctiveness, virtue or blessedness of Mary herself but the utterly unique and unanalyzable characteristics of Jesus Christ to which we have alluded.

There have always been denials of this doctrine in the history of theology. Most such denials, in keeping with the church doctrine, indicate a theological point larger than the physiological issue. The exception of course is the general point of view that rules out the miraculous, the unique and the unanalyzable as a prolegomenon to any biblical interpretation or theological reflection. There are ways this kind of objection can be met by believers, but there is a mound of resources available for this without me going into it also. (C. S. Lewis's *Miracles* is as good a place as any to start, but it shouldn't be mistaken for the final word on the subject.) This is a theoretical objection that can only be met with another theory or with multiple counterinstances. So without attempting to address the principle here, I will simply argue that however this theory may have it, the doctrine of the virgin conception makes sense. Moreover, the implications of *denying* it are worse by far for Christian theology than the "embarrassment," if such it is, of affirming it in a scientific and religiously pluralist context.

In my view we can neither flatly assert nor flatly deny the virgin conception as an empirically established genetic and physiological fact because the relevant, scientifically controllable evidence is not available to be examined and never will be. The only possibilities open to us are to grant marginal control to the scientific unlikelihood or to allow marginal control to the confession of faith.

---

[13]John H. Leith, *Crisis in the Church* (Louisville, Ky.: Westminster John Knox, 1997).

Which one will do is not simply a matter of fideistic or rationalistic decision, as though there were no other criterion. I believe some rational controls are placed on who or what we believe God is and how we find out what we think we know about God and his dealings with the world. In the Christian tradition this means asking how we weigh natural and special revelation and how we suppose we ought to evaluate them using our human capacity for rationality (on the status of which we may also hold varying opinions). I affirm this doctrine and insist that Christians must not deny it, not because I think I am able to answer unanswerable questions about Mary's body but because the doctrine is functioning in a certain way in the web of Christian beliefs. The Bible seems to think of itself as reporting straightforwardly on the facts about the relationship between Mary and Joseph, and about Jesus' conception, but it shows no anxiety or apprehensiveness about the issues that arise for us when we think to ask about that relationship and its bodily implications apart from the report.

The doctrine of virgin conception or, as the creeds put it less technically, virgin birth, is then less a statement about Mary than it is a statement about Jesus Christ. As such it is one element in the christology or christologies of the New Testament that Jesus Christ is first *truly God* (in whatever way the Father is God) because he was conceived by the Holy Spirit in a woman whose pregnancy is otherwise inexplicable; second, that he is *truly human* (in whatever way we are human, except for sin) because he was carried by and born to a human mother; and third, he is nevertheless a single, integrated person. Most importantly, seen against the background of the ancient (as well as modern) understanding that births to virgins do not happen, it depicts the conviction of the apostles that the incarnation, the embodiment of God in a particular human life, is a totally unique, history-transforming event, utterly without analogy, otherwise unexampled in human history and experience. When we confess this clause in a creed, we are saying something, not so much about Mary, about whom we can know very little that is relevant to decide the question, but rather about the mighty act of God in Jesus Christ.

Likewise, questions about whether and how this could be credible in a postmodern, scientific world also miss the point. The first question, *whether* it is credible, is empirically testable, and the flat assertion that it is not credible is empirically falsifiable. It seems to me that in many American cities hosts of intelligent, well-educated, thoroughly modern people are finding the basic questions of life more intelligently answered in the most conservative churches than in any other framework or institution with which they have been involved. That is to say, an even more traditional version of Christian theology than I have defended here, to say nothing of Peacocke's, is in empirical fact successfully appealing to, being credible to and believed by large numbers of people who live every day in an educated, scientific world. Many people in that world are skeptical about the Christian faith, but they doubt not so much what we believe than our seriousness and integrity in believing it. They tend to think we are hypocrites rather than dupes. What we need in order to make Christian faith credible in the modern world, rather than a faith defined down to a "believable" but not very substantial core, is to show in our lives what we mean by what we say in our special language and practices.

This doctrine is always going to be an issue in Christian theology. Its innate problems will always raise questions. At the same time, though, it is precisely the recognition that Jesus Christ is uniquely God living a particular human life that is the meaning of the doctrine of virgin conception from the New Testament forward. The ground for the most prominent and intuitive objection, which Peacocke states so clearly, turns out to be identical or almost so with the theoretical grounds for the Christian affirmation of the doctrine: it indicates that Jesus Christ is fully human, and yet he is also the appearance in creation of the Creator, and God's presence in Jesus Christ is without analogy among the natural facts and phenomena of creation.

9

CAN A MALE SAVIOR SAVE WOMEN?

JAY WESLEY RICHARDS

IN THIS CHAPTER I CONSIDER A CONTEMPORARY CHALLENGE TO THE SAVING efficacy of the incarnation, namely, the question posed by Rosemary Ruether: "Can a male savior save women?" For a traditional locus I concentrate on Gregory of Nazianzus's famous axiom that in the incarnation *the unassumed is the unhealed, and the assumed is the healed.* Insofar as this axiom implicitly animated the early christological debates to defend a traditional understanding of the saving effects of the incarnation, this axiom must be defended. I concentrate specifically on (1) Gregory's *intent* in this claim (as an argument against Apollinarianism), (2) what he means by *nature* and (3) what it means for such a nature to be *assumed* by God the Son.

Although Gregory obviously does not consider Ruether's question, I argue that, armed with a few conceptual distinctions, we can maintain his commitment while partially accommodating a concern implicit in questions such as Ruether's. My strategy is to argue that the notion of a *nature* is still a very meaningful and truth-preserving concept to retain in an understanding of the incarnation and that retaining it assures the articulation of the saving efficacy of the incarnation better than substitutes offered by some feminist theologians such as Ruether.

To apply Gregory's dictum to this question I introduce a few distinctions, including necessary but essential properties or attributes, contingent or accidental properties, universal but contingent properties, and properties designated by inclusive disjunctions in English, and suggest a way they all might be thought to relate to a *nature*. I suspect that the easiest way to deflect the challenge is to deny that maleness or femaleness is a necessary property of the human being (and so part of human nature). However, in order to accommodate the intuition that our sexuality is not merely a contingent aspect of our existence, I propose that we view a property expressed by an inclusive disjunction—*male or female*—as one of the properties comprising human nature.

Gregory on the Logos's Assumption of Human Nature

Gregory of Nazianzus (d. 389), one of the three Cappadocian Fathers, is generally credited with the famous christological principle that, in the incarnation, the unassumed is the unhealed. This actual phrase comes from his letter to Cledonius against Apollinaris (Epistle 101), written about 382. But its influence as a presupposition in patristic christological formulations is nearly ubiquitous, and the idea is clearly employed by Origen and Tertullian.[1] Gregory's primary concern in this letter is to defend Christ's full humanity against the arguments of Apollinaris because of his conviction that the salvation wrought in Christ depended on Christ's full humanity. While his argument is *christological,* his motivation is clearly *soteriological.*

He is concerned specifically with Apollinarianism, which taught that the divine Logos "took the place of" the human mind of Christ. But he is also at pains to avoid the error of Nestorianism, which so emphasized the distinctness of the divine and human natures of Christ as to threaten the unity of his person. (Christ's full divinity is the other christological axiom that stood behind the debates. That is, only God can save humanity from its condition. But both Apollinaris and Gregory share this axiom.) He is here grappling with terms that would preserve both Christ's full humanity and the unity of his person, but without the benefit of the terminology of *two natures in one person* finally adopted in the Chalcedonian Definition in 451. So he argues against Apollinaris:

---

[1] M. F. Wiles, "Soteriological Arguments in the Fathers," in *Studia Patristica,* 9 vols. (Berlin: Academie Verlag, 1966), p. 322.

If anyone has put trust in him as a man without a human mind, he is really bereft of mind, and quite unworthy of salvation. For that which he has not assumed he has not healed; but that which is united to his Godhead he has also saved. If only half Adam fell, then that which Christ assumes and saves may be half also; but if the whole of his nature fell, it must be united to the whole nature of Him that was begotten, and so be saved as a whole. Let them not, then, begrudge us our complete salvation, or clothe the Saviour only with bones and nerves and the portraiture of humanity.[2]

The phrase *to gar aproslepton, atherapeuton* employs a medical metaphor (with the English word *therapeutic* obviously derived from the verb *therapeuein),* which we can take as an expression for salvation.[3] For salvation to be realized, all of human nature must be assumed: "For Godhead joined to flesh alone is not man, nor to soul alone, nor both apart from intellect, which is the most essential part of man."[4]

If a person is to insist that any part of human nature must be assumed by the Logos, the mind is surely not the part to leave out since it is the part from which sin came and so is in most need of redemption. If we were to conclude that the human mind was not assumed by the Son, then we could infer that it was not capable of being healed:

If the mind was utterly rejected, as prone to sin and subject to damnation, and for this reason he assumed a body but left out the mind, then there was an excuse for them who sin with the mind; for the witness of God—according to you—has shown the impossibility of healing it.[5]

Like must be sanctified by like[6] *in order for our salvation to be achieved.*

Gregory anticipates the arguments of the Apollinarians, who might appeal to divine omnipotence, arguing that God is surely capable of saving humanity without assuming a human mind. Also they might contend, "Does not Scripture say, 'The Word was made *flesh* and dwelt among us'?"

---

[2]In Edward R. Hardy, ed., *Christology of the Later Fathers* (Philadelphia: Westminster Press, 1954), pp. 218-19. All English quotes of the text in this chapter are from Hardy.

[3]M. F. Wiles takes this up in more detail in "The Unassumed Is the Unhealed," *Religious Studies* 4, no. 1 (1969): 50-51.

[4]Hardy, *Christology of the Later Fathers*, p. 219.

[5]Ibid., p. 220.

[6]Ibid., p. 221.

The implication is that taking on human flesh need not entail taking on a human mind. But if their appeal to divine omnipotence is legitimate, then why would the Apollinarians insist that the Logos take on the human *body?* Would it not be more consistent just to abandon all this talk about the divine and human in Jesus, since God need not bother in the first place? "Take away, then, the flesh as well as the mind, that your monstrous folly may be complete."[7] As for the Word taking on flesh alone, it is clear that Scripture is not removing the human mind from Christ as the Apollinarians would have it but is merely speaking synecdochically, taking a part to signify the whole.[8]

Understanding how the Logos could take on a human mind while remaining one person might be difficult, but Gregory sees a partial analogy in the way his own personality "can contain soul and reason and mind and Holy Spirit"[9] while still remaining one person (of course, this analogy is dangerous, since it could be susceptible to Apollinarian appropriation). If this is possible—which everyone concedes—then such an assumption should be possible. Just because a greater mind takes on a human mind does not mean the human mind ceases to exist or cannot be assumed. And since we know (1) we are saved in Christ, (2) the unassumed is the unsaved and (3) the human mind needs saving, we should conclude not only that such an assumption is possible but that it has in fact taken place in the incarnation of the divine Logos.

As it stands, a person might wonder what Apollinaris's complaint is with Gregory's way of articulating the incarnation. Notice that both Gregory and Apollinaris share the tripartite distinctions of body, soul and mind in the human being. However one negotiates these distinctions, they agree that the human is a composite creature. We might say, a little pedantically, that they would both concur with the universally quantified conditional:

(1) For all *h*, if *h* is a human, then *h* has (or is) a body, a soul and a mind.

In fact, Gregory and Apollinaris could agree on more than this. Namely, both would submit to

(1′) For all *h*, if *h* is a human, then *h* has (or is) a human body, a human soul and a mind.

---

[7]Ibid.
[8]Ibid., p. 222.
[9]Ibid., p. 219.

But while (1) and (1´) are necessary conditions for *h* to be a human, they are not sufficient. Gregory requires *more* than this for human nature to be assumed. He requires something like

> (1´´) For all *h*, if *h* is a human, then *h* has (or is) a human body, a human soul and a *human* mind.

So why would Apollinaris refuse to submit to (1´´)? Presumably something about his understanding of *nous* prevented or proscribed it. Kenneth Paul Wesche has recently argued quite plausibly that the source of Apollinaris's difficulty lay in his inability to conceive of a mind *(nous)* as distinct from a self *(ho autos)*. In the fourth-century milieu the mind was considered the essential part of the person. More strongly, it was identified with the *self*.[10] Given this assumption it is quite clear why Apollinaris objected to the Logos assuming a *human* mind. This would have left Christ with two selves, two subjects, two *whos*. Such a state would obviously have compromised the unity of Christ's person.

Gregory also insists with Apollinaris that the mind "is the most essential part of man."[11] At the same time he is capable of distinguishing between this most essential part of human nature and the actual self.[12] Gregory, while he did not have the terminology of Chalcedon, nevertheless exhibits the christological intuition that the Chalcedonian definition codified. In Chalcedon the term *autos* is used repeatedly to emphasize the "one actor," the one subject of Jesus Christ.[13]

---

[10]Kenneth Paul Wesche, " 'Mind' and 'Self' in the Christology of Saint Gregory the Theologian: Saint Gregory's Contribution to Christology and Christian Anthropology," *The Greek Orthodox Review* 39, no. 1 (1994): 36.

[11]Hardy, *Christology of the Later Fathers*, p. 219.

[12]"In the union of . . . the anthropological and the Christological, there emerges a distinction between mind and self which will enable Saint Gregory to affirm against Apollinaris the assumption of a full human mind by the divine Logos without thereby implying the assumption of a human self" (Wesche, " 'Mind' and 'Self,' " p. 50). Wesche also sees this as evidence that Gregory's anthropology is more Hebraic than is usually recognized: "The distinction between mind and self which emerges out of the Christology of Saint Gregory shows how fundamentally Hebraic is his Neoplatonism. Since the self or person is no longer identified as the soul, the real man is not conceived as being joined to the body, as though the body were an accidental appendage to the real man, but as containing both soul and body. The human self both transcends, and exists in, its human nature so that the whole composite is essential to the real man" (Wesche, " 'Mind' and 'Self,' " p. 59).

[13]Ibid., p. 57. Significantly, this letter to Cledonius against Apollinaris was adopted "*en toto* by the Synod of Chalcedon" (Wesche, " 'Mind' and 'Self,' " p. 51).

This distinction between *mind* and *self* appears tacitly in our distinction between (1´) and (1´´). Gregory apparently had some notion of the predicate *human* that transcended *mind*, since the qualification of a *human* mind was the bone of contention between Apollinaris and him. Gregory could ascribe a human mind to the part of human nature that the Logos assumed (and still remain orthodox), just in case the Logos could do this in one self. But since the Logos is himself one self, one subject, this would only be possible if the Logos could assume a human mind without assuming an accompanying human self.

If this is a correct reading of Gregory's debate with Apollinaris, then we can accurately say that in Gregory's reflection on the reality of the incarnation of the Logos in the one man Jesus Christ, he modified a very basic anthropological assumption—one he presumably shared with his contemporaries. Gregory did not simply adopt the anthropological presuppositions of his *Zeitgeist* to articulate the incarnation. Rather he transformed such presuppositions in light of the wider reality of the incarnation. He obviously employed terminology and concepts that were broadly *Hellenistic;* however, when some of those concepts made a correct articulation of the incarnation impossible (or at least very difficult), they were forced to budge in light of the reality of the incarnation. He did not merely hold Christ's assumption of human nature before the bar of a prior definition of human nature; rather the reality of the incarnation shaped his definition of human nature. This is not to say that his intuitions and prior concepts on such matters were demolished. They clearly were not. But in Gregory's reflection Christ's assumption of human nature took priority over such concepts. We should remember the order of this priority when we take up a contemporary concern of our own below.

So goes Gregory's argument. We can put his articulation of the principle—that the unassumed is the unhealed and that the assumed is the healed—more formally and apply it to human nature, which was obviously his concern. It consists of two conditionals:

(2) If human nature is fully assumed (by the Logos), then it is healed.

(3) If human nature is not fully assumed (by the Logos), then it is not fully healed.

For simplicity we can combine (2) and (3) into a single biconditional:

(4) Human nature is fully healed if and only if human nature is fully assumed (by the Logos).

Perhaps we should say that for Gregory, Christ must fully assume human *nature* so that it could be *healed*, so that humanity, which includes human *individuals*, could be *saved*. But I take *healed* and *saved* to be roughly synonymous here.

Many difficult and important questions should be asked of (4): How do we know it is true? How can we infer it from the fact of the incarnation? What sort of necessity attaches to it? Does it constrain God? We will not consider these matters here but will only consider something of what it would mean for the right side of this biconditional to obtain or be satisfied. Since this part is required for human nature to be healed [assuming the truth of (4)], a defense of the cogency of this requirement is preliminary to a defense of (4) as a whole. The reason for defending it should be clear to the Christian who affirms the Nicene and Chalcedonian formulations. For although the principle is not explicitly found in these documents, something very much like it is a guiding motivation behind the developments in christology from Nicaea to Chalcedon. This is apparent in the orthodox insistence that Jesus Christ be confessed as fully human and fully divine. If the contemporary Christian were to abandon (4)—or something similar—as an illegitimate or incorrect claim, it would be difficult to understand if he or she still insisted on Christian adherence to Chalcedon or to the christological parts of Nicaea. On the contrary, if such a person denied (4), he or she would be unlikely to see the urgency or soteriological significance of affirming that Jesus is fully human and fully divine.[14]

Can A Male Savior Save Women?

As I noted, Gregory struggled with how to maintain the conviction that the divine Logos, the Second Person of the triune Godhead, could become incarnate, that is, could assume human nature. Gregory could not avoid the understanding of human nature that his contemporaries held and that

---

[14]M. F. Wiles is a fitting example. He dissolves the traditional aspect of the incarnation and atonement that sees them as effecting a reconciliation and healing between sinful and fallen humanity and a righteous and holy God. In its place he emphasizes a personal relationship between God and humanity. While personal relationship is surely a part of the incarnation and atonement, he emphasizes it to the detriment of these other aspects, and consequently he sees no soteriological need for insisting that Jesus be fully human and fully divine (see Wiles, "Unassumed Is the Unhealed," p. 55). Of course, a person should not affirm the Chalcedonian Definition only because it satisfies the requirement of principle (4). A person should affirm it because he or she thinks it is *true*.

he generally shared. But this struggle is one we cannot avoid ourselves. In
recent years a challenge to the claim that Christ fully assumed human
nature has come from some feminist theologians and may be exemplified
in the title of an essay by Rosemary Ruether: "Can a Male Saviour Save
Women?"[15] In the remainder of this chapter I put this question to Gregory's
way of understanding the incarnation.

Ruether's own arguments in support of this concern are weak, although
a plausible way of formulating the objection can be constructed. Nevertheless, we should consider her argument. She introduces her essay by con-
curring with feminist theologian Mary Daly's fallacious dictum: "When
God is male, the male is God."[16] We should ask: Has Christian orthodoxy
ever said God is male? Probably not. Of course, since Jesus is male, a
Christian would say that the Second Person of the Trinity became incarnate as a human male. But even if we agreed that God *is* male, *the male is
God* still does not follow from it. Daly's claim suffers from a *false conversion* of the subject and predicate, and hides an equivocation of terms from
the predicate *male* to the corporate or abstract term *the male*. It is akin to
the claim that *if God is incorporeal, the incorporeal is God*. This would
mean that, say, propositions, states of affairs and numbers are God. Unfortunately Daly's dictum has enjoyed more currency in feminist literature
than its logic merits.

Ruether also notes (correctly) that many thinkers in Christian history
have viewed the male as the bearer of the generic human nature, as the
norm, which the female has not attained. Augustine even saw the *imago
Dei* as having a "male generic character."[17] Ruether detects this same bias
in recent pronouncements in Roman Catholic, Orthodox and Anglican
churches on the ordination of women. Women are denied ordination into
the priesthood because they do not sufficiently resemble Christ. This is a
bad argument against women's ordination, but it is far from clear what this
problem has to do with women's *salvation*. As far as I can tell, no influential leader in the history of Christianity who denied women the right of
ordination has concluded, with Ruether, that this implies that Christ's

---

[15]In Rosemary Radford Reuther, *To Change the World: Christology and Cultural Criticism*
  (New York: Crossroad, 1981), p. 45. This book is a collection of essays originally delivered in September 1980 as the Kuyper Lectures at the Free University in Amsterdam.
[16]Ibid., p. 45. Daly's quote can be found in *Beyond God the Father* (Boston: Beacon,
  1973), p. 19.
[17]Reuther, *Change the World*, p. 45.

work does not *save* women. And she provides us with no argument for the connection between ordination and salvation.

She then dismisses the christological developments from Nicaea to Chalcedon in a page and a half under the caricatured subtitle *The Imperial Christ*, moving on to consider *androgynous christologies* that have emerged in the history of Christianity (which have been judged heretical). Of these proposals she observes: "The root of these christologies lies in the basic Christian affirmation that Christ redeems the whole of human nature, male and female. In Paul's words, in Christ there is 'neither male or female.' "[18] Of course, the basic Christian affirmation has always been that a *male* Christ effected such redemption. Moreover, these christologies look more like theological constructions (particularly in their contemporary forms) concerned with what sort of Redeemer some would *like* to have rather than the *truth* of whether there is such a Redeemer. And insisting on an androgynous Christ would require separating the Redeemer from the man Jesus, a move not very congenial to the bulk of the Christian tradition.

Although not for these reasons, Ruether concludes that androgynous christologies—while perhaps promising—are an "ambivalent heritage" since some—such as Gnostic androgyny and the mysticism of Jacob Boehme—have been androcentric: "Maleness and femaleness are still seen as opposite principles standing for mind and spirit *versus* sense, body and sexuality. The two are brought together in a male-centred concept of the self in which the female is neutralized."[19] She prefers what she calls the prophetic iconoclastic Christ in which there is not a concern for "the dualism of male and female." On this view of the "salvation" wrought by Christ, a male savior *can* save women. Unfortunately, her Savior and Redeemer puts on Bolshevik garb, and salvation is more or less reduced to political emancipation: "His ability to be liberator does not reside in his maleness, but on the contrary, in the fact that he has renounced this system of domination and seeks to embody in his person the new humanity of service and mutual empowerment."[20] She resolves the dilemma posed by her question by drastically *redefining* what most mean by Christ's redemption and salvation. This is more a dissolution of the dilemma than a resolution of it.

---

[18]Ibid., p. 49.

[19]Ibid., pp. 50, 52-53.

[20]Ibid., p. 56.

She also contends that the prophetic iconoclastic view avoids what she takes to be an illegitimate "abstraction" of male and female as *opposite principles*: "To abstract these definitions into eternal essences is to miss the social context in which these definitions arise."[21] While this construal of male and female may be objectionable, others are surely possible. *Opposite principles* might just fail to capture the *correct* distinction between male and female. This does not mean there is no such correct "abstract" distinction. Moreover, dismissing a truth claim by noting the social context in which it arises is to commit the genetic fallacy. Every view has a social origin, but this is no logical fact about the truth or falsity of any particular view. For these reasons I find Ruether's arguments uncompelling.

Nevertheless I think her question can generate an argument that raises some systematic concerns for the Nazianzen view of the incarnation. Since the forms of this question and answers to it are as varied as are feminist theologians themselves, we consider her question here as an ideal type for the multitude of challenges that arise from some feminist quarters.

The presupposition that seems to guide the question is: If divine assumption is necessary for healing and salvation, since Christ did not assume femaleness or womanness, does this not put women's salvation in jeopardy? In a more recent work Elizabeth Johnson considers this issue more carefully than Ruether. As with Ruether, Johnson's concerns include a Roman Catholic document that denies ordination to women because they do not sufficiently resemble the male Christ, whom the priest is to represent. She observes:

> As a logical outcome of this exacerbated stress on Jesus' maleness in the context of dualistic anthropology that essentially divorces male from female humanity, women's salvation is implicitly put in jeopardy, at least theoretically. The Christian story of salvation involves not only God's compassionate will to save, but also the method by which this will becomes effective, namely, by God's plunging into sinful human history and transforming it from within. The early Christian aphorism "What is not assumed is not redeemed, but what is assumed is saved by union with God" sums up the insight that God's saving solidarity with all of humanity is what is crucial for the birth of the new creation. *Et homo factus est:* thus does the Nicene creed confess the universal relevance of the incarnation by the use of the inclusive "homo." But if in fact what is meant is *et vir factus est,* with stress on sexual

---

[21]Ibid., p. 55.

manhood, if maleness is essential for the christic role, then women are cut
out of the loop of salvation, for female sexuality is not taken on by the Word
made flesh. If maleness is constitutive for the incarnation and redemption,
female humanity is not assumed and therefore not saved.[22]

These are clearly cogent and relevant worries. Just what is "constitutive
for the incarnation and redemption"? Is maleness "essential for the christic role"? What exactly needs to be assumed for universal healing to occur?

Natures in general. As with Gregory and Apollinaris, the central issue
seems to be the notion of a *nature,* which is implicit in Gregory's famous
quote. The coherence of the claim that Christ *assumed human nature*
presupposes some sort of realism with respect to *properties,* because a
nature consists of a cluster of essential properties that makes a person or
entity *what it is.* Nature is often used synonymously with essence, the
sine qua non of an entity. Gregory's discussion betrays his belief that
there is some distinct *human* nature, a cluster of properties that must
obtain for an individual to qualify as a member of the kind *human.* He
mentions at least three such essential properties (which exhibit his tripartite anthropology): human body, human soul and human mind. Thus
he complains about Apollinarianism: "For Godhead joined to flesh alone
is not man, nor to soul alone, nor to both apart from intellect, which is
the most essential part of man."[23] The sense is clear: mind is an essential
property for the kind *human.* So if the Son did not assume a human
mind, it would be false to say he has assumed *human* form (as we confess in the Nicene Creed), and the unassumed "he has not healed . . ." So
affirming salvation in this way seems to presuppose that there are such
things as natures.

At this point someone is bound to object that this way of putting things
is hopelessly antiquated and naively pre-Kantian. As such it is not useful
to a contemporary defense of the incarnation. Gregory's reasoning assumes
two contentious premises. First, he assumes that there is some sort of connection between an Adam whose sin has some ontological effect on his
progeny (as in Romans). Second, he at least implies that there is some eternal Platonic form of *humanness* that exists separately from individual
human beings, with a greater reality than those individuals, and which

---

[22]Elizabeth Johnson, *She Who Is: The Mystery of God in Feminist Theological Discourse*
(New York: Crossroad, 1994), p. 153.

[23]Hardy, *Christology of the Later Fathers,* p. 219.

such individuals reflect only imperfectly.[24]

There is a sense in which such a charge is accurate. If the nominalist is correct, and there just is no referent to what we normally call *human nature*, then this way of articulating the efficacy of the incarnation will have to be abandoned like physicists abandoned phlogiston and ether. But does belief in natures require, or even depend on, caricatured theories about hyper-Platonic forms that float untethered in some celestial realm? I do not think this is at all the case.

Arguments about the existence of universals such as natures are as old as Western civilization itself. Even when disputants concede their existence, there has been bitter disagreement as to their *nature*. Are they real abstractions that are exemplified by individuals but actually have a greater reality than any exemplification of them? Do they have a reality but *only* as instantiated in individuals? These are valuable questions on which I have an opinion, but I think these theoretical matters are secondary to the primary, pretheoretical claim. In christology the pretheoretical claim is that the divine Logos *became human*. Correct or not, this claim is no more tendentious than any use of the "human predicate" in everyday English, or talk about *humanity*, as Johnson puts it. (Of course, there are special questions about how *God* can become human, but the predicate *became human* is not by itself particularly troubling). Orthodox Christian theologians are bound to assent to this pretheoretical claim. This does not mean they are automatically shackled to, say, a "Platonic" or "Aristotelian" view of natures. It does mean such theologians are bound to a theory of natures that adequately accommodates the claim that the Logos became human in the man Jesus Christ. This does not require that orthodox Christian claims always be philosophical claims; it does imply that such claims have philosophical *implications* that different theoretical proposals will accommodate more or less adequately. Theologians search for the most willing philosophical hostess available. If they need some view of the reality of natures for the central incarnational claim, then Christian theologians have an interest in defending and developing theories that allow for natures.

While developing and defending such a theory obviously lies beyond the

---

[24]Again M. F. Wiles fits the bill: "Our principle must have seemed much more convincing to people who thought in terms of the Hebraic conception of a real solidarity of all mankind in Adam or who were thorough-going Platonists" ("Unassumed Is the Unhealed," p. 53).

scope of this essay, I think there are several contemporary theories that capture intuitions about natures quite adequately and, to my mind, plausibly. I briefly mention one: the well-developed conceptual apparatus of possible-worlds semantics.[25] In possible-worlds terminology we can conceive of an essence or nature of a thing as that set of properties that will be borne by an entity in any and every world in which it exists (an entity does not have any properties in worlds in which it does not exist, since existence is not taken as a property but as a necessary condition for something to have properties).[26] A possible world is a complete state of affairs, a compossible way the world could have been, a possible but nonactual world. This is a formalized expression of our everyday use of modal terms such as *could possibly have, could not possibly have* and *it is necessary that.*

Accidental or contingent properties are those properties that an entity has in some possible worlds in which it exists but not all. For example, *being a person* is probably essential to the individual designated as *Socrates.* There is no possible world in which Socrates exists but is not a person. More formally, we could put this as follows:

(5) There is no possible world *w,* such that it is true in *w* both that *p is Socrates and p is not a person.*

A contingent property for Socrates, such as *being brown eyed* (let us assume he was in fact brown eyed in the actual world) could be expressed as:

(6) There is some possible world *w,* such that it is true in *w* both that *p is Socrates and p is not brown-eyed.*

More to our concern, Gregory could voice his objection to Apollinaris quite succinctly by insisting on (7):

(7) There is no possible world *w,* such that it is true in *w* both that *p is fully human and p does not have a human mind.*

For Gregory, *having a human mind* is a necessary or essential property for the kind human. This obviously falls short of establishing the reality of natures, but I think this shows that talk of natures and essences is still a meaningful and useful way of speaking in our contemporary setting. The

---

[25]See, for example, the collection of essays in Michael Loux, *The Possible and the Actual* (Ithaca, N.Y.: Cornell University Press, 1979); Richard Cartwright, "Some Remarks on Essentialism," in *Philosophical Essays* (Cambridge, Mass.: MIT Press, 1987); and Alvin Plantinga, *The Nature of Necessity* (Oxford: Clarendon Press, 1973).

[26]The way I put things here relies heavily on Plantinga's theory in *Nature of Necessity.*

theologian who believes that such talk is vital to preserving the incarnational claim does not need to be intimidated by any half-baked invocation of Kant for the obsolescence of such "metaphysical language."

Human natures in particular. Interestingly, feminist theologians in general tend to shy away from such metaphysical doctrines, often implying that they are at least implausible or even that they tend to harm the concerns of women. But Ruether's question that we are considering takes on greater clarity when put in these terms. Ruether does not put it this way, but her nagging intuition seems to be captured by the following biconditional:

(8) Female nature is fully healed if and only if female nature is fully assumed.

Apart from the essential properties that comprise a nature, there are (as mentioned above) *contingent* or *accidental* properties that subgroups and individuals of the kind human may possess but which do not go into the definition of human. These may be essential properties for some subkind but contingent with respect to qualification for the kind human. For example, *being an American* may be essential for *being a Texan* but nonessential or contingent for *being a human* (although non-Texans are no doubt subhuman in some sense). Moreover, some such properties may be very important, even *universally* possessed by the relevant constituency, without being *essential* properties. For example, until recently all human beings were conceived in the wombs (fallopian tube, uterus, etc.) of their mothers. *Conception in the womb* was then a *universal* property of human beings, but it was not essential, as the existence of test-tube conceptions made apparent.[27] So we need to make a distinction between necessary properties of some entity or kind (which go into a nature and are thus universal for that kind) and merely universal properties that are not essential and so do not go into the definition of the nature of the relevant kind. This is important because it exposes the inadequacy of attempts to reduce language about natures and necessity to empirical conclusions about traits everyone seems to have. Universality ranging over a relevant kind is necessary for a property to be *essential* to that kind, but it is not sufficient.[28]

Now consider Ruether's query: Can a male Savior save women? Assum-

---

[27]I guess Adam and Eve might count as exceptions as well, but that is another matter.

[28]For more on this, see Thomas V. Morris, *The Logic of God Incarnate* (Ithaca, N.Y.: Cornell University Press, 1986), pp. 62-70.

ing a certain view about natures, this is clearly a cogent question. How might Gregory of Nazianzus answer it, and how might we answer it? Without some belief in the existence of properties and natures, I think the answer is either No! or Huh? That is, salvation as explained by Gregory makes no sense if there is not a human nature that Christ assumed (whether there is a salvation in another sense is another matter for another time). However, if we assume the existence of natures and properties, I think Gregory would answer unequivocally Yes! How might he justify such a claim in his own terms? He could simply deny that *maleness* and *femaleness* are essential human properties in the requisite sense (and so are not part of human nature). Thus the assumption of either property by the Son is not necessary for our salvation. His maleness is an *accidental* or *contingent* property.

And in other texts he does display belief in the contingency of our sexual designations. He quotes Galatians 3:28 as evidence that there will be no distinction between male and female in heaven and claims that sexual differences apply to the body and flesh, and not to the soul.[29] So he evinces a willingness to make sexuality an accidental or contingent property of human individuals, which is not a member of that set of essential properties that make up human *nature*. This type of reasoning has some *apparent* biblical support in Jesus' claim that in the kingdom of God we will neither marry nor be given in marriage. But this by itself does not warrant the conclusion that our sexuality will be obliterated. And if reports of the Lord's resurrection body are any indication, this does not seem to be a correct inference.

Unfortunately, such a relegation of our sexuality to the contingent may provide grist for the feminist mill as evidence that Gregory was illegitimately influenced by a Platonic culture, which denigrated the physical and material and exalted the intellectual and immaterial. This way of partitioning human properties could be seen as downright misogynous if the female were identified with the lowly physical and the male with the "higher" intellectual and spiritual.

Whether this accusation is warranted, I think something like this designation of our sexuality to an accidental property runs afoul of the intuition

---

[29]See discussion and sources from Gregory's Orations in Donald F. Winslow, *The Dynamics of Salvation: A Study in Gregory of Nazianzus* (Cambridge, Mass.: Philadelphia Patristics Foundation, 1979), p. 175.

embedded in Ruether's query. This intuition might arise from the conviction that our sexuality is so fundamental to our being that it should not be consigned to the nonessential realm. After all, according to Scripture our sexuality is central to the divine intention for human beings (Gen 1:27). Being female is as important as being enfleshed, or as having intellectual or moral capacity, or as any other essential human property. If this argument is correct, then even on Gregory's terms it is difficult to see how women's *nature* could be assumed and therefore healed.

This is a sensible objection if maleness and femaleness are essential properties in such a way that Christ's male nature prevents his saving efficacy for women. It should give the systematic theologian some pause, but making a person's sexual identity essential has some very troubling implications that its advocates should consider. Most significantly, it makes our *sexuality* a more transcendent property than our *humanity*. This disturbing claim does have plausibility since there are nonhuman things (such as animals) with the properties of maleness and femaleness but apparently no human beings that are simply nonsexual. On this view, human nature must always be sex indexed, so that one man or woman could never *stand in*, as Christ has traditionally been understood to do, for the race as a whole. This would seem to gut a significant portion of Christian theology.

Moreover (it could be argued), what about all those dynamic properties (as opposed to those stiff, static Greek properties) such as human suffering and experience in general? Does not Christ have to assume those as well? Even Gregory talked as if the Logos's assumption of things like hunger and thirst was important.[30] In fact, the feminist complaint usually is not expressed in terms of natures but in terms of experience, such as women's experience. But if a generic human or female nature is difficult to determine, surely something like women's experience is even more so. Even if God had become incarnate as a woman, it is not at all clear that he could have assumed something like women's experience. After all, what is more distinct, various, individual and less susceptible to generalization than *experience*?

Once this strategy of piling on essential properties for the Logos's assumption is employed, it is hard to see where it would end. For example, what about a person's culture, ethnicity, historical and social context? Surely no human beings can exist without these things. Are they not just

---

[30]Ibid., pp. 92-93.

as "essential" as maleness or femaleness? So I might argue: Jesus was a first-century Jew. He did not assume the "nature" of a twentieth-century, white, nearsighted, left-handed Presbyterian. How then can he save me?

Before long we are all right back to dying for our own sins—the state of affairs for which the Logos became incarnate in the first place. Therefore, if we are going to make any sense of Christ's assumption of human nature, we are going to have to distinguish between essential and contingent properties. And it appears that this division of human nature along sexual lines comes into significant conflict with the Cappadocian conception of the incarnation. Insofar as this conception was a central motivation for the early christological debates and for the codification of orthodoxy at Nicaea and Chalcedon, there seems to be a conflict between this view of human nature and Christian orthodoxy itself.

This brings us to what I think is the crucial dilemma our discussion reveals: *Should we allow the reality of the incarnation to govern our view of human nature, including maleness and femaleness, or should we allow our disparate intuitions about human nature to trump the Nazianzen and traditional view of the incarnation?* When there is a conflict, should we allow present concerns to override fundamental principles of the faith, such as Christ's full and sufficient humanity assumed to make possible the salvation of the entire race—male and female—or should we let those theological principles challenge, shape and guide our present reflection and theorizing on human nature? As we have seen, this problem is similar to the one Gregory himself had to face in the interaction between the anthropological assumptions of his age and his commitment to the reality of the incarnation. This dilemma is not uniquely modern. If we choose the priority of the incarnation of the Logos in the man Jesus Christ, we will seek a definition of human nature that permits a male to stand in for humanity as a whole.

Some residual doubt. Having said this, I think there is something correct in the intuition that exhibits discomfort at consigning our sexuality to the merely contingent. A counterexample can be proposed to challenge this consignment. For is it altogether clear that I, a distinct person and a male, could still exist but be a female? This question could resurface however we decide what goes into our definitions of maleness and femaleness (assuming they are sufficiently robust), including all relevant genetic, social, parental, hormonal, metaphysical and theological components. Assume that *Jay* designates the primitive *person* I am and is not a mere shorthand description of my empirically accessible characteristics. Now suppose I consider:

(9) There is some possible world *w*, such that it is true in *w* that *p is Jay and p is a female.*

Or

(10) There is some possible world *w*, such that it is true in *w* that *p is Jay and p is not a male.*

Although I am not certain, I think it quite conceivable that neither (9) nor (10) is true. Being a male does seem to be part of my essential identity in a way different from, say, my cursed myopia. If I awoke tomorrow to find I had 20/20 vision, I would be grateful but would not think my nature or essential identity had changed. But if I awoke as a female or with no sexual identity whatever—androgynous or otherwise—I would probably have significant doubt as to my identity. So it does seem to be a plausible claim that, at least for humans, our sexual status is more than a mere contingent property. Even those who argue for more than two "genders" tend to insist that our sex is more than that. Ruether herself, while criticizing the dualism that makes male and female opposite principles, nevertheless objects to those androgynous christologies "in which the female is neutralized." So she retains some distinct notion of what the female *is*. But if our sexuality is somehow essential, and the Logos did not assume it, this makes hash of Gregory's claim. It seems we either hold on to the incarnational claim and deny the truth of this intuition or vice versa, but we cannot have both. Is this an unresolvable conflict?

A possible solution. Perhaps we *can* have both and do it consistently with a biblical view of our sexuality (in light of Gen 1:27). Instead of making maleness or femaleness into essential properties themselves, perhaps we should construe an essential, even divinely intended property of human nature to consist of an *inclusive disjunction* of these two categories. That is, one of the many essential human properties that the Logos assumed in taking on human nature is the property *essentially male or essentially female.*[31] As with any inclusive disjunction the disjunction as a whole is satisfied if either of the two sides obtains. Every human female exemplifies this property, as does every male. Both instantiate the "generic" human nature. Both are equally normative and need not be

---

[31]Needless to say, this solution will not be satisfactory to those who wish to claim there are five or even seven "genders." But, alas, every dilemma is not so easily resolved.

viewed as opposite principles. This would accommodate our intuitions
that there are important distinctions to be made between the male and
female. Ruether and many feminists object to identifying the male with
the mind and the female with the body and emotions. This objection is
well founded. Nevertheless, their objection does not negate the conviction
that maleness and femaleness are distinct. Moreover, the distinction has
significant biblical precedent. This way of construing the sexual property
allows us to preserve the obvious historical connection that the *male* Jesus
fully exemplified *human* nature and releases the pressure to require an
androgynous Christ (whom we do not have anyway). Of course, any
androgynous individual who, say, possessed both sets of sexual organs
would still instantiate human nature, since an inclusive disjunction is also
satisfied if *both* disjuncts obtain.[32]

At the same time we could affirm that it is the divine intention for
human nature to have the property *essentially male or essentially female*
without reading this or any specifically sexual characteristic into the Godhead. (This conception might have the added benefit of resolving the question: Who properly bears the divine image, individual males and females,
or the two in a marital union? The answer is, both individuals and the
couple bear the divine image, since the property that distributes that
image is an inclusive disjunctive property. But these divisions reflect the
way that image is distributed in *human* nature and are not necessarily
themselves reflective of the divine nature.)

On the other hand, this conception does not free us to claim that God
did not have significant reasons for becoming incarnate as a *man*. He no
doubt did, even if we do not have access to his reasons. But we need not
claim that he became a man *instead* of a woman *in order to assume human
nature*. As far as this requirement is concerned, the Logos could equally
have satisfied it as a female. This distinction helps us deflect the feminist
complaint that God's incarnation as a male implies that maleness is normative for humanity, whereas femaleness is derivative. The sonship of the
Logos would then have more to do with his procession (not birth) from the
Father, rather than the fact that Jesus was a male. Nevertheless, given the
distinction between male and female, the fact that the Logos became incarnate as a male gives us warrant to refer to him as God's *Son* and to use

---

[32]The inclusive disjunction *male or female* does not mean *only male or female, but not
male and female*. Rather, it means *male or female, or male and female*.

masculine pronouns in referring to him. Alternating between masculine and feminine pronouns would introduce an ambiguity that would obscure the particular way God chose to become incarnate. It would also depart from the biblical language for the Logos.

Conclusion

The question, Can a male savior save women? raises important questions about the relationship of our sexual identities to our human nature. It also constitutes a significant contemporary challenge to the incarnational claim that Christ fully assumed human nature and that he saves men *and* women in so doing. But, like the Hellenistic anthropology with which Gregory had to deal, it presents no insuperable difficulties to the Christian convinced of the truth of the incarnation. Moreover, there is a way of including our sexuality within human nature—and partially accommodating the concern that seems to inspire this challenge—which is compatible with this claim. To the question, Can a male savior save women? the Christian can confidently answer yes.

PART 4

THEOLOGY

10

CHRISTIANITY OR FEMINISM?

LESLIE ZEIGLER

MOST OF THE FEMINIST THEOLOGIANS ARE GIVING US *NOT* THE CHRIS-
tian faith but a quite different religion.[1] And unfortunately their efforts are
being aided and abetted, as well as camouflaged, by the churches themselves, particularly by the mainline Protestant churches. It is generally recognized today that these churches are in trouble—some would say in a
mess. Basically the problem is one of uncertainty about their true function, accompanied by and actually resulting from a general theological disarray.

The feminists, of course, not only find this unnerved church (or unbelieving church) a very receptive medium for promoting their agenda, but
their agenda also serves as a very effective catalyst for magnifying the
theological disarray in the churches.

Of course, if an individual is going to speak of the Christian gospel
being replaced by other gospels, he or she has to be clear about what is

---

[1]This is a vast and complicated subject. I will therefore try to present my position as
briefly and simply as possible. This essay will essentially be an outline. Although I am
well aware of the differences that exist among the various feminist writers, I will limit
myself to those issues on which they all essentially agree.

meant by the Christian gospel. I am assuming at least the following param-
eters must be acknowledged if a person is legitimately to claim to be
within the Christian tradition:

1. The authority of the Scriptures must be recognized. Without the
Bible there can be no church.

2. The crucial significance of Jesus Christ must be recognized. The
Christian faith stands or falls with God's self-revelation in Jesus of Nazareth.

3. This self-revelation requires speaking of God as Trinity. If we wish to
speak of the Christian God and not some other god, we must be clear
regarding the significance of the trinitarian name for God—Father, Son and
Holy Spirit.

Each of these statements could easily require a large volume for its
development. I will only mention very briefly some of the basic issues
involved. Each of these issues is very significant for understanding the
theological crisis we face today and the place of feminism in that crisis.

First, we need to consider a very important statement by John Calvin, a
statement that has been repeated by generations of theologians since his
time. He wrote that the word *God* is merely an empty term, flapping
around in our brains, with no relation to reality, unless and until we attain
some knowledge of God as he has made himself known, as he has imaged
and designated himself.[2] The term *God* is simply a general, abstract, empty
term flapping around in our heads until it is given some definite referent—
until we know *which* god we are talking about.

For the Christian the Scriptures, the ancient creeds and the historical
Christian faith have been very clear that God has made himself known in
his Son, Jesus Christ, and has designated himself through that event as the
triune One—Father, Son and Holy Spirit.

This historical faith rules out as inappropriate certain specific ways of
referring to God. God is *not* to be referred to as some "spirit of love" or as a
"concern for life." Instead the Christian faith affirms, along with the early
members of the community that gave us the Scriptures, that Jesus is "Lord
and Christ" (Acts 2:36 NIV). This is both a theological and historical statement. It says that God has done something for human beings at a particular
time, in a particular place and in a particular manner. It also involves the
affirmation that as a Christian a believer understands himself or herself as

---

[2]John Calvin *Institutes* 1.13.2.

a member of that particular historical community that has its origin in that particular act of God—the life, work, death and resurrection of Jesus of Nazareth.

This historical Christian faith does *not* begin with some phenomenon of the world and deduce God from it; it does *not* begin with some human value or activity and define God by elevating that value or activity to *divinity.* Doing so is making God in our own image—concocting the God we want. The most common and insidious form of this is "role-model" theology—concocting a God who "is like me" and hence one to whom I can relate.

What's more, the historical Christian faith does *not* begin with the claim that the term *God* refers to the "Great Unknown," thereby implying that we must invent language for this Unknown—language that then can be changed at will since it was invented at will. Rather, we begin with the understanding that the Christian God has made himself known, identified himself in the biblical story—the story of redemption and the promise of salvation as given in the history of Israel and the event of Jesus Christ. And that particular God is specifically identified by the trinitarian name— Father, Son and Holy Spirit—which distinguishes him from all other gods. The Christian answer to the question *Who is God?* is simply *the Father of our Lord Jesus Christ.*

But this gospel is under heavy attack today throughout the churches— particularly in the mainline Protestant churches. This attack appears under different banners, usually involving the promotion of some favorite cause, and the feminists are in the frontlines in this respect. This God who tells Moses "I AM WHO I AM" (Ex 3:14), who enters into contingent relationships with human beings at particular times and in particular places, who approves of certain actions and not of others, has always been, to say the least, hard to live with. Human beings have always preferred gods for whom they can write the job descriptions themselves.

Scripture refers to these preferred gods as idols, and Isaiah 44:9-20 gives us as clear a description as has ever been written of the idol maker and his idol. The craftsman cuts down a good, healthy tree, uses part of it for a fire to warm himself and to cook his dinner. Then from part of it he makes a graven image, to which he falls down and worships, praying— "Save me, for you are my god!" (Is 44:17).

It's only at this point that Isaiah delivers his punch line, a punch line that is all too often overlooked. He tells us of the awesome power of the idol. That piece of wood that the craftsman himself has formed has deceived him—has led him astray to the point that he no longer recognizes it as his own creation. He has been blinded—blinded by his own creativity—so that he no longer recognizes that he is worshiping a delusion and hence is no longer able to deliver himself. He is unable to ask himself, "Is not this thing in my right hand a fraud?" (Is 44:20).

Other Old Testament passages speak eloquently of the idols as being useless, unable to do anything, unable to support their people, instead having to be carried around and being a burden to them. But Isaiah puts his finger on a far more dangerous characteristic: they have the power to delude and deceive their makers.

The work of those attempting to craft a god of their own making, the god *we* want and for whom *we* can provide the job description, is rampant within the church today. The feminists are not alone. They have built on a foundation provided by many others, but they lead the pack. The foundation on which feminists build is the widespread view that not just what Isaiah calls idols are made in the carpenter shop but that *all* gods—including the Christian God—have their origin in somebody's carpenter shop.

One of the leading spokesmen for this view is Gordon Kaufman, professor at Harvard University. Kaufman argues that we need to recognize that Scripture, like all texts, is a culturally bound product of humanly created concepts.[3] *It does not* refer to a reality with whom we must deal and who deals with us—One with whom we must come to terms. The central concepts of Scripture, the concepts of God and Jesus Christ, come out of an ancient carpenter shop. And while they may have served a useful function at one time, we need to recognize that they are now badly disintegrated— they are actually misleading and dangerous, destructive to human well being today. So the task of today's theologians is to get back to the carpenter shop, to work on producing new images—new symbols that will serve a useful function for our time.

The feminists lead the workforces that have gotten busy in this way. Their carpenter shops are very energetically turning out replacements for the traditional *images* of God and Jesus Christ. The basic material being fashioned in their carpenter shops is not the wood of an oak tree but something referred to as "women's experience," or more specifically, "women's

---

[3]See, for example, Gordon Kaufman, *An Essay on Theological Method* (Missoula, Mont.: Scholars Press, 1989).

experience in the struggle for liberation from oppression." The blueprints that guide the carpenters in their work carry the title "guidelines for promoting the full humanity of women." And the tools they employ are designed for the express purpose of liberating women from all forms of patriarchal oppression in both church and society.

Within this program, "patriarchal" is the expression of ultimate evil. It encapsulates all forms of racism, classism and, above all, sexism. And in all these forms of oppression it is the men who dominate the women. Patriarchy permeates all of our social, political, cultural and economic structures. All of the evils of these structures can ultimately be laid at its door. And for the feminist theologian the chief culprit in this respect is the Christian faith, with its Bible, its tradition and its churches saturated with patriarchy.

The first hurdle to be overcome then is the Bible, since it is regarded as essentially androcentric and thoroughly pervaded by patriarchy. It was written by men living in a patriarchal society, has been interpreted throughout the centuries solely by men and has been used in the church to subordinate women to men. Moreover, its influence is regarded as a major reason for the oppressive patriarchal structures and attitudes within modern Western society.

This understanding of the Bible leads to the obvious conclusion that what needs to be done, if possible, is to find something in it that will support the goal of promoting the full humanity of women and to reject any aspect of it that denies or diminishes the full humanity of women. Any such passages cannot be true to the new image being fashioned. Or as Rosemary Ruether puts it, such passages "must *not* be presumed to reflect the divine will or the authentic nature of things."[4] In this vein Elisabeth Schüssler Fiorenza proposes that all such texts should *not* be retained in the lectionary, should *not* be proclaimed in Christian worship and should *not* be used in catechism classes.[5] Obviously the authority of the Scriptures in any traditional sense has been rejected. They do not speak authoritatively *to us—we* control them.

The function of the feminist's carpenter shop is to turn out images that

---

[4]Rosemary Ruether, "Feminist Interpretation: A Method of Correlation," in *Feminist Interpretation of the Bible,* ed. Letty M. Russell (Philadelphia: Westminster Press, 1985), p. 115, emphasis mine.

[5]Elisabeth Schüssler Fiorenza, *Bread not Stone: The Challenge of Feminist Biblical Interpretation* (Boston: Beacon, 1984), p. 18.

promote the full humanity of women, and the Scriptures are only useful to the extent that they serve that purpose, and as just indicated, they don't do that very well. A number of shops have claimed to have found other sources, other traditions, that serve their purpose better.

According to the owners of these shops, the fundamental problem with the images produced in the ancient carpenter shops is that they were male. The traditional Christian God is a male God, and according to Mary Daly "If God is male, the male is God."[6] The Bible's use of masculine language for the deity serves to legitimate the domination of women by men. It legitimates patriarchy. Hence the first order of business in the task of producing new images is to "feminize" God. And the solution would seem to be obvious—just turn out female images instead of male. Some shops are willing to settle for about a 50-50 ratio as being sufficient, others have decided upon a genderless or neuter image, and others have opted for nothing less than 100 percent female images. After all, this is the better product—the one that will serve more effectively to correct the oppressiveness found in our churches and our society.

It's time to take a closer look at the basic theological issues that are at stake here. Specifically, we need to inquire into the theological legitimacy of the premises upon which the feminist workshops are organized and that are responsible for the work being carried out. Assumptions are being made not only about the use of language but about the nature of the Christian God himself, that are being regarded as almost self-evident and frequently being accepted without question as axiomatic.

Crucial, of course, is the view that the Christian God is male. When it is pointed out that usage of masculine language does *not* mean that the biblical God is male (that never has been the teaching of either the central Christian or Jewish faith), the feminist response is usually, *But that is the way it is heard, and hence it is exclusive and offensive to women*. It may be that some people have heard it that way, but if so, that is a misconception—a misunderstanding. Misunderstandings can only be corrected by improving our understanding, by arriving at a better understanding. We cannot correct a misconception by further contributing to that misconception, by reinforcing it and making it appear valid even though it is invalid.

Attempts to correct this misconception by employing female images and language to speak of God (i.e., attempts to counteract the maleness of

---

[6]Mary Daly, *Beyond God the Father* (Boston: Beacon, 1973), p. 19.

God by "feminizing" the deity) are based upon a further assumption, namely, the claim that the Bible itself makes frequent use of female images for God, and this justifies the use of female language as a literary device to overcome the sexism of the patriarchal tradition.

This assumption is based on a fundamental linguistic and literary mistake. The nature of this mistake is dealt with specifically by several authors in *Speaking the Christian God*, most directly by Roland Frye. As Frye puts it, this mistake consists in a confusion about two central uses of language, two figures of speech, which he refers to as "metaphor" and "simile."[7]

We don't need to get into a debate over what a metaphor is and how it functions. That is not the issue. The issue is simply this: whatever term you use to indicate them, you have two different uses of language (or figures of speech) that are being employed. One merely states a resemblance, saying that something may be like something else under certain conditions. This figure of speech Frye calls a *simile*, and the way in which something may be like something else is clarified or explained by the context in which it is used. The other form of speech, which Frye calls a *metaphor*, makes a bold statement that the one thing represents or predicates the other. This form of speech stretches language, so to speak, as a means of providing a fuller and more direct understanding of the subject in question.

The Bible is filled with statements that say that God, in certain situations—under certain conditions and in specific contexts—*acts* like something else or may be compared to something else. And some of these involve feminine activities or subjects. Thus God in the Scriptures is said to act like a comforting mother [Is 66:13], cry out like a woman in childbirth (Is 42:14), act like a mother eagle (Deut 32:11) and rage like a mother bear robbed of her cubs [Hos 13:8]. But God is never addressed as mother. To say that God acts like a mother bear robbed of her cubs is vividly meaningful, to say that God *is* a mother bear is ludicrous.

It is also very generally assumed that the biblical language is sexist, and of course the prime examples are "Father" and "Son." Obviously Jesus of Nazareth is male. But *are* these terms sexist? A number of authors have shown, very convincingly, that the relation between the Father and the

---

[7]Roland Frye, "Language for God and Feminist Language: Problems and Principles," in *Speaking the Christian God*, ed. Alvin Kimel (Grand Rapids, Mich.: Eerdmans, 1992).

Son as provided in Scripture has nothing to do with sexuality.[8]

To call God *Father* in the Christian tradition is always shorthand for "the Father of our Lord Jesus Christ." In other words, it does not refer to *a* father, but it addresses God in solidarity with Jesus as "our Father." Hence the meaning of the metaphor has to be sought in the story of *the One whom Jesus called Father.* Immersion in that story—immersion in Scripture—provides the means for eventually recognizing that those images we have made in our own workshops to serve our own purposes are lies that we hold in our hands.

We need to close our carpenter shops—all of them—and immerse ourselves in Scripture. Then we will meet the Christian God, the Father of our Lord Jesus Christ, and our Father.

Further Reading

Kassian, Mary A. *The Feminist Gospel: The Movement to Unite Feminism with the Church* (Wheaton, Ill.: Crossway, 1992).

Keck, Leander E. *The Church Confident* (Nashville: Abingdon, 1993).

Kimel, Alvin, ed., *Speaking the Christian God* (Grand Rapids, Mich.: Eerdmans, 1992). Kimel's book deals specifically and in detail with the relationship of feminism to Christianity. It includes an article of mine that is distinct from the present essay but has the same title, "Christianity or Feminism?"

---

[8]Here I simply refer you to some sources that argue this point very clearly, such as the articles in *Speaking the Christian God* by Garrett Green and Colin Gunton, as well as those by Elizabeth Achtemeier and Roland Frye. These all provide references to additional sources.

JESUS' PARADIGM FOR RELATING HUMAN EXPERIENCE & LANGUAGE ABOUT GOD

GARY W. DEDDO

T HE PROBLEM OF THEOLOGICAL LANGUAGE IN WORSHIP HAS NOW BECOME an issue debated even within individual congregations. It is no longer confined to secular academia or seminaries where the contemporary debate has been going on for some time. The most basic issues underlying the contemporary debate have been with us, in the West, at least since the time of Plato and Aristotle. It was central to the debates of the early church in dealing with Arianism, and it surfaced in an obvious way in the medieval realist and nominalist controversy. In modern times it was Ludwig Feuerbach who raised this problem so forcefully. However, the root issues were already dealt with in the laws of ancient Israel. What we are going through now is an old problem in a contemporary form. How can we and how should we speak of God?

The present focus of debate falls on the use of gender related issues of language in reference to persons and to God. In this essay I would like to restrict discussion to the problem of our language about God that at this point in time centers on the issue of the use of gendered terms. I will also discuss how our approach to handling concerns of gendered language has enormous implications for our referring to God at all. I want to suggest that the biblical record of Jesus' teaching in Matthew 23:9 is crucial for this debate and that his teaching offers a radical alternative to the solution most often recommended today.[1] In fact, it is so distinct that it could be designated an alternative paradigm for understanding and resolving the issue of relating our language of God to our experience.

An Assumption and a Hermeneutical Paradigm

Most proposed solutions to the problem of traditional speech about God and issues of sexism seem to be based on a common assumption made within a common paradigm to be used for relating human language to language about God. Masculine language about God is judged problematic because of the kinds of negative associations and even sinful experiences persons have suffered, poor relationships between women and their fathers being cited most often to make the point. This perspective was poignantly illustrated in a presbytery debate where a woman recounted a story of young girl whose father had deserted her and her mother. The conclusion of her argument for the proposed inclusive language policy (which was subsequently adopted) was that, by speaking and writing of God under these "gender-inclusive and gendered-balanced" guidelines, this girl could be spared from being led to think that God was like her unfaithful father and rather led to think that God was more like her mother. It was assumed that masculine language about God would only serve to tear at her wound and drive her away from the true God and that, given her experience, feminine language would avoid this problem. The girl's experience of a faithless relationship with her father was assumed to be the determinative factor for her point of view and thus rendered masculine language of God unacceptable. At a more general level it is often argued that it is the evil of patriarchalism experienced throughout society at large that makes masculine language problematic for many.

---

[1]See for example, Anne E. Carr, *Transforming Grace: Tradition and Women's Experience* (San Francisco: Continuum, 1988); Rosemary Ruether, *Sexism and God-Talk: Toward a Feminist Theology* (Boston: Beacon, 1983); Sallie McFague, *Metaphorical Theology: Models of God in Religious Language* (Philadelphia: Fortress, 1997); and Mary Daly, *Beyond God the Father: Toward a Philosophy of Women's Liberation* (Boston: Beacon, 1973).

Having such an experience with a father or other male authority figure is assumed to have such a powerful and unchangeable character that it serves as a permanent lens through which all talk of God must be interpreted. Such negative experiences are judged to distort permanently any concept of God whenever it is communicated in language that an individual might associate with that painful experience. Thus for those who have had painful experiences with men, masculine words, images or concepts could only serve to distort communication about God. It is this assumption of the determinative quality of such painful experiences that underlies most contemporary demands for a change in the language of our worship, prayer and theology.

The assumption regarding the power of past experience to play the determinative role in any subsequent approach to God has an even deeper assumption upon which it is built. The conditioning force of past experi-ence can be assumed to have determinative power only when the much more comprehensive assumption is made that no other influence can be greater. This assumption is rarely if ever articulated, much less debated, but is clearly required to sustain the more obvious assumption. These two assumptions together form the basis for most contemporary arguments for changing how we speak of God.

These assumptions have coalesced into the establishment of a norm for approaching the problem of relating our experience to language about God, which we will call a paradigm. This paradigm stipulates how to solve the problem of the proper relationship between our language about God and our experiences in the human created realm. It seems to assert this: whenever our human experience might misconstrue our understanding of our language about God, our theology and liturgy ought to be adjusted to accommodate it, since it is our experience that is fixed and unchangeable. Our theology and liturgy should be relativized in the light of our experience.

The assumption of the determinative power of past experience is thereby conjoined with a normative or paradigmatic approach to relating our experience and speech about God. The often hidden assumption of a determinative power for our experiences is thus codified through the prescription of a particular hermeneutical paradigm that tells us we ought to move from our experiences, which serve as incorrigible criteria, to our interpretation of any proper reference to God.[2]

---

[2]The Freudian and perhaps Marxist overtones of this argument deserve treatment, although I will not take it up here.

The argument runs: since such painful experiences are irremediable, we can only act and speak in terms of our past experiences, even or especially when it comes to speaking of God. Since there is no other possibility, we ought to condition our language about God by our experiences. To recommend an alternative, in this framework, is regarded both as a delusion and as cruel.

This paradigm assumes and legitimizes the sovereignty of a given individual's experience for formulating speech about God. Consequently we will designate this pervasive contemporary orientation to the problem as the anthropocentric paradigm.

A Shared Concern but a Faithful and Compassionate Alternative

Although I think we must question the assumptions and the interpretive paradigm that follows in such arguments, I want to acknowledge one thing first. There is a real problem here and a real call for a responsible decision regarding language. The fact that many women have been shamefully treated by their biological fathers or other male authorities must be acknowledged, and we must anticipate that such experiences will indeed have implications for their spiritual journey toward God. Such faithless relationships do present serious obstacles to the comprehension of God's true character. A false witness is a lie against God, and for those who have been subjected to such distortions there will be serious pastoral implications that should not be minimized.

The reason I raise the question about the anthropocentric paradigm is not to ignore or deny the experience of such persons, but because I believe that the assumptions are false and that this paradigm will not in the end be truly helpful to those very persons who have been injured.

First, I want to present an alternative way to relate our experience and language about God based on the example and teaching of Jesus. My second concern is to demonstrate that if we follow the now predominant anthropocentric paradigm we may perhaps avoid further irritating people's wounds, but we will leave them still bleeding and unhealed in their experience and captive of it. Consequently, they will be defenseless against further abuse and perhaps liable to pass it on to others. But third, and worse yet, the anthropocentric paradigm leaves all of us without any reason or hope of having any valid knowledge of God. It is a self-defeating hermeneutic that calls into question not only gendered language about God but *all* language about God. This solution invalidates all theological statements that purport to refer to God, not just masculine language. In sum, I argue that true compassion for those used and abused calls for a different solution that holds out the possibility of freedom from the domination of past injury and also a freedom from mere self-projection, thus opening a way to a true and healing knowledge of God and renewed relationships with others.

Jesus' Paradigm, Assumption and Compassion

The passage in Matthew 23:1-12 is an interesting one to consider in the light of the issue of language about God, even gendered language about God. In this context Jesus criticizes the scribes and Pharisees of his day for being hypocritical spiritual leaders of the people. "They bind heavy burdens, hard to bear . . . but they themselves will not move them with their finger" (Mt 23:4 RSV). Here Jesus is concerned that what they do betrays who God is. They misrepresent God in their actions and set up obstacles to people's grasping God's true character. This is a situation very much like we see today when, as is most often pointed out, biological fathers are unfaithful in their responsibility to rightly reflect God's character in their own parenting. Jesus sees and acknowledges that our experience of another person's behavior can indeed create obstacles to our trust in God. There can be a great distortion of the truth of God as it comes to be reflected in human relations.

However, Jesus' solution works in exactly the opposite direction than the one most often urged on us today. Rather than adjusting our language of God to our experience of human relations, Jesus directs us to change our language about human relations in the light of our language about God. Jesus tells them we are not to be called rabbi, master or father, and the reason he gives is because ultimately there is but one Teacher, Master and Father, namely, God. If human beings have betrayed the true meaning of these names, it is human beings who should be deprived of their assumption of the names, not God.

Jesus relativizes the language about persons in terms of language about God, not vice versa. If Jesus were to follow the contemporary paradigm, he would have insisted that they not call him Teacher, that they not call God Father, nor Master. For Jesus, the solution to the unfaithfulness of human witness to the true character of God was to reverse the direction of adaptation. We must adapt our language about our human experiences to the language about God given to us by Jesus

Christic.[3] If humans are unfaithful to their calling to represent the fatherhood of God, the title should be revoked from them, not God.

Furthermore, although he did recognize an influence of others on us
that constituted a genuine obstacle to faith, Jesus did not assume that our
experience has determinative power to condition our knowledge of God.
Rather he assumed that there is a greater influence that can reach into our
lives with the power to set us free from the prison of ourselves and our
past. He assumed the determinative power of God's grace by the Holy
Spirit to be sovereign over us. Consequently, when it came to speaking
faithfully of God, his greatest concern was not to avoid using words or
concepts that might possibly be associated with unfaithful human relationships. Rather he continued to use humanly misused terms such as
Father, Master and *Lord* for God, assuming that the true word about God
would judge and overcome any misrepresentation in their human relationships. Here he commands his listeners to do just this.

Finally, we can assume that it was the same compassion manifest everywhere else in his ministry that led him to direct us to this paradigm rather
than the other. For Jesus, true reconciliation and healing can be found only
when we first use language that is faithful to God, and second, let this shed
light on all other usages, faithful or unfaithful. The true original word is to
be used to interpret all its representations. Jesus' teaching thus orders the
direction of the hermeneutical task. We will designate this approach as the
theocentric paradigm for relating human experience and speech about
God.[4]

The problem that human unfaithfulness poses for our ability to talk

---

[3]Thus although God does "adapt" his truth to us that we might grasp it, we too are called
to adapt our thought and language to God's adaptation to us in Christ. Otherwise there
would be no revelation at all, and there certainly would never be repentance or *meta-
noia*, a radical change of mind about God. If God's adaptation to us was absolute, this
would then amount merely to a confirmation of us as we are and as we think; it would
make unnecessary not only any change on our part but any need for a revealing or justifying act of God in the first place.

[4]We could have called this the christocentric paradigm, but that might have been misleading for some. The revelation of the whole triune God was focused in the person and
life of the Son of God incarnate. However, the Son reveals the Father and sends us the
Spirit. Thus a christocentrism, while proper, leads to a trinitarian theocentrism, and not
to a so-called christomonism. In an orthodox trinitarian frame, calling it a christocentric
paradigm would have the value of indicating that the demand to have to choose
between a theology "from above" or "from below" presents a false dichotomy. Strictly
speaking then, it is this *trinitarian* theocentrism to which we refer.

about God faithfully is not new. Jesus acknowledged it in the first century
A.D., the passage above being a prime example.[5] Persons in human history
from beginning to end have experienced the wrenching pain of human
unfaithfulness in the most intimate of relations. Given the universal experience of the human failure of fathers (and everyone else) to faithfully represent God, it is curious that it has taken this long for the demand to
minimize or eliminate (at least for some persons) masculine speech about
God to become so insistent and widespread.

The problem of human unfaithfulness and language about God has been
recognized throughout the history of religious and philosophical reflection. From Jesus' time onward the church has been consciously wrestling
with it.[6] What is new is the prescribed solution to it and the two assumptions brought together and made prior to our approach to the perennial
problem of language about God.

Unfortunately, in the contemporary phase of this debate the assumption
about the incorrigibility of past personal experience is seldom questioned.
However, the force of the argument rests entirely on it. If they are false, the
proposed anthropocentric solution loses its ground. The assumption is
called into question by the fact that Jesus' teaching assumes the opposite,
namely that the truth of God as presented in and by him has the power to
reorient us to it. Thus the anthropocentric assumption cannot stand as the
only option within the framework of Christian faith.

---

[5]When Jesus asks the question "Why do you call me good?" (Mk 10:18), the same issue is
involved. On what basis will they form their definitions?

[6]Athanasius' fourth-century debate with Arius involves the same rival assumptions and
hermeneutical paradigms. Do we call God Father on the basis of our experience of
human fatherhood or on the basis of Jesus' own sonship? Do we call God Father
because God is like us, one member of the class of beings called fathers, or do we refer
to ourselves as fathers because God is first of all the Father of Jesus Christ and so we too
may bear witness to that original, true and faithful fatherhood in some of our own relationships? Athanasius was clear; we name God according to the revelation in the Son,
not according to our human experience. The alternatives for him were mythology and
idolatry (Athanasius *De Synodis* 42, in *Athanasius: Select Writings and Letters*, NPNF,
ed. Philip Schaff, 2nd series [Buffalo, N.Y.: Christian Literature, 1892], 4:472. See also
Karl Barth, *Church Dogmatics*, 1/1, 386ff. Behind Athanasius' thought lies the Patristic
recognition of the *apophatic* nature of theological statements. It anticipated the classical formulation that no reference to God can be regarded as *univocal*. That is, no word
proper to human experience (such as "good," "wise," "present" or "alive") can be said
to be attributed to God in exactly the same way. But there are words that are not *equivo-
cal* (have no proper reference to God) but are properly *analogical* (are first true of God
and then are in a derived way appropriate to human existence).

Furthermore, those who reject the presently reigning anthropocentric solution have often been accused of denying the human problem and pain and even of perpetuating it. However, to insist that any alternative must be a cruel one also runs into the obstacle that Jesus' theocentric solution arises out of his full sympathy with those spiritually harmed by those he himself criticizes. Our approach must do no less.

True Compassion: Beyond Sympathy to Healing

Perhaps a few words about the nature of Jesus' compassion will clarify the true nature of his solution compared to the contemporary one. It seems that Jesus' compassion involved a concern that went beyond merely helping people avoid more immediate pain. In fact, he made it clear to those who followed him that certain kinds of suffering were intrinsic to his call. They would have to lose their lives (Mk 8:35), cut certain things out of their lives (Mt 5:29) and suffer persecution (Mk 10:30). Jesus did not spare people's false pride but rather exposed it, all the while preserving their true integrity. Even those caught in the most shameful situations were not spared his straightforward evaluation of their behavior and given a warning ("Neither do I condemn you. Go and sin no more" [Jn 8:11]). Yet he would preserve them from any self-righteous condemnation. Jesus would not condone wrong to spare people's feelings (egos) but rather did everything to spare their lives for God. And that's the point. Jesus, as a faithful incarnate representative of God, was moved by his own compassion to lead people to full life in him even if this meant exposing a wound, either self-inflicted or caused by others. Healing for the first called for the pain of repentance; the second required the agony of giving forgiveness. Jesus would not limit his compassion to a kindness that would allow the avoidance of the additional pain of forgiveness or repentance but rather pursued people's full restoration from the wound of the past by means of telling them to repent and forgive.[7]

Let me venture to draw out how the dynamic of Jesus' compassion calls for an alternative paradigm for speaking about God in painful situations. Those who have been sinned against have not only been betrayed on a human level but also on a spiritual level. Human relationships when distorted and broken are themselves a source of pain. But beyond that, God's

---

[7]Of course Jesus' own suffering on our behalf demonstrates the true depth of the Father and Son's love for humanity and all creation.

true character is obscured by that human sin. The severity of the wound inflicted cannot be assessed merely by an analysis of the particular act of unfaithfulness exhibited and the immediate pain experienced. It can be fully grasped only by perceiving the deeper wounding that involves the defacement of the image of God entrusted to, say, a father. The gift of human fatherhood is a God-given trust meant to bear witness to God's love for his Son and their love for us in him. Its purpose is to be a means to lead others to trust in God's love.

Such human failure tempts people to misunderstand or mistrust the living God. That this is especially true in the context of the family is underscored in the special biblical commands, warnings and promised blessings directed to parent-child relationships. The victims of such treatment are robbed of a true witness to the character of God, a responsibility uniquely entrusted to that one person. Such unfaithfulness disrupts the child's relationship with God, leading him or her into temptation to not trust God.

If earthly fathers have betrayed that God-given task, not only is the human relationship broken but the God relationship is at least threatened, if not broken. Thus it too must be restored if full healing is to be accomplished. The question arises as to what could possibly replace the false witness implanted in a child's heart? On the human plane only a true witness by another could possibly serve, but this has its limitations. Persons only have one earthly father, and a subsequent experience cannot of itself become a norm but only an additional experience that may at most relativize the former unfaithfulness. Full restoration must, therefore, involve a reapprehension of the true fatherhood that invites a renewed trust in God. Without this deeper dimension of reconciliation all other healing remains relatively superficial and leaves the person vulnerable to further harm. The deepest healing is required *at the wound*. Only a true witness to the character of God could bring this about. Full restoration for such a person would certainly involve a healing in both dimensions, but it must essentially involve the restored knowledge of true fatherhood.

This explains Jesus' response. The leaders have been unfaithful in their witness to the character of the true God. They have abused people by misrepresenting in themselves the reality behind the titles Master, Rabbi and Father. However, these words, in Jesus' view, cannot be thrown out of the theological dictionary. Their degradation calls for their restoration. Their true meaning must be restored by reference to

God, for God is the norm by which to grasp the true meaning of these words.[8] To cease speaking of the fatherhood of God because of human unfaithfulness would avoid reminding someone of their pain, but such a strategy precludes the possibility of the renewal of their grasp of the character of God at the very point at which it is most distorted. Out of his compassion Jesus' primary concern is to have their knowledge of God's true character restored at the very point where pain and deception were experienced.

This dynamic has been born out many times in my own ministry. I have had a number of persons (men and women) testify that their own restoration at the deepest level came when they discovered that they did have a faithful father, after all, in the Father of our Lord Jesus Christ. Proclamation of the true father character of God did not prove to be an unsurmountable obstacle to approaching God but was vital to their healing.[9]

---

[8]In several notable cases it has become obvious that New Testament authors had to wrestle with the selection and meaning of certain words to convey the unique revelatory meaning of their message. The words and meanings of love *(agapē)*, fellowship/participation *(koinōnia)*, truth *(alētheia)* and even Messiah are clear examples. During the first four centuries of theological reflection, which came to be summarized in the statements of the ecumenical councils, could be characterized as essentially discovering, defining and redefining within the Greek philosophical framework key terminology adequate to the Christian revelation (e.g., *being, person, nature, substance*) and coordinating their meanings in at least two languages, Latin and Greek.

[9]This essay is essentially about ascertaining the proper relationship between our experience and language about God in general. It argues that at their intersection the biblical content should serve as the criteria to regulate our usage. However, it primarily makes use of a particular instance of the problem: namely the problem of speaking of God as Father.

This particular issue was chosen because of the contemporary concern and the biblical parallel in Matthew 23. The force of the argument, as it relates to the particular title *Father*, leads to the conclusion that it is theologically and pastorally crucial to maintain this particular designation, and a proper understanding of it, for God. It cannot and should not be minimized or eliminated.

This argument does not directly address the issue of the propriety of addressing God additionally with feminine pronouns or as *she* or *Mother*. However, its conclusion indicates that if we are to avoid mythology or idolatry and benefit from the revelational content of Scripture, then our usage and practice should follow the biblical pattern of usage centered in Jesus Christ.

Thus the determination of whether God should be addressed as she or Mother or with feminine pronouns would require a comparative analysis of the various ways that God is addressed in the biblical material, especially as given to us by Jesus in addressing God as Father and explicitly instructing his disciples to do so as well (Mt 6:9). This has been expertly done by a number of persons. (See below.)

The conclusions of those studies and my own work are that certain aspects of God's

Two Further Dimensions of Healing: Forgiveness with Discernment and Stronger Defenses Against Abuse and Abusing

But faithful speech about God, in the face of human failure, brings with it the possibility of another dimension of healing. On the horizontal plane of relationships an understanding of the nature of abuse seems to contribute to the healing process involving both forgiveness and a growing capacity to avoid (where possible) future abuse. Human sin involves in large part deceit, not just immediate harm. A crucial aspect of evil is its power to call into question the victim's ability to discern the truth, to undermine a person's trust in his or her own capacity to judge good from evil. It is well documented that a frequent response to abuse is for the victim to blame himself or herself. In my own ministry I have found persons to be amazingly resistant to acknowledging mistreatment by others, especially parents. Such persons experience a profound inner turmoil and confusion when betrayed by an intimate. This often produces a further lack of confidence in their own powers of discernment, even in matters of their own experience! The persons who have wronged them often appear to them at worst as blameless monsters or at best as huge unanswerable question

---

character are indeed *illustrated* by a few but nevertheless explicit associations with the exclusively feminine attribute of motherhood (Is 42:14; 45:10; 49:15; 66:13; see also Dt 32:11; Is 31:5; Hos 13:8; Mt 23:37). These comparisons are made exclusively through the figure of simile ("God is like a . . .") and not through the use of metaphor or by names of address that make for much stronger and direct comparison. The numerous metaphorical and vocative usages are reserved for fathering and the name Father. God is said to *be* the Father of Israel and is called by the name Father. By contrast, God is never said to be a mother and is never addressed as she. So our usage should follow.

Nevertheless, if the feminine-like comparisons and characteristics of God have been neglected in the church's preaching and worship, as I am inclined to think they have, then it is appropriate to see that they are properly noted so as to faithfully reflect the biblical witness to the fullness of God's character. Reference to certain aspects of God's character that could be compared to those we might associate with the feminine go far beyond those limited to the explicitly feminine ones such as motherhood. Conveying this fullness will be helpful to those who may think that God is somehow essentially male or masculine.

However, since God is never addressed as Mother or she, our doing so would be quite a different matter and crucially misleading. Further exploration as to why this might be so is beyond the scope of this essay but may be explored by the reader elsewhere. See my "Speaking of God," *Religious and Theological Studies Fellowship Bulletin* 7 (April-May 1995): 10-13, 23. Also the essays "Exchanging God for 'No Gods': A Discussion of Female Language for God" by Elizabeth Achtemeier, "Language for God and Feminist Language: Problems and Principles" by Roland Frye and "The Gender of God and the Theology of Metaphor" by Garret Green, all in Alvin F. Kimel Jr., ed., *Speaking the Christian God* (Grand Rapids, Mich.: Eerdmans, 1992).

marks, leaving them in fear and anger, which they sometimes direct at themselves.

Abused persons arrive at a significant turning point when they come to see clearly what parents or others did both faithfully and unfaithfully. The clear presentation of true love and service in Christ's revelation of his heavenly Father serves to provide the norm, the light by which to discern the true state of affairs in a person's own experience. Coming to such a place is indeed painful. However, it leads to a greater clarity about the true character of their relationships, and this in turn opens a door to the offering of genuine forgiveness. Forgiveness and a sober, honest recognition as to how and when a person was abused seem to be often linked. A deep forgiveness may follow upon the clear identity of the evil experienced (even if anger interposes itself first). And forgiveness, following the New Testament teaching, is crucial to our restoration. Forgiving another calls for the acknowledgment of the sin and leads to healing not only the relationship but also leads to a cleansing of the pollution of deceit and the subsequent insecurity it breeds. The deception is broken, and the evil nature of the wrong is exposed for what it is.

The light of a norm beyond an individual's past experience brings a restored power of discernment. Gaining a clear grasp of the nature of the evil done strengthens his or her capacity to recognize and avoid being abused in the same way again.

A crucial element in the process of healing involves persons grasping clear criteria for recognizing wrong behavior when directed against them by persons close to them. Their own broken experiences cannot serve as the norm, but a reapprehension of the truth of God in Christ can. In the light of this norm, persons can better evaluate the treatment they are receiving from others and take measures to minimize or avoid that which they have come to recognize as harmful. And it does so in a way that mere anger and unforgiveness can never provide. In this way they can overcome their fear of remaining a victim and take some responsibility for the maintenance of their own health.

Such discernment of healthy relationships will also contribute to a person's resistance to passing on any harmful behavior to his or her children or others. And as numerous studies show, persons abused are those most likely to abuse their own children.

Jesus' insistence that those who have been harmed by the mistreatment of others should look to their God for a true grasp of the normative pattern for their relationships arises from his compassion. He assumes that there is a possibility for us to transcend our own experience graciously granted to us by God through Christ. This self-transcendence is necessary if our broken relationships with God are to be restored, if we are to have the possibility of extending forgiveness to others, to avoid being further abused and also to escape passing on abusive patterns of behavior. If persons are left with only the painful experiences of fatherhood and are denied access to a positive and true pattern of relating, then healing can only be delayed. Surely hopelessness about their own capacity to be any more faithful than their own parents will threaten to overwhelm them.

Jesus cannot leave them confined within the walls of their own broken experience and so calls them out of their own immediate experiences to grasp a greater truth that sheds light on their experience. The paradigm of Jesus' solution is that we are not to interpret God in terms of our previous experience understood apart from Christ, but we are to interpret our experience in terms of the revelation of God in Jesus Christ. It is on the basis of our grasp of the true fatherhood of God that we can most clearly discern the normative pattern by which to evaluate and conduct our relationships.

Furthermore, this is a call for people to resist the contemporary skepticism that assumes our experiences, and their prima facie interpretations are permanently and necessarily determinative for our perspective on life and thereby deny the possibility of any growth beyond them. If we are to be true to the gospel, we must present an alternative and opposite paradigm. Who we are is not essentially determined by our past experience understood apart from God in Christ but is determined by the grace of God in Christ. Thus ultimately we are to interpret our own experience in the light of that grace made visible in the relationship of the Father and Son in the Spirit. True compassion and hope for the healing of others cannot settle for anything less than this if it is to be reflective of the compassion of Jesus.

A Few Implications for Ministry in a Changing Context

The implication of such a proper theology is not that we force people at all times and places to blindly speak of God as Father. Rather we should continually encourage persons to struggle with the meaning of God's own fatherhood as a crucial element leading toward their own healing. It is important to recognize the shifting cultural context away from masculine reference to God. I believe it signals in part the legitimate rejection of a distorted and unfaithful human masculinity. Ultimately what is needed is a restoration in idea and practice of a true redeemed human masculinity. Such will not be a threat to true human femininity but rather a blessing.

But how will we get there? When dealing with those new to Christian faith who come with a negative bias toward the masculine, it would not be advisable to start with an announcement of an obligation to call God "Father." We may, of course, begin by having them address God as merely "God." From there the true full character of God must be uncovered and explored as it is revealed in God's relationship with Israel, and especially in the relationship of the incarnate Son with his heavenly Father as depicted in the New Testament. Where we can see true fatherhood and sonship being lived out is in the relationship Jesus had with his heavenly Father. People need to have the particulars of this glorious relationship narrated for them. The exposition of Jesus' treatment of women would also be especially important in this connection. This process may continue with initiates by perhaps speaking of "the Father *of our Lord Jesus Christ*," or qualifying our address by saying "Our *heavenly* Father," thus preserving the unique, normative and prior fatherhood of God over our human experience of fatherhood. In a pastoral situation it may be advisable to encourage persons to duly note the unfaithfulness of a human father or the betrayal of masculinity in a given situation by way of comparison with God's true fatherly care.

Ultimately, however, the issue cannot and should not be avoided. We can expect great difficulty in dealing those who wish to address God as she or who refuse to call God Father. There can be no shortcuts. Demonstrating how and in what way it is essential in the end to come to recognize God as the Father of our Lord Jesus Christ and why we are baptized in the triune name must become a matter of Christian maturity. Ultimately the cultural shift unavoidably demands the additional theological education of our congregations as to why we address God as Father at all and what we mean by it. We must show that we do so because he is the Father of the Son of God and because our speech about God is not derived from ourselves but rather our speech about ourselves is derived and interpreted in terms of God's truth and reality. How and why this is also compassionate and helpful is the burden of part of this essay. We will no longer be able to assume a proper understanding and acceptance of this way of addressing God.

Furthermore, we will have to make explicit the fact that God is not a sexual being, although up till now, in general, this could be assumed.

Many who argue against Christianity in general and against its masculine religious language in particular have asserted that what is meant by such language is that God is male, even though God's being a sexual being always has been denied and never affirmed. People will have to be led, instructed and encouraged to take on a proper biblical way of speaking of God.[10] Our theology will have to be decidedly and explicitly more trinitar-

---

[10]Another issue, far beyond the scope of this essay, is whether persons who are female can relate to the God revealed in Jesus Christ. On the basis of this essay we can point out that the primary issue is not whether men or women can relate to God but whether God can and has related to us. To insist that the most important question is whether God is like me is to assume the anthropocentric orientation. Its result can only be the projection of God according to our own individual images. Females would be led to create a god(dess), which would justify them as they are, and men would do the same. If the anthropocentric paradigm is all that is possible, then both would be justified in doing so and neither could call the other into question.

However, out of the theocentric and christocentric orientation we first see that God through the Son, the Word, creates male and female for the purpose of imaging God in Christ. As their creator, God knows the humanly feminine and masculine. God created them and their relation for a good purpose, to be a complementary channel of blessing to each other and to give glory to God. That is, men and women, in right relationship, are to be in their relations creaturely reflections of the fullness of the character of the triune relations within the Godhead. Masculinity and femininity provide a foundation, not an obstacle, for relationship to God and each other. As such they are not separate and unrelated realities but exist only in and for relationship with each other in God. While God is not a sexual being, it is more proper to say that God's character is "genderful," rather than "genderless." See my "Grammar of Barth's Theology of Personal Relations," *Scottish Journal of Theology* 47, no. 2 (1996): 183-222.

God in Christ and by the Spirit also reconciles male and female to himself and to each other. This has been accomplished in God's identification with us in our humanity by way of the incarnation and crucifixion. If Jesus were neither male nor female, or he was both, his existence would have been alien to ours altogether, because in our humanity we are particularly one or the other as he was. God in Christ can and has identified with us in a reconciling way. We in turn may identify with God through Christ at the level of our humanity, a humanity that is shared by men and women.

Through creation in Christ and the incarnation of the Son we learn that the differences between God and humanity and between male and female do not constitute separate and unrelatable realities. On the contrary, humans have their existence, their life, by being covenantally related to God and each other. We were created and reconciled for relationship with God in Christ and for right relationship between women and men. Recall the apostle Paul's admonition: "Nevertheless, in the Lord woman is not independent of man or man independent of woman. For just as woman came from man, so man comes through woman; but all things come from God" (1 Cor 11:11-12; cf. Gal 3:28).

In Christ the differences are not a threat to love and understanding but serve as a good foundation for right relationship which may image or reflect the glory of God. God can identify and has identified himself with us in Christ through creation and reconciliation. The only question is whether we will meet and know God where he has met and known us.

ian. It will also have to be much more theological rather than anthropo-logical, explicitly distinguishing it more deliberately from all mythologizing and other systems of self-projection and self-justification. It will be our burden to demonstrate what exactly is at stake if we refuse to follow the biblical pattern and assert alien patterns in our language and liturgy. For the implications of our assumptions and paradigms for relating language and experience go far beyond the concerns of Christian theological method or even of Christian ministry we have so far considered.

The Self-Defeating Nature of the Anthropocentric Assumption and Paradigm

Up to this point we have been considering how Jesus' directive for us to maintain faithful language about God as Father is compassionate because it leads to a reconciliation with God and with others, and brings a healing in ourselves. However, much more than this is at stake if the theocentric paradigm is rejected. In fact, I would go so far as to say that the gospel itself is at stake. Consider this. If indeed our understanding of God is determined (not merely influenced in a way that could eventually be over-come by grace) by our experiences of human relationships, then the question arises, On what basis could there ever be any true knowledge of God, any true worship of God?

The anthropocentric paradigm is grounded on an apprehension of human limitations and problems. It assumes that we are influenced by our experience. Well enough. But when such influence is assumed to be determinative for all subsequent experience, then it has the effect of relativizing or even eliminating a confidence in God's own ability to break into our experience to enable us to distinguish between the faith-fulness of God and faithlessness of human persons. What must be pointed out is that while the anthropocentric paradigm begins with a recognition of human limitation, it entails an assertion also of what *God* can and cannot do. God is rendered impotent in the sight of our limitations. This constitutes the denial of the efficacy of the grace of God. Jesus' intention to make the Father known as he knows the Father to those to whom he chooses, is nullified by such a paradigm. God's own purposes in Christ are thereby essentially circumscribed by human sin. There can be no overcoming of evil by God's good in this framework. Human sin obliterates our apprehension of God's character, and thus it serves as the most fundamental reality that orients how we think and speak of God. What begins as a humble concern about our own limitations turns out to constitute a powerful assertion about the impotence of God.

The anthropocentric paradigm also entails that it is not just our language about the fatherhood of God that is rendered useless but that *all* our language about God is irrelevant and misleading. If the brokenness of a relationship with a father rules out the possibility of knowing God in terms of fatherhood, then we must ask, What unbroken relationships are capable of use for our knowledge of God? All our relationships are broken to some degree even if we prefer one over another. All our knowledge of God in this paradigm becomes problematic because it is all essentially reduced to an unavoidable projection of our own experiences on a cosmic screen.[11] Our broken experiences serve to disqualify all our talk about God. Once we have eliminated all language that offends anyone in the church on the basis of their experience of some human relationship, what would be left? Do we have undistorted and perfectly faithful relationships with our mothers, our brothers or sisters, our legislators, our ministers, our lovers, our employers, our computers, our . . . ? Language about God would have to become more and more abstract and impersonal to avoid its association with any of our broken relationships. But then language of God would have been forced to the meaningless margins of our lives. Alternatively, we could substantially shift our thinking regarding the significance of our *God-talk* thereby reducing it to represent mere projections of ourselves. In either case the anthropocentric paradigm condemns us to being mythologizers and idolaters who have no meaningful or valid language by which to know God; or it leaves us consigned to hopelessly projecting ourselves out of the brokenness of our relationships, unhealed.

The anthropocentric assumption and paradigm asserts that all our language about God, including Christ's own language, is merely culturally or psychologically determined mythological projection. It denies the possibility of obeying the commands neither to make graven images of God nor

---

[11]This is, of course, the exact claim of Ludwig Feuerbach (*The Essence of Christianity*, trans. George Eliot [1841; reprint, New York: Prometheus, 1989] and *Lectures on the Essence of Religion*, trans. Ralph Manheim [1851; reprint, San Fancisco: Harper & Row, 1967]). He marks the involution of theology into anthropology. His conclusions can be seen as the working out of the religious skepticism reaching back to Hume and Kant.

to use God's name in vain.[12] It must construe Jesus himself as just another idolater or mythologizer of his day. We can be no more. There is no room for the gospel of grace here; the anthropocentric paradigm has excluded it from the outset. This is the deepest reason that Jesus rejects the solution of relativizing our language about God to our experience. To deny that this is possible and right is to deny the grace of God and to make our experience of evil sovereign. It is to make an idol of our broken experiences and thereby enslave us to them for eternity. It renders all our talk of God idolatry, mythology.

Thus the anthropocentric paradigm is not merely an argument against calling God Father but is essentially an argument against the Christian faith as a whole, and further, a denial of the possible truth of any religion at all.[13] All religious claims are thereby reduced to psychologically or sociologically based mythologies, none having any validity beyond its own bald assertions.

What alternative does Jesus offer us?—a life of exposing *all* our language and every one of our relationships to the light of the holiness revealed in the relationship of Jesus with his heavenly Father by the Spirit. All our language and experiences must be relativized, reinterpreted, in the light of a norm that has come to us from beyond our immediate past experience. A mental and emotional repentance on our part is called for at every turn. This is a crucial aspect of our dying to ourselves in order to follow Jesus. The

---

[12]Exodus 20. Indeed the recognition both that human beings are indeed inveterate mythologizers *and* that there is held out for us a gracious possibility and obligation for us to not be idolaters who make God in our own image is enshrined in the Decalogue of ancient Israel as well as the New Testament, for example, Paul's warning about those who exchange the glory of the immortal God for the image of some aspect of creation (Rom 1:22-25). The awareness of the human propensity to project out of its own subjectivity is not a new insight but an ancient one. Even Plato rejected the pantheon of Greek gods on this basis.

[13]And indeed, there are those who argue for some kind of post-Christian religion or goddess worship. Most notable is Daly, *Beyond God the Father*. But also see Daphne Hampson, *Theology and Feminism* (Oxford: Blackwell, 1990); Ruether, *Sexism and God-Talk*; and Carol Christ, "Symbols of Goddess and God in Feminist Theology" in *The Book of the Goddess Past and Present: An Introduction to Her Religion*, ed. Carl Olson (New York: Crossroad, 1983). What is still not widely recognized is that their critique of Christianity ultimately nullifies the truthfulness or normativity of any religion whatsoever. All religion becomes merely self-projection. And, of course, if this is so, then *all* religion is, on the one hand, intrinsically self-worship, equally valid and already self-justified (and therefore in no need of reformation or justification), or, on the other, is all self-deceit and therefore ought to be rejected in every form altogether.

false sovereignty of our own experience must be overthrown in the power of the gospel. This is the theological task of the church in its teaching and preaching. There are no words or concepts in any language or culture that need no reinterpretation in the light of the gospel. It all must come under judgment. The true meaning of love, justice, holiness, reconciliation, faithfulness, goodness, being persons, being human, being masculine or feminine, and so forth can be discerned only in the light of the gospel. This is always a painful process and yet is the only way forward to the healing of our relationships with God and with each other. All our language, not just gendered language, is broken and needs healing. Jesus calls us all to the same task; we are all under this gracious burden. This possibility is not a human one apart from the gracious action of God; it is the possibility of God given to us in his Word and by his Spirit.[14]

The theocentric alternative is altogether excluded by the presently promoted anthropocentric paradigm of how to relate our experience to our speaking of God. This is the ultimate reason why the anthropocentric paradigm must be rejected. It is God's grace that is sovereign, not my broken experience. It is God's grace alone that calls us out of our brokenness and refuses to leave us deceived about the unfaithfulness of human persons and the faithfulness of God. It is God's grace that calls us to repent of our sin-conditioned grasp of God, even when it is conditioned by the sin of others against us. The anthropocentric paradigm, built on seemingly self-evident assumptions and allegedly promoted on the basis of compassion, actually constitutes a denial of the sovereign grace of God and leaves persons enslaved to themselves, their diminished comprehension of God, and enslaved to their brokenness. The theocentric paradigm in Jesus' teaching demonstrates a true compassion that refuses to be restricted to mere kindness and demonstrates the truth of the surpassing power of the gospel to reach and transform us that we might enter into the healing of our apprehension of God and our broken relationships.

Conclusion

Ultimately there are two opposite alternatives for relating our experience to our language of God, with radically different assumptions—the anthro-

---

[14]The most comprehensive and helpful source I am aware of for critical discussions on the theological issues involved in language about God, especially in light of the challenges of feminism, is Alvin F. Kimel's *Speaking the Christian God*.

pocentric and theocentric paradigms. We stand at a crisis point. We will all have to determine which paradigm is the more compassionate and which embodies the truth of the gospel of Jesus Christ. Will we cease to call people to wrestle with the meaning of the fatherhood of God and concede to the assumption of the determinative and incorrigible nature of our painful experiences that thereby have the effect of insulating us even from God's own working? Or will we cease to give the name of father to those who were unfaithful to their calling and resist the temptation to allow those experiences to define for us the meaning of fatherhood? Will we open ourselves up to receiving the healing that comes in letting God fill his name with the meaning of the fatherhood revealed in Christ and delivered to us in the gospel by the Spirit?

12

A PASCALIAN ARGUMENT AGAINST UNIVERSALISM

JAY WESLEY RICHARDS

M̲Y ASPIRATIONS FOR THIS CHAPTER ARE MODEST. AFTER DEFINING some terms, I present one of the better arguments for the doctrine of universalism. Then I consider the primary grounds for our knowledge of this doctrine (namely, Scripture). Given the nature of these grounds I then attempt a cost and benefit analysis to reveal that the benefits of teaching this doctrine are so meager and the costs so immense (if we are mistaken) that we can never justify teaching it. Thus I conclude that Christians act imprudently and irresponsibly whenever they do teach universalism. All my arguments presuppose readers who are broadly speaking members of the Reformed tradition, or who at least commit themselves to the belief that Scripture should be a person's primary source for constructing Christian doctrine. This does not require a denial of all other sources of doctrinal authority such as tradition, philosophical argument, moral intuitions or even "personal experience," but the argument does require the commitment to Scripture as the *primary* authority for Christian theology. For this reason, the only case for universalism I consider is one that has some exegetical strength and some foothold in the Christian tradition. My argument will be unconvincing for the individual who deems biblical texts as secondary or irrelevant for doing Christian theology.

Some Definitions

For the sake of clarity, we should agree on some definitions of terms.

Salvation. By salvation I mean at least this (though not necessarily only this): that state of affairs in which a sinful person is brought into right relationship with the just and loving God, in which eternal dwelling in the presence of God is made an actuality.

Let us also assume that whatever Christ accomplished by his incarnation and death on the cross, this accomplishment was the event that made such salvation possible. So Christ's work (as the Son of God, the Word, the Second Person of the Trinity and the man Jesus) wrought or *effected* salvation. The saved (whomever they may be) are saved by virtue of this work.

Universalism. By the doctrine of universalism I mean that Christ's atoning work on the cross in securing salvation for sinners is not only *sufficient* to save every sinner, but it is also (or will be) *actual.*

That is, for the universalist, by Christ's death all people are not only given the opportunity to be saved, they are in fact saved. So in the final consummation there will be *no one* who does not enjoy the full benefits of this saving work. Ultimately everyone will be saved. No one will be barred from God's eternal presence.

Particularism. Although Christ's work on the cross in securing salvation for sinners is in some sense sufficient to save every sinner, such salvation will not finally be actual.

That is, for whatever reason not every person will eternally enjoy the presence of God at the final consummation. Some will not partake of the beatific vision. And by *damnation* or *hell* let's mean that state of affairs in which a person does not so enjoy the divine presence.

These definitions are obviously bare boned and do not come close to accommodating all of the biblical allusions and images concerning Christ's work and our salvation. But I choose these minimalist definitions in order to concede as much as possible to the position I am attempting to defeat. So we will adopt only a *privative* definition of hell, given only in terms of what it is *not* with respect to salvation. I will not depend on any of the "positive" portrayals of hell found either in Scripture or the common conception. If I were to include such positive elements my argument would only be stronger. But for irenic purposes I will avoid images of fire, eternal darkness, weeping and gnashing of teeth, and immortal worms.

A Pretty Good Argument for Universalism

While there are many arguments for universalism, I will only consider one. To avoid combatting a straw man, it seems appropriate to consider the strongest one that can be mustered. Instead of some generic argument the one I think has the most bite is one that proceeds from specifically Christian and at least partly biblical premises. It has even more force for those within the Reformed tradition. Let's schematize it for simplicity.

The first premise we must assume we might call the *principle of double jeopardy* (PDJ). It states that: If a due penalty has been paid for a sin (or crime), that penalty shall not be exacted again.

To use a mundane example, if I (or someone else) pay the required fine for a speeding ticket, this fine will not have to be paid again. This is not so much a deep metaphysical principle as it is a simple exposition of what it means to pay a fine. If I still owed the fine after paying it, either I didn't really pay the fine or someone at the Department of Motor Vehicles is pulling a fast one. Part of the meaning of *paying the due penalty* is that after I have paid it, I will no longer be in debt for that offense. Analogously, if we are to express anything true when we say that Christ paid the debt for our sins on the cross, something like the principle of double jeopardy must apply. If my *entire* debt is paid, I can't still be liable for the punishment due as a result of my many sins.

Given the principle of double jeopardy, we can formulate the rest of this defense of universalism as follows. To avoid undue complexity, take a particular individual as a representative for all human individuals. Let's call her Gehenna, or Henny for short. Now

(P1) If Henny has her debt paid (or her sins atoned), she will not be punished for her sins.

(P2) Every person has had his or her sins paid by Christ's work on the cross (see, e.g., 1 Tim 2:6 and 1 Jn 2:2).

(C1) Therefore Henny has had her sins paid for.

(C2) Therefore Henny will not be punished for her sins.

(P3) But hell is a punishment for unatoned sins.

(C3) Therefore, Henny will not go to hell.

(P4) Henny stands in for every person (from our stated premise).

(C4) Therefore no one will go to hell.

This sort of argument is especially compelling for those in the Reformed tradition who resist separation between the work of atonement and its effects. For others, such as Wesleyan Arminians, Orthodox and Catholics, Christ's work on the cross may be conceived (usually implicitly) as making the salvation of everyone *possible* but not necessarily *actual*. To Reformed ears this can sound like a denial of the full sufficiency of Christ's work. So it is very natural in the Reformed tradition to tie the work of the cross very closely to its effects in justifying the believer, leaving little slack for doctrines such as human self-determination or individual freedom. Of course, most Reformed thinkers acknowledge the importance of repentance for individual appropriation of the work of the cross but not in such a way that repentance is a causal condition for that work. Rather, repentance is itself *evidence* that an individual is in fact part of the elect for whom the forgiveness of sins is intended.

It was probably the pressure of this view of the atonement that led the Reformed scholastics to develop explicitly the doctrine of *limited atonement*. They would have conceded the reasoning of the argument above, except for one of the premises, namely, the claim that Henny could represent *every person*. For the Reformed scholastic, Henny could exemplify the *elect* but not the entire race. Why would the scholastics have been so stingy with the salvific effects of the cross? We should not ascribe to them ignoble motivations, such as the desire to make sure unbelievers got what was coming to them. Rather, we should see that they *deduced* it from the particular Reformed understanding of the complete sufficiency of the cross for salvation *plus* the clear biblical evidence that not all will be saved. If some are to be consigned to perdition, they reasoned, then the work of the cross must not extend to every human being. If you remove this premise, which the Reformed scholastics culled from Scripture, but retain their view of the atonement, you get essentially the argument for universalism described above.

I say this neither to deny nor defend this scholastic view but to draw attention to the fact that this is likely a reason this argument for universalism is popular in Reformed circles and to note that a turn toward universalism at Princeton Theological Seminary is not *simply* a movement toward liberalism (even if it is partly that). At least this form of universalism has some specifically Christian premises.

This argument can be strengthened with additional premises, such as reference to passages of Scripture that, at least in isolation, seem to imply universalism. So in Colossians Paul says that through Christ "God was pleased to reconcile to himself all things, whether on earth or in heaven, by making peace through the blood of his cross" (Col 1:20). There are others, such as 1 Corinthians 15:20-28, Acts 3:21 and 1 Timothy 4:10. Also there are passages such as 1 Timothy 2:4, which expresses God's desire for *all* to be saved. Conjoin these passages with some philosophical objections against hell and an appeal to moral intuitions about its unfairness, and you've got a pretty good argument for universalism.

Types of Systematic Theological Arguments

At this point many will protest that I have given too rosy a picture of the biblical support for this doctrine, but before we consider that, we should concede that there is a case to be made for universalism that is not simply an expression of twentieth-century sentimentalism.

Nevertheless, we should recognize this argument for what it is: a *systematic theological argument*. As an argument of the systematic theological species, it should be granted the same status as all such arguments and judged accordingly. So what are our criteria for evaluating systematic theological arguments? Surely coherence and proper logic will be included in our list. But in the Reformed tradition and Protestantism generally, the primary criterion is of course *sola Scriptura*. We need not take this criterion in the most restrictive and implausible way, which would require that we deny the force of any other source than the express words of Scripture. But I think as a bare minimum this criterion requires that we give Scripture the primary place among our sources for systematic theological arguments.

Some arguments are given clear and unambiguous warrant from Scripture, such as the claim that God exists and created the world. Such claims, if we trust the testimony of Scripture, we may say are biblically *established*. (I'm not saying this establishes God's existence.) Other arguments are *underdetermined* by Scripture. That is, a theory might be consistent with and even derived from Scripture, but a different theory might be more or less consistent with it as well. In such a case neither theory is *required* as the only legitimate interpretation of Scripture. Sincere exegetes may disagree without impugning one another's piety or intellectual integrity. I tend to think the dispute between infant and believer's baptism falls into this category. If this is correct, then an exact theory of baptism is underdetermined by Scripture.

On the other hand, some arguments are just not compatible with Scripture. I count some of Rudolf Bultmann's attempted compromises between naturalism and biblical language as fairly obvious examples (of course, I'm not claiming that such arguments are always easy to recognize).[1] Finally, there are *hybrid* theological arguments, which are clearly compatible with some portions of Scripture and might even be derived from such portions, but which are in either apparent or actual conflict with other parts. In this type, some conclusions of an argument may seem to follow validly from biblically warranted premises but tend to go far beyond or even violate what Scripture says elsewhere. Such an argument will have textual anomalies that it cannot account for. Usually the advocate of such a theory will attempt to explain away such anomalies or to interpret them in a way that is compatible with the main argument. Evaluation of such arguments can be very difficult, even giving rise to new Protestant denominations in the process (I say this in all seriousness). There may be an alternate argument that accounts well for the anomalies of the other argument but that has different textual anomalies itself. So passages like 1 John 2:2 and 1 Timothy 2:6 may be irritating anomalies for the Calvinist who affirms a doctrine of limited atonement, and all those "election" passages in Romans and Ephesians may function similarly for the Arminian. I do not wish to defend any of these points here, but I think we need these distinctions in order to evaluate the argument for universalism.

Let's count systematic theological arguments as falling roughly into one of these four categories: (1) *established*, (2) *underdetermined*, (3) *incompatible* or (4) *hybrid*. These obviously exist on a spectrum, but for simplicity let's define these four as set-theoretical complements, so that any such argument will fall somewhere into one of these four categories, even though each one may vary in its degree of biblical support. Of course, an argument might be incorrectly categorized at some point. A passage might appear to be an anomaly for some theory, making it a hybrid. But perhaps the passage was misinterpreted, and when it is correctly interpreted, we discover that the theory is fully compatible but just underdetermined by Scripture. So we should leave room for this possibility.

Now equipped we can consider our argument for universalism. Which category should it be placed in? To be *established*, no alternate theory can

---

[1]As in Rudolf Bultmann, *Jesus Christ and Mythology* (New York: Macmillan, 1996).

be compatible with all the textual "data." This is clearly not the case with universalism. Just a single example is sufficient to bar the universalist argument from membership in the club of established theological arguments. Revelation 20:7-15 and Matthew 25:31-46 (the parable of the sheep and the goats) should suffice. Moreover, these passages, and many similar ones from the Gospels and elsewhere, exclude the doctrine from the set of merely underdetermined theories. How about the category of incompatible arguments? The uncharitable might defend this, but the passages mentioned above suggest that there is at least some biblical warrant for the argument for universalism. How much support is another matter. So, at least for the sake of argument and peace, let's place universalism among those systematic theological arguments and theories that are deemed *hybrid* with respect to biblical support. It seems to have some support, but it also seems to contradict significant portions of Scripture as well. Less contentiously we could say that it has many textual anomalies it cannot easily account for.

Although an extensive survey and exegesis of relevant passages is needed to confirm this claim, for the sake of brevity I will assume that most readers are sufficiently familiar with Scripture to know that the New Testament is replete with references to judgment, condemnation and the like. I personally located fifty such references in the Gospels alone, although we haven't the time to consider these here. As a generalization, an urgency for repentance marked Jesus' ministry as recorded in the Gospels; his parables often served to warn others to be prepared for the coming of God's kingdom and its judgment. There seems to be a lot of fuss and anxiety as if people's very lives and destinies were dependent on their response to his message, as if our actions have eternal significance: "I tell you that men will have to give account on the day of judgment for every careless word they have spoken. For by your words you will be acquitted, and by your words you will be condemned" (Mt 12:36-37 NIV). Many parables speak of everlasting fire and of the outer darkness. These all serve as likely anomalies for the doctrine of universalism.

To point out that scriptural language about hell and damnation (and so for particularism) is picturesque, metaphorical and geographical is beside the point. We could easily concede that Jesus and the authors of the New Testament used such language. We need not expect a biblical treatment of hell to conform to the images of perdition depicted in Gary Larson's *Far Side*. But what relevance does this have? How can a person infer from the fact that language about the condemned state is picturesque to the conclusion that this state does not really exist? Isn't this usually the intended implication for such arguments? But if colorful or metaphorically descriptive language were evidence that a place or state did not exist, this would be an equally valid argument against the reality of heaven and the kingdom of God as well. After all, much of the description of these places we receive from Scripture is also couched in geographic and parabolic language. Should we therefore conclude that there is no such state and that salvation is not really relevant to it? If so, then the universalist's argument is undercut as well since he presumably wants to maintain not that there is *no* state to which the saved are ushered at death or the consummation of all things but rather that *everyone* is ushered into that blissful state.

The abundance of references to damnation and especially its urgency throughout the New Testament suggests that our previous argument for universalism is incompatible with Scripture. But a few passages we've mentioned lead me to designate it as a *hybrid* theory. Now for the sake of argument let's assume that the doctrine of particularism, as defined above, is also a hybrid argument. In fact, I think it is very close to a confirmed but underdetermined doctrine. But let's concede as much as is plausible to universalism. Let's even say they are equally possible alternatives, given our primary basis for knowledge of such things (namely Scripture). Let's assume, like Buridan's ass caught between two stables, that these alternatives look to us like equally balanced exegetical options. Which one ought we to believe, and which one ought we to teach?

If this *were* the case, someone might counsel that we all be good pluralists and advocate the doctrine "to each his own." But this seems to me manifest foolishness. It is here that a cost-benefit analysis becomes appropriate. For if we really are trapped between these two major alternatives, the relative costs and benefits for teaching each one become profoundly important and may compel us to move in one way rather than the other.

If we're committed to scriptural authority, then whatever Scripture in fact teaches, and whatever the Spirit intends us to learn from it, is what we should teach. At the least, if there is a discoverable truth to the matter concerning the extent of salvation, then we will discover this truth from Scripture. So the Reformed commitment, at least formally, is to believe and advocate the truth and to treat Scripture as our primary source for teaching certain truths (particularly theological ones). But sometimes we have only a hint concerning the truth about things. Let us assume that the facts of the matter concerning the ultimate destiny of some people is an area about which we are uncertain. We are unable to decide whether universalism or particularism is true. And so as Christians we are unable to decide which doctrine to teach. I will now argue that even if we were in such a state of equipoise between these two alternatives, we would still be nowhere near justified in teaching universalism as the truth. In fact we would be grossly irresponsible if we did so. We can see this most easily by running a cost-benefit analysis.

Universalism and Particularism: A Cost-Benefit Analysis

For simplicity, let's assume *universalism* and *particularism* are our primary alternatives but that we are unable to decide because of the ambiguity of our epistemic base (i.e., the basis of our knowledge of this question). Even if our evidence for them were equal, the costs and benefits of the respective doctrines are anything but equal.

We should distinguish this from two similar but less respectable types of arguments. The first is the argument *ad misericordiam*. This argument is actually fallacious and would go as follows: *the results of teaching universalism are bad; therefore it's not true.* Put so baldly, no bright person would fall for it. Nevertheless, this form is apt to hide among a bluster of big words, so it is important that we not construe our argument this way. A more deceptively similar but still different argument would be the pragmatic one. It might go like this: *the results of teaching universalism are bad; therefore we ought not teach it.* This might be a legitimate argument for some things. However, it is unworthy of theological pursuits because we should be primarily concerned with knowing and teaching what we take to be true. Concerns about the results of such teaching should always be secondary. Truth and consequences are not synonymous. Of course we hope that teaching the truth will produce desirable consequences. But if we seek results at the expense of truth, we make ourselves objects of the wrath of the One who is the Author of truth.

My argument here assumes that we want to teach what we think is true. However, the basis for our knowledge of a certain truth—namely the extent of salvation—looks a little ambiguous (or so I'm allowing for the sake of argument). Given such a dilemma, pragmatic questions of cost and benefit become permissible, and in this case I think decisive. With these provisos, let's list some of the costs and benefits of our alternative doctrines.

First, universalism. What are some generic benefits to teaching it? If we were correct, the greatest benefit is that we would be teaching the truth. What other benefits might accrue (irrespective of its truth or falsity)? Well, it would surely comfort our consciences as Christians. We would not need worry about the fact that we have never witnessed to our agnostic and unrepentant colleagues at work. We need not fret too much that people are dying in Tibet without ever having heard the name of Jesus Christ. No doubt the level of anxiety among Christians would significantly diminish. We might reduce high blood pressure, ulcers and many other stress related-illnesses among the Christian constituency privy to this nice teaching. On a less trivial note, we would have a far more felicitous answer to skeptics who deny God's goodness because of the problem of evil, of which damnation is perhaps the worst example. In fact, there might even be some individuals, such as Bertrand Russell, who would be willing to consider becoming Christians if we dropped the doctrine of damnation from the Christian canon. In *Why I Am Not a Christian* Russell cites Jesus' teachings about hell as one of his reasons for doubting that Christ spoke divine truth.[2] And perhaps Europe could have avoided such unfortunate events as the Thirty Years' War and the Crusades if this doctrine had caught on sooner.

Concerning costs: If we are honest, we should admit that there would probably be fewer Christians than there are now. This doesn't mean that all missionary activity and evangelism would cease. But it would surely be less common, since its urgency would be greatly diminished. After all, what missionary would be willing to die in his or her own pool of blood at the hands of pagan tribes if the salvation of such tribes were in no way dependent on such risk? In fact, if I were to be realistic, probably neither my family nor I would have been Christians, since I suspect no missionaries would have risked life and limb to bring the gospel to my undoubtedly bloodthirsty northern European ancestors. Of course, this fact would not redound to any of our damnations (if our teaching were correct); we would just probably not have experienced the joy that often accompanies the Christian life. While hardship often follows it, and for some even martyrdom, I have no doubt that the overall benefit of the Christian life makes for healthier and happier social and economic experiences, at least at a societal level. So some of the spread of Christianity would likely have been stunted.

---

[2]Bertrand Russell, *Why I Am Not a Christian* (New York: Simon & Schuster, 1957), p. 17.

Now, what about the costs of teaching particularism (irrespective of its truth or falsity)? Well, we could probably expect the opposite of the benefits listed above. Christians would be likely to suffer no small dose of torment over their lukewarm witness to their fellow human beings. The (presumably) lost in Tibet might haunt the dreams of the more thoughtful Christians. Theological arguments and fights might be more prominent, and missionary zeal might foster obsessive-compulsive disorders of many varieties. We would be strapped with some troubling questions concerning the problem of evil and no easy answers for the skeptic. And Bertrand Russell would have stayed the same intransigent atheist he was. On the other hand, the benefits would at least equal whatever worldly benefits do in fact accrue from the spread of Christian thought and belief.

But now we need to consider the costs that would result if we teach universalism, *and we are wrong.* For, we admitted earlier that our knowledge of this comforting doctrine is tenuous and uncertain. Need I ask what the costs would be if we propagated this notion and we were mistaken? What if the things we say and do in this life do have eternal consequences, not only for our own lives but for the lives of our fellow human beings? What if Jesus had a very strong motivation for commanding us to go and make disciples of all nations? What if God has so constructed the world that our obedience to his command is part of his eternal plan and is in some inscrutable way a (divinely ordained) contingency? What if our arrogance in denying the obvious tenor of the Gospels results in a lessening of evangelistic zeal and a decrease of repentance and saving knowledge of God? Universalists uniformly deny this connection, but common sense and study of denominational missionary activities clearly confirm a very high correlation between the teaching of universalism and a diluting or redefining of the Great Commission. Universalism does not logically entail a repudiation of a call to repentance and acceptance of Christ's lordship, but these certainly do seem to follow as a historical fact. And besides all this, the cost of teaching universalism if it is not true is that *we will be teaching a falsehood.*

Conclusion

Compared to these costs, the benefits of teaching universalism and the costs of teaching particularism seem too meager to countenance. For both are concerned with the temporary things of this life. If we teach universalism and we're right, the *infinite* good that will follow is the same as if we do not teach it. For the ultimate salvation of all is not at stake and will result either way. If we teach particularism and we're wrong, the infinite good of universalism will still result—so there's no infinite *cost*. After all, no one's salvation is at stake just because Christians teach erroneous doctrines. But if we teach universalism and we're *wrong*, the cost of so doing is as infinite as the good of enjoying the eternal presence of the living God, and surely this is a cost greater than any other. So the costs of teaching universalism erroneously are infinite, whereas the costs of teaching particularism erroneously are a mere finite pittance. Therefore, short of certainty concerning the truth of universalism, the prudent will not teach universalism and will teach particularism. Of course, this is not yet a positive case for the truth of particularism, which goes beyond the scope of this essay. My intention here is only to nip the teaching of universalism in the bud. And for these reasons I conclude that it is foolish for the Christian to teach this doctrine.

Postscript

We should note that there are different forms that universalism might take, and we might wonder whether this critique applies to all of them. Obviously we will have to take it case by case. Let's consider just one. What ought we to say about systematic theological theories containing premises that seem to lead to universalist conclusions, even though the theorists repudiate such conclusions? For instance, some judge that Barth's view, in which everyone is both elect and reprobate in Christ, implies universalism. But Barth himself repudiated this doctrine and insisted that Holy Scripture did not teach such a view. But what if someone argued the equivalent of premises (1) through (4) in our ideal argument above but just denied that conclusion (4) followed from it? Perhaps they conscript a category such as divine freedom in order to block the inference. How should we judge such a move? I would suggest that we study such proposals very carefully to decide if they really resolve the dilemma or just avoid it by a sleight of hand. If the implications of a theory are clearly universalist, I think it would be susceptible to the critique suggested here. But whether or not any particular theory has such implications is a decision that all young theologians will prayerfully have to decide for themselves.

PART 5

SCIENCE

13

WHAT EVERY THEOLOGIAN SHOULD KNOW ABOUT CREATION, EVOLUTION & DESIGN

WILLIAM A. DEMBSKI

F ROM ITS INCEPTION DARWINISM POSED A CHALLENGE TO CHRISTIAN THE-
ology by threatening to undo the church's understanding of creation and
therewith her understanding of the origin of human life. Nor did the challenge of Darwinism stop here. With human beings the result of a brutal,
competitive process that systematically rooted out the weak and favored
only the strong (we might say it is the strong who constitute the elect
within Darwinism), the church's understanding of the Fall, redemption,
the nature of morality, the veracity of the Scriptures and the ultimate end
of humanity were all in a fundamental way called into question. Without
exaggeration, no aspect of theology escaped the need for reevaluation in
the light of Darwinism.

A lot has happened since the publication of Charles Darwin's *Origin of
Species*. Theology that is academically respectable has long since made its
peace with Darwinism. Indeed, respectable theologians have long since
had their understanding of the origin of life thoroughly informed by Dar-

winism and its interpretation of natural history. Thus when a group of Christian scholars who call themselves *design theorists* begin to raise doubts about Darwinism and propose an alternative paradigm for understanding biological systems, it is the design theorists and not Darwin who end up posing the challenge to theology.

At the heart of the creation-evolution controversy is the question, What evidence is there of God interacting with the world? As Christians we know that naturalism is false—nature is not all there is. God created nature as well as any laws by which nature operates. Not only has God created the world, but God upholds the world moment by moment. Daniel's words to Belshazzar hold equally for the dyed-in-the-wool naturalist: "You have praised the gods of silver and gold, of bronze, iron, wood, and stone, which do not see or hear or know; but the God in whose power is your very breath, and to whom belong all your ways, you have not honored" (Dan 5:23). The world is in God's hand and never leaves his hand. Christians are not deists. God is not an absentee landlord.

That said, the question remains as to what evidence God has given of his interacting with the world. Because God is intimately involved with the world moment by moment, there is no question that God interacts with the world. This is a tenet of our faith that brooks no controversy. Controversy arises, however, once we ask whether God's interaction with the world is *empirically detectable*. It is one thing as a matter of faith to hold that God exists, interacts with and sovereignly rules the world. Alternatively, it may be argued on philosophical grounds that the world and its laws are not self-explanatory and therefore point to a transcendent source. But it is another matter entirely to assert that empirical evidence supports God's interaction with the world, rendering God's interaction empirically detectable. Theology and philosophy are perfectly legitimate ways for understanding God's interaction with the world. Nonetheless, neither theology nor philosophy can answer the evidential question whether God's interaction with the world is empirically detectable.

To answer this question we must to look to science. The science we look to, however, needs to be unencumbered by naturalistic philosophy. If we prescribe in advance that science must be limited to undirected natural causes, then science will necessarily be incapable of investigating God's interaction with the world. But if we permit science to investigate intelligent causes (as many special sciences already do, e.g., forensic science and artificial intelligence), then God's interaction with the world, insofar as it manifests the characteristic features of intelligent causation, becomes a legitimate domain for scientific investigation.

There's an important contrast to keep in mind here. Science, we are told, studies natural causes, whereas to introduce God is to invoke supernatural causes. This is the wrong contrast. The proper contrast is between *undirected natural causes* on the one hand and *intelligent causes* on the other. Intelligent causes can do things that undirected natural causes cannot. Undirected natural causes can throw scrabble pieces on a board but cannot arrange the pieces to form meaningful words or sentences. To obtain a meaningful arrangement requires an intelligent cause. Whether an intelligent cause operates within or outside nature (i.e., is respectively natural or supernatural) is a separate question entirely from whether an intelligent cause has operated. For instance, we can reliably infer that a Shakespearean sonnet has an intelligent cause independently of whether Shakespeare actually lived, whether a space alien moved Shakespeare's quill or whether an angel made the sonnet materialize magically.

Intelligent Design

This distinction between undirected natural causes on the one hand and intelligent causes on the other has underlain the design arguments of past centuries. Throughout the centuries theologians have argued that nature exhibits features that nature itself cannot explain but that instead require an intelligence beyond nature. From church fathers like Minucius Felix and Gregory of Nazianzus (third and fourth centuries) to medieval scholars like Moses Maimonides and Thomas Aquinas (twelfth and thirteenth centuries) to Reformed thinkers like Thomas Reid and Charles Hodge (eighteenth and nineteenth centuries), we find theologians making design arguments, arguing from the data of nature to an intelligence that transcends nature.

Design arguments are old hat. Indeed, design arguments continue to be a staple of philosophy and religion courses. The most famous of the design arguments is William Paley's watchmaker argument.[1] According to Paley, if we find a watch in a field, the watch's adaptation of means to ends (i.e., the adaptation of its parts to telling time) ensure that it is the product of an intelligence and not simply the result of undirected natural processes. So

---

[1]See William Paley, *Natural Theology* (1802; reprint, Charlottesville, Va.: Rembrandt-Lincoln, 1986).

too the marvelous adaptations of means to ends in organisms, whether at the level of whole organisms or at the level of various subsystems (Paley focused especially on the mammalian eye), ensure that organisms are the product of an intelligence.

Though intuitively appealing, design arguments had until recently fallen into disuse. This is now changing. Indeed, design is experiencing an explosive resurgence. Scientists are beginning to realize that design can be rigorously formulated as a scientific theory. What has kept design outside the scientific mainstream these last 140 years is the absence of precise methods for distinguishing intelligently caused objects from unintelligently caused ones. For design to be a fruitful scientific theory, scientists have to be sure they can reliably determine whether something is designed. Johannes Kepler, for instance, thought the craters on the moon were intelligently designed by moon dwellers.[2] We now know that the craters were formed naturally. It is this fear of falsely attributing something to design only to have it overturned later that has prevented design from entering science proper. With precise methods for discriminating intelligently from unintelligently caused objects, scientists are now able to avoid Kepler's mistake.

What has emerged is a new program for scientific research known as *intelligent design*. Within biology, intelligent design is a theory of biological origins and development. Its fundamental claim is that intelligent causes are necessary to explain the complex, information-rich structures of biology, and that these causes are empirically detectable. To say intelligent causes are empirically detectable is to say there exist well-defined methods that, on the basis of observational features of the world, are capable of reliably distinguishing intelligent causes from undirected natural causes. Many special sciences have already developed such methods for drawing this distinction—notably forensic science, artificial intelligence (cf. the Turing test), cryptography, archeology and the search for extraterrestrial intelligence (cf. the movie *Contact*).

Whenever these methods detect intelligent causation, the underlying entity they uncover is information. Intelligent design properly formulated is a theory of information. Within such a theory, information becomes a reliable indicator of intelligent causation as well as a proper object for sci-

---

[2]Steven J. Dick, *Plurality of Worlds: The Origins of the Extraterrestrial Life Debate from Democritus to Kant* (Cambridge: Cambridge University Press, 1982), p. 179.

entific investigation. Intelligent design thereby becomes a theory for detecting and measuring information, explaining its origin and tracing its flow. Intelligent design is therefore not the study of intelligent causes per se but of informational pathways induced by intelligent causes. As a result, intelligent design presupposes neither a creator nor miracles. Intelligent design is theologically minimalist. It detects intelligence without speculating about the nature of the intelligence. Biochemist Michael Behe's "irreducible complexity" mathematician Marcel Schützenberger's "functional complexity" and my own "complex specified information" are alternate routes to the same reality.

It is the empirical detectability of intelligent causes that renders intelligent design a fully scientific theory and distinguishes it from the design arguments of philosophers, or what has traditionally been called *natural theology*. Natural theology reasons from the data of nature directly to the existence and attributes of God—typically the trinitarian God of Christianity with all the usual perfections. Perhaps the weakest part of Paley's *Natural Theology* was his closing chapter where he sings the praises of nature's delicate balance and how only a beneficent deity could have arranged so happy a creation. Darwin turned this argument on its head, focusing instead on the brutality of nature and seeing anything but the hand of a beneficent deity.

Intelligent design is at once more modest and more powerful than natural theology. From observable features of the natural world, intelligent design infers to an intelligence responsible for those features. The world contains events, objects and structures that exhaust the explanatory resources of undirected natural causes and that can be adequately explained only by recourse to intelligent causes. This is not an argument from ignorance. Precisely because of what we know about undirected natural causes and their limitations, science is now in a position to demonstrate design rigorously (see my chapter "Reinstating Design Within Science" in this volume). Thus what has been a longstanding but fuzzy philosophical intuition can now be cashed out as a robust program of scientific research. At the same time, intelligent design resists speculating about the nature, moral character or purposes of this intelligence (here rather is a task for the theologian—to connect the intelligence inferred by the design theorist with the God of Scripture). Indeed, this is one of the great strengths of intelligent design, that it distinguishes design from purpose. We can know that something is designed without knowing the ultimate or even proximate purpose for which it was designed. The Smithsonian has a collection of human artifacts whose design is obvious but whose purpose remains a mystery.

What will science look like once intelligent causes are readmitted to full scientific status? The worry is that intelligent design will stultify scientific inquiry. For after determining that something is designed, what remains for the scientist to do? Even if there are reliable methods for deciding when something is designed, and even if those methods tell us that some natural object is designed, so what? Suppose Paley was right about the mammalian eye exhibiting sure marks of intelligent causation. How would this recognition help us understand the eye any better as scientists? Actually it would help quite a bit. For one thing, it would put a stop to all those unsubstantiated just-so stories that evolutionists spin out in trying to account for the eye through a gradual succession of undirected natural causes. By telling us the mammalian eye requires an intelligent cause, intelligent design precludes certain types of scientific explanation. This is a contribution to science, albeit a negative one.

Even so, intelligent design is hardly finished once it answers whether an object was designed. Another question immediately presents itself, namely, *how* was the object produced? Consider a Stradivarius violin. Not only do we know that it is designed, but we also know the designer—Stradivarius. Nevertheless, to this day we are unable to answer the "how" question: we no longer know how to manufacture a violin as good as a Stradivarius, much less how Stradivarius himself actually went about making his violins. Lost arts are lost precisely because we are no longer able to answer the "how" question, not because we have lost the ability to detect design. Now the problem of lost arts is the problem of reverse engineering. Unlike the ordinary engineer who constructs an object from scratch, the reverse engineer is first given an object (in this case a violin) and then must show how it could have been constructed.

Intelligent design's positive contribution to science is to reverse engineer objects shown to be designed. Indeed, the design theorist is a reverse engineer. Unconstrained by naturalism the design theorist finds plenty of natural objects attributable to design (this is especially true with biological objects). Having determined that certain natural objects are designed, the design theorist next investigates how they were produced. Yet because evidence of how they were produced is typically lacking (at least for natural objects), the design theorist is left instead with investigating how these objects could have been produced. This is reverse engineering.

In this vein consider again the Stradivarius example. In attempting to reconstruct Stradivarius's art of violinmaking, the contemporary violinmaker does well to learn as much as possible about Stradivarius's actual methods for producing violins. Nonetheless, because the extant account of Stradivarius's methods is incomplete, the contemporary violinmaker can do no better than try to reinvent Stradivarius's methods. Without a complete record of Stradivarius's actual methods, the contemporary violinmaker can never be sure of reconstructing his methods exactly. Still, a person can legitimately claim to have reinvented Stradivarius's methods if he or she is able to produce a violin as good as his.

To sum up, intelligent design consists in empirically detecting design and then reverse engineering those objects detected to be designed. The worry that intelligent design stifles scientific inquiry is therefore ill founded. Indeed, it can be argued that many scientists are design theorists already, albeit in naturalistic clothing. In biology, for instance, very few researchers confine themselves to Miller-Urey type experiments, attempting to generate biological complexity solely through undirected natural processes. No, most researchers studying biological complexity bring all their expertise and technological prowess to bear, especially when trying to reconstruct complex biological systems. As Paul Nelson aptly remarks, scientists ought to line their labs with mirrors to remind themselves that at every point they are in the labs designing and conducting their experiments. Intelligent design is one intelligence determining what another intelligence has done. There's nothing mysterious about this. The only reason it seems mysterious is because naturalism so pollutes our intellectual life.

Theistic Evolution

Where does intelligent design fit within the creation-evolution debate? Logically, intelligent design is compatible with everything from utterly discontinuous creation (e.g., God intervening at every conceivable point to create new species) to the most far-ranging evolution (e.g., God seamlessly melding all organisms together into one great tree of life). For intelligent design the first question is not how organisms came to be (though, as we've just seen, this is a vital question for intelligent design), but whether organisms demonstrate clear, empirically detectable marks of being intelligently caused. In principle, an evolutionary process can exhibit such "marks of intelligence" as much as any act of special creation.

That said, intelligent design is incompatible with what typically is meant by theistic evolution. Theistic evolution takes the Darwinian picture of the biological world and baptizes it, identifying this picture with the way God created life. When boiled down to its scientific content, however, theistic evolution is no different from atheistic evolution, treating only undirected natural processes in the origin and development of life. Theistic evolution places *theism* and *evolution* in an odd tension. If God purposely created life through Darwinian means, then God's purpose was to make it seem as though life was created without purpose. Within theistic evolution, God is a master of stealth who constantly eludes our best efforts to detect him empirically. Yes, the theistic evolutionist believes that the universe is designed. Yet insofar as there is design in the universe, it is design we recognize strictly through the eyes of faith. Accordingly, the natural world in itself provides no evidence that life is designed. For all we can tell through our natural intellect, our appearance on planet earth is an accident.

Now it may be that God has so arranged the physical world that our natural intellect can discover no reliable evidence of him. Yet if this is so, how could we know it? Scripture and church tradition are hardly univocal here. Throughout church history we find Christian thinkers who regard our natural intellect as hopelessly inadequate for finding even a scrap of reliable knowledge about God from nature and others who regard our natural intellect as able to extract certain limited, though still reliable, knowledge about God from nature. Thus in the early church we find Tertullian inveighing against our natural intellect; Basil the Great and Gregory of Nazianzus defending it. In the Middle Ages we find Ockham's occasionalism undermining the powers of our natural intellect; Thomas Aquinas raising it to new heights. In the modern era we find Blaise Pascal, Søren Kierkegaard and Karl Barth making the *Deus absconditus* a fundamental plank of their theology; Isaac Newton, Thomas Reid and Charles Hodge asserting how wonderfully God is revealed in nature. Sadly, the current theological fashion prefers an evolutionary God inaccessible to scientific scrutiny over a designer God whose actions in nature are clearly detectable.

How then do we determine whether God has so arranged the physical world that our natural intellect can discover reliable evidence of him? The answer is obvious: put our natural intellect to the task and see whether indeed it produces conclusive evidence of design in nature. Doing so poses no threat to the Christian faith. It challenges neither the cross, the tomb, the resurrection on the third day, the ascension into heaven, the sitting at the right hand of the Father nor the second coming of Christ. Indeed, nature is silent about the revelation of Christ in Scripture. On the other hand, nothing prevents nature from independently testifying to the God revealed in the Scripture.[3] Now intelligent design does just this—it puts our natural intellect to work and thereby confirms that a designer of remarkable talents is responsible for the natural world. How this designer connects with the God of Scripture is then for theology to determine.

Intelligent design and theistic evolution therefore differ fundamentally about whether the design of the universe is accessible to our natural intellect. Design theorists say yes, theistic evolutionists say no. Why the disagreement? To be sure, there is a scientific disagreement: Design theorists think the scientific evidence favors design whereas theistic evolutionists think it favors Darwin or one of his naturalistic successors. Nonetheless, in discounting intelligent design, theistic evolutionists tend also to appeal to philosophical and theological considerations. Pessimism about the powers of the natural intellect to transcend nature is a dominant theme in certain theological traditions (cf. the theology of Karl Barth). Often aesthetic criteria for how God should create or interact with the world take precedence—*a worthy deity wouldn't have done it that way!* My own view is that it is much more shaky to speculate about what God would have done or what nature might in principle reveal than simply to go to nature and see what nature actually does reveal.

If theistic evolution finds no solace from intelligent design, neither does it find solace from the Darwinian establishment. For the Darwinian establishment the "theism" in theistic evolution is superfluous. For the hardcore naturalist, theistic evolution at best includes God as an unnecessary rider in an otherwise purely naturalistic account of life. Thus by Ockham's razor, since God is an unnecessary rider in our understanding of the natural world, theistic evolution ought to dispense with all talk of God outright and get rid of the useless adjective *theistic*. This, at any rate, is the received view within the Darwinian establishment.

It is for failing to take Ockham's razor seriously that the Darwinian establishment despises theistic evolution. Not to put too fine a point on it,

---

[3]See Thomas Aquinas *Summa Contra Gentiles* 3.38.

the Darwinian establishment views theistic evolution as a weak-kneed sycophant that desperately wants the respectability that comes with being a full-blooded Darwinist but refuses to follow the logic of Darwinism through to the end. It takes courage to give up the comforting belief that life on earth has a purpose. It takes courage to live without the consolation of an afterlife. Theistic evolutionists lack the stomach to face the ultimate meaninglessness of life, and it is this failure of courage that makes them contemptible in the eyes of full-blooded Darwinists. (Richard Dawkins is a case in point.)

Unlike full-blooded Darwinists, however, the design theorists' objection to theistic evolution rests not with what the term *theistic* is doing in the phrase "theistic evolution" but rather with what the term *evolution* is doing there. The design theorists' objection to theistic evolution is not in the end that theistic evolution retains God as an unnecessary rider in an otherwise perfectly acceptable scientific theory of life's origins. Rather, the design theorists' objection is that the scientific theory that is supposed to undergird theistic evolution, typically called the neo-Darwinian synthesis, is itself problematic.

The design theorists' critique of Darwinism begins with Darwinism's failure as an empirically adequate scientific theory and not with its supposed incompatibility with some system of religious belief. This point is vital to keep in mind in assessing intelligent design's contribution to the creation-evolution controversy. Critiques of Darwinism by creationists have tended to conflate science and theology. Design theorists want none of this. Their critique of Darwinism is not based on any supposed incompatibility between Christian revelation and Darwinism. Rather, they begin their critique by arguing that Darwinism is *on its own terms* a failed scientific research program—that it does not constitute a well-supported scientific theory, that its explanatory power is severely limited and that it fails abysmally when it tries to account for the grand sweep of natural history.

Darwinists will no doubt object to this characterization of their theory. For them Darwinism continues to be a fruitful theory and one whose imminent demise I am greatly exaggerating. There is no question that Darwin's mutation-selection mechanism constitutes a fruitful idea for biology and one whose fruits have yet to be fully plundered. But Darwinism is more than just this mechanism. Darwinism is the totalizing claim that this mechanism accounts for all the diversity of life. The evidence simply doesn't support this claim. What evidence there is supports limited variation within fixed boundaries, or what typically is called microevolution. Macroevolution—the unlimited plasticity of organisms to diversify across all boundaries—even if true, cannot legitimately be attributed to the mutation-selection mechanism. To do so is to extrapolate the theory beyond its evidential base. This is always a temptation in science—to think that one's theory encompasses a far bigger domain than it actually does. In the heady early days of Newtonian mechanics, physicists thought Newton's laws provided a total account of the constitution and dynamics of the universe. Maxwell, Einstein and Heisenberg each showed that the proper domain of Newtonian mechanics was far more constricted. So too the proper domain of the mutation-selection mechanism is far more constricted than most Darwinists would like to admit.

Indeed, the following problems have proven utterly intractable not only for the mutation-selection mechanism but also for any other undirected natural process proposed to date: the origin of life, the origin of the genetic code, the origin of multicellular life, the origin of sexuality, the scarcity of transitional forms in the fossil record, the biological big bang that occurred in the Cambrian era, the development of complex organ systems and the development of irreducibly complex molecular machines. These are just a few of the more serious difficulties that confront every theory of evolution that posits only undirected natural processes. It is thus sheer arrogance for Darwinists like Richard Dawkins and Daniel Dennett to charge design theorists with being ignorant or stupid or wicked or insane for denying the all-sufficiency of undirected natural processes in biology or to compare challenging Darwinism with arguing for a flat earth.

The strength of the design theorists' critique against Darwinism, however, rests not in the end with their ability to find holes in the theory. To be sure, the holes are there and they create serious difficulties for the theory. The point at which the design theorists' critique becomes interesting and novel is when they begin raising the following sorts of questions: Why does Darwinism, despite being so inadequately supported as a scientific theory, continue to garner the full support of the academic establishment? What is it that continues to keep Darwinism afloat despite its many glaring faults? Why are alternatives that introduce design ruled out of court by fiat? Why must science explain solely by recourse to undirected natural processes? Who determines the rules of science? Is there a code of scientific correctness that instead of helping lead us into truth actively prevents us from asking certain questions and thereby coming to the truth?

We are dealing here with something more than a straightforward determination of scientific facts or confirmation of scientific theories. Rather we are dealing with competing worldviews and incompatible metaphysical systems. In the creation-evolution controversy we are dealing with a naturalistic metaphysic that shapes and controls what theories of biological origins are permitted on the playing field in advance of any discussion or weighing of evidence. This metaphysic is so pervasive and powerful that it not only rules alternative views out of court, but it cannot even permit itself to be criticized. The fallibilism and tentativeness that are supposed to be part of science find no place in the naturalistic metaphysic that undergirds Darwinism. It is this metaphysic then that constitutes the main target of the design theorists' critique of Darwinism and to which we turn next.

The Importance of Definitions

The design theorists' critique of the naturalistic metaphysic that undergirds Darwinism can be reduced to an analysis of three words. They are *creation, evolution* and *science.* Let us start with the words *creation* and *evolution.* Suppose you are on a witness stand and required to respond yes or no to two questions. The questions are these: (1) Do you believe in creation? (2) Do you believe in evolution? Could you respond to these questions with a simple yes or no and still feel satisfied that you had expressed yourself adequately? Probably not. The problem is that the words *creation* and *evolution* both have multiple senses.

For instance, *creation* can be construed in the narrow sense of a literal six-day creation as presented in Genesis 1 and 2. On the other hand, *creation* can also be construed in the broad sense of simply asserting that God has created the world, where the question of how God created the world is simply set to one side. Similarly, *evolution* can be construed as a fully naturalistic, purposeless process that by means of natural selection and mutation has produced all living things. On the other hand, *evolution* can mean nothing more than organisms have changed over time (leaving the extent and mechanism of change unspecified). Depending on how a person construes the words *creation* and *evolution*, his or her answer to the questions Do you believe in creation? and Do you believe in evolution? are likely to show quite a bit of variability.

Now it is the design theorists' contention that the Darwinian establishment, in order to maintain its political, cultural and intellectual authority, consistently engages in a fallacy of equivocation when it uses the terms *creation* and *evolution*. The fallacy of equivocation is the fallacy of speaking out of both sides of your mouth. It is the deliberate confusing of two senses of a term, using the sense that's convenient to promote the speaker's agenda. For instance, when Michael Ruse, in one of his defenses of Darwinism, writes, "Evolution is Fact, Fact, Fact!"[4] how is he using the term evolution? Is it a fact that organisms have changed over time? There is plenty of evidence to confirm that organisms have experienced limited change over time. Is it a fact that the full panoply of life has evolved through purposeless naturalistic processes? This might be a fact, but whether it is a fact is very much open to debate.

Suppose you don't accept the Darwinian picture of natural history; that is, you don't believe that the vast panoply of life evolved through undirected naturalistic processes. Presumably, then, you are a creationist. But does this make you a young-earth creationist? Ever since the publication of *Origin of Species* Darwinists have cast the debate in these terms: either you're with us or you're a creationist, by which they mean a young-earth creationist. But of course it doesn't follow, logically or otherwise, that by rejecting fully naturalistic evolution you automatically embrace a literal reading of Genesis 1—2. Rejecting fully naturalistic evolution does not entail accepting young-earth creationism. The only thing that can be said for certain is that to reject fully naturalistic evolution is to accept some form of creation broadly construed, that is, the belief that God or some intelligent designer is responsible for life. Young-earth creationism certainly falls under this broad construal of creation but is hardly coextensive with it.

Let us now assume we've got our terms straight. No more terminological confusions. No more fallacies of equivocation. No more straw-man arguments. From here on in we're going to concentrate on the substance of the creation-evolution debate. Henceforth this debate will be over whether life exhibits nothing more than the outcome of undirected natural processes or whether life exhibits the activity of an intelligent cause—usually called a designer—who in creating life has impressed on it clear marks of intelligence. For simplicity, let us refer to the first view as *naturalistic evolution*. As for the second view, we already know it as intelligent design. Now the key question to be resolved in the creation-evolution controversy is decid-

---

[4]Michael Ruse, *Darwinism Defended* (Reading, Mass.: Addison-Wesley, 1982), p. 58.

ing which of these views is correct. How then to resolve this question?

The first thing to notice is that naturalistic evolution and intelligent design both make definite assertions of fact. To see this, let's get personal. Here you are. You had parents. They in turn had parents. They too had parents. And so on. If we run the video camera back in time, generation upon generation, what do we see? Do we see a continuous chain of natural causes that go from apes to small furry mammals to reptiles to slugs to slime molds to blue-green algae and finally all the way back to a prebiotic soup, with no event in the chain ever signaling the activity of an intelligent cause? Or as we trace back the genealogy, do we find events that clearly signal the activity of an intelligent cause? There exist reliable criteria for inferring the activity of intelligent causes. Does natural history display clear marks of intelligence and thereby warrant a design inference or doesn't it? To answer this question one way is to embrace intelligent design; to answer it the other way is to embrace naturalistic evolution.

Now Darwinists are quite clear about rejecting intelligent design and affirming naturalistic evolution. For instance, in *The Meaning of Evolution* George Gaylord Simpson, one of the founders of the neo-Darwinian synthesis, asserts:

> Although many details remain to be worked out, it is already evident that all the objective phenomena of the history of life can be explained by purely naturalistic or, in a proper sense of the sometimes abused word, materialistic factors. They [that is, the objective phenomena of the history of life] are readily explicable on the basis of differential reproduction in populations [that's natural selection], and the mainly random interplay of the known processes of heredity [that's random mutation, the other major element in the Darwinian picture]. Therefore, man is the result of a purposeless and natural process that did not have him in mind.[5]

Where does Simpson derive his confidence that naturalistic evolution is correct and intelligent design is incorrect? How can Simpson so easily elide the weaknesses in his theory and then with perfect equanimity assert "it is already evident that all the objective phenomena of the history of life can be explained by purely naturalistic factors"? And how does he know that when the "many details that remain to be worked out" actually do get worked out that they won't overthrow naturalistic evolution and instead

---

[5]George Gaylord Simpson, *The Meaning of Evolution,* rev. ed. (New Haven, Conn.: Yale University Press, 1967), p. 345.

confirm intelligent design? Science is after all a fallible enterprise. Where then does Simpson get his certainty?

To answer this question we need to examine how the Darwinian establishment employs the third word in our trio, namely, *science.* Although design theorists take the question Which is correct, naturalistic evolution or intelligent design? as a perfectly legitimate question, it is not treated as a legitimate question by the Darwinian establishment. According to the Darwinian establishment, naturalistic evolution addresses a *scientific* question, whereas intelligent design addresses a *religious* question. Thus for the Darwinian establishment, intelligent design is a nonstarter. Yes, naturalistic evolution and intelligent design taken together may be mutually exclusive and exhaustive, but naturalistic evolution is the only viable scientific option. Intelligent design must therefore be ruled out of court.

Why is this? The answer is quite simple. Science, according to the Darwinian establishment, by definition excludes everything except the material and the natural. It follows that all talk of purpose, design and intelligence is barred entry from the start. By defining science as a form of inquiry restricted solely to what can be explained in terms of undirected natural processes, the Darwinian establishment has ruled intelligent design outside of science. But suppose now that a design theorist comes along and like most Americans thinks intelligent design is correct and naturalistic evolution is incorrect. (According to a Gallup poll close to 50 percent of Americans are creationists of a stricter sort, thinking that God specially created human beings; another 40 percent believe in some form of God-guided evolution; and only 10 percent are full-blooded Darwinists.[6] It is this 10 percent, however, that controls the academy and the media.) The design theorist's first inclination might be to say, "No big deal. Intelligent design is at least as good an answer to biological origins as naturalistic evolution. Science just happens to be limited in the questions it can pose and the answers it can give." Any such concession is deadly and turns science into the lapdog of naturalistic philosophy.

The problem is this. As Phillip Johnson rightly observes, science is the only universally valid form of knowledge within our culture. This is not to say that scientific knowledge is true or infallible. But within our culture whatever is purportedly the best scientific account of a given phenomenon

---

[6]Ronald Numbers, *Darwin Comes to America* (Cambridge, Mass.: Harvard University Press, 1985), pp. 9, 11.

demands our immediate and unconditional assent. This is regarded as a matter of intellectual honesty. Thus to consciously resist what is currently the best scientific theory in a given area is, in the words of Richard Dawkins, to be either ignorant, stupid, wicked or insane. Thankfully, Richard Dawkins is more explicit than most of his colleagues in making this point and therefore does us the service of not papering over the contempt with which the Darwinian establishment regards those who question its naturalistic bias.

It bears repeating: the only universally valid form of knowledge within our culture is science. Within late-twentieth-century Western society neither religion nor philosophy nor literature nor music nor art makes any such cognitive claim. Religion in particular is seen as making no universal claims that are obligatory across the board. The contrast with science here is stark. Science has given us technology—computers that work as much here as they do in the Third World. Science has cured our diseases. Whether we are black, red, yellow or white, the same antibiotics cure the same infections. It is therefore clear why relegating intelligent design to any realm other than science (e.g., religion) ensures that naturalistic evolution will remain the only intellectually respectable option for the explanation of life.

But there is a problem here. Intelligent design and naturalistic evolution both inquire into definite matters of fact. If every cell were to have emblazoned on it the phrase "made by Yahweh," there would be no question about intelligent design being correct and naturalistic evolution being incorrect. Granted, cells don't have "made by Yahweh" emblazoned on them. But that's not the point. The point is that we wouldn't know this unless we actually looked at cells under the microscope. It is for precisely this reason that both intelligent design and naturalistic evolution must remain live scientific options, unfettered by artificial, a priori requirements about what can count as legitimate explanations in biology.

Logically, naturalistic evolution and intelligent design are real possibilities. What's more, as mutually exclusive and exhaustive possibilities, one of these positions has to be correct. Now the Darwinian establishment so defines science that naturalistic evolution alone can constitute a legitimate scientific answer to the question How did life originate and develop? Nonetheless, when Stephen Jay Gould, Michael Ruse, Richard Dawkins, George Gaylord Simpson and their disciples assert that naturalistic evolution is true; they purport that naturalistic evolution is the conclusion of a scientific argument based on empirical evidence. But it is nothing of the sort. The empirical evidence is in fact weak, and the conclusion follows necessarily as a strict logical deduction once science is as a matter of definition restricted to undirected natural processes. Naturalistic evolution is therefore built directly into a naturalistic construal of science.

Logicians have names for this—circular reasoning and begging the question being the best known. The view that science must be restricted solely to undirected natural processes also has a name. It is called *methodological naturalism*. So long as methodological naturalism sets the ground rules for how the game of science is to be played, intelligent design has no chance of success. Phillip Johnson makes this point eloquently. So does Alvin Plantinga. In his work on methodological naturalism, Plantinga remarks that if a person accepts methodological naturalism, then naturalistic evolution is the only game in town.

Therefore, since naturalistic evolution is so poorly supported empirically and since intelligent design is having such a hard time passing for science, what's wrong with a simple profession of ignorance? In response to the question How did life originate and develop? what's wrong with simply saying, We don't know? (Such a profession of ignorance, by the way, was the reason Michael Denton's book *Evolution: A Theory in Crisis* was panned by the Darwinian establishment.) As philosophers of science Thomas Kuhn and Larry Laudan have pointed out, for scientific paradigms to shift there has to be a new paradigm in place ready to be shifted into. You can't shift into a vacuum. Napoleon III put it this way: "One never really destroys a thing till one has replaced it." If you are going to reject a reigning paradigm, you have to have a new-improved paradigm with which to replace it. Naturalistic evolution is the reigning paradigm. But what alternative is there to naturalistic evolution? Logically, the only alternative is intelligent design. But intelligent design, we are told, isn't part of science.

There is a simple way out of this impasse: *dump methodological naturalism*. We need to realize that methodological naturalism is the functional equivalent of a full-blown metaphysical naturalism. Metaphysical naturalism asserts that nature is self-sufficient. Methodological naturalism asks us for the sake of science to pretend that nature is self-sufficient. But once science is taken as the only universally valid form of knowledge within a culture, it follows that methodological and metaphysical naturalism become functionally equivalent. What needs to be done, therefore, is to break the grip of naturalism in both guises, methodological and meta-physical. And this happens once we realize that it was not empirical evidence but the power of a metaphysical worldview that was urging us all along to adopt methodological naturalism in the first place.

14

REINSTATING DESIGN
WITHIN SCIENCE

WILLIAM A. DEMBSKI

SHOULD DESIGN BE PERMITTED BACK INTO SCIENCE GENERALLY AND BIOL-
ogy in particular? Scientists bristle at the very thought. For scientists who
are atheists, design is an accident of natural history. Indeed, with no
divine architect to start creation on its course, any designing agents,
including ourselves, must result from a long evolutionary process that
itself was not designed. For the atheist, design occurs at the end of an
undesigned natural process and cannot be prior to it.

What about scientists who are not atheists? Sadly, most scientists who
are theists agree with their atheist colleagues that design should be
excluded from science. It's not that they agree with their atheist colleagues
that the universe is not designed. Indeed, as good theists they believe
wholeheartedly that the universe is designed—and not just by any
designer but by the God of some particular religious creed. Nevertheless,
as a matter of scientific integrity they believe that science is best served by
excluding design. The worry always is that invoking design will stifle scientific inquiry, substituting a supernatural cause where scientists should
be seeking an ordinary natural cause.

Against this received view I want to argue that design should be readmitted to full scientific status. To make this argument, let me begin by briefly reviewing why design was removed from science in the first place. Design in the form of Aristotle's formal and final causes had, after all, once occupied a perfectly legitimate role within natural philosophy—or what we now call science. With the rise of modern science, however, these causes fell into disrepute.

We can see how this happened by considering Francis Bacon. Bacon, a contemporary of Galileo and Kepler, though himself not a scientist, was a terrific propagandist for science. Bacon concerned himself much about the proper conduct of science, providing detailed canons for experimental observation, recording of data and inferences from data. What is interesting here, however, is what he did with Aristotle's four causes. For Aristotle, to understand any phenomenon properly an individual had to understand its four causes, namely, its material, efficient, formal and final cause.

A standard example philosophers use to illustrate Aristotle's four causes is to consider a statue—say Michelangelo's *David*. The material cause is what it is made of—marble. The efficient cause is the immediate activity that produced the statue—Michelangelo's actual chipping away at a marble slab with hammer and chisel. The formal cause is its structure— it is a representation of David and not some random chunk of marble. And lastly, the final cause is its purpose—presumably, to beautify some Florentine palace.

Although much more can be said about Aristotle's four causes than is evident from this illustration, two points are relevant to this discussion. First, Aristotle gave equal weight to all four causes. In particular, Aristotle would have regarded any inquiry that omitted one of his causes as fundamentally deficient. Second, Bacon adamantly opposed including formal and final causes within science (see his *Advancement of Learning*). For Bacon, formal and final causes belong to metaphysics and not to science. Science, according to Bacon, needs to limit itself to material and efficient causes, thereby freeing science from the sterility that inevitably results when science and metaphysics are conflated. This was Bacon's line, and he argued it forcefully.

We see Bacon's line championed in our own day by atheists and theists alike. In *Chance and Necessity* biologist and Nobel laureate Jacques Monod argues that chance and necessity alone suffice to account for every aspect of the universe. Now whatever else we might want to say about chance and necessity, they provide at best a reductive account of Aristotle's formal causes and leave no room whatever for Aristotle's final causes. Indeed, Monod explicitly denies any place for purpose within science.[1]

Monod was an outspoken atheist. Nevertheless, as outspoken a theist as Stanley Jaki will agree with Monod about the nature of science. Jaki is as theologically conservative a historian of science and Catholic priest as one is likely to find. Yet in his published work he explicitly states that purpose is a purely metaphysical notion and cannot legitimately be included within science. Jaki's exclusion of purpose, and more generally design, from science has practical implications. For instance, it leads him to regard Michael Behe's project of inferring biological design from irreducibly complex biochemical systems as hopelessly misguided.[2]

I don't want to give the impression that I am advocating a return to Aristotle's theory of causation. There are problems with Aristotle's theory, and it needed to be replaced. My concern, however, is with what replaced it. By limiting scientific inquiry to material and efficient causes, Bacon fed into a mechanistic understanding of the universe that was soon to dominate science.

To be sure, mechanism has its advantages. Back in the seventeenth century the French playwright Molière ridiculed Aristotelians for explaining the medicinal properties of opium in terms of its "dormitive power."[3] Appealing to a final cause like "dormitive power" is of course totally unenlightening. Much better is to know the chemical properties of opium and how those properties take advantage of certain nerve centers in the brain. Mechanistic explanations that describe how something works without speculating about its ultimate meaning or purpose seemed a much safer course for science and one that promised to and in fact did yield much fruit.

Mechanism is still with us, though not the deterministic form that dom-

---

[1]Monod writes, "The cornerstone of the scientific method is the postulate that nature is objective. In other words, the *systematic* denial that 'true' knowledge can be got at by interpreting phenomena in terms of final causes—that is to say, of 'purpose'" (Jacques Monod, *Chance and Necessity* [New York: Vintage, 1972], p. 21).

[2]Jaki writes, "I want no part whatever with the position . . . in which science is surreptitiously taken for a means of elucidating the utterly metaphysical question of purpose" (Stanley Jaki, *Chesterton: A Seer of Science* [Urbana: University of Illinois Press, 1986], pp. 139-40 n. 2).

[3]*Le Malade Imaginaire*, in *The Principal Comedies of Molière*, ed. Fredrick K. Turgeon and Arthur C. Gilligan (New York: Macmillan, 1935), pp. 941-1037.

inated from Newton to the quantum revolution. In our own day scientists concentrate on undirected natural causes and take as their preferred mode of scientific explanation a combination of deterministic laws and chance processes. Chance and necessity, to use Monod's phrase, set the boundaries of scientific explanation, and woe to anyone who would reintroduce a sterile and moribund teleology into science.

Why Reinstate Design?

Faced with a discredited Aristotelian science, a marvelously successful modern science, and an entrenched opposition within the scientific community against design, why should anyone want to reintroduce design into science? The short answer is that chance and necessity have proven too thin an explanatory soup on which to nourish a robust science. In fact, by dogmatically excluding design from science, scientists are themselves stifling scientific inquiry. To a generation suckled on naturalism's teat, this will no doubt seem counterintuitive. Nevertheless, the case for reintroducing design within science becomes compelling as soon as we attend to certain relevant facts.

The first glimmers that excluding design artificially restricts science come from admissions by scientists opposed to design. The arch-Darwinist Richard Dawkins begins his book *The Blind Watchmaker* by stating, "Biology is the study of complicated things that give the appearance of having been designed for a purpose."[4] Statements like this echo throughout the biological literature. In *What Mad Pursuit* Francis Crick, Nobel laureate and codiscoverer of the structure of DNA, writes, "Biologists must constantly keep in mind that what they see was not designed, but rather evolved."[5]

Granted, the biological community thinks it has accounted for the apparent design in nature apart from any actual design (typically through the Darwinian mechanism of mutation and selection). The point to appreciate, however, is that in accounting for the apparent design in nature, biologists regard themselves as having made a successful *scientific* argument against actual design. Scientific refutation is a double-edged sword. Claims that are refuted scientifically may be wrong, but they are not necessarily wrong. Alternatively, for a claim to be scientifi-

---

[4]Richard Dawkins, *The Blind Watchmaker* (New York: W. W. Norton, 1986), p. 1.
[5]Francis Crick, *What Mad Pursuit* (New York: BasicBooks, 1988), p. 138.

cally falsifiable, it must have the possibility of being true.

As suggested in the previous chapter, consider the possibility that microscopic examination revealed that every cell was inscribed with the phrase "Made by Yahweh." Although cells don't have "Made by Yahweh" inscribed on them, we wouldn't know this unless we actually looked at cells under the microscope. It is a contingent fact which could have been otherwise.

Design always remains a live option in biology. A priori prohibitions against design are easily countered, especially in an age of diversity and multiculturalism where it is all too easy to ask Who sets the rules for science? Nonetheless, once we admit that design cannot be excluded from science on first principles, a weightier question remains: Why should we want to reinstate design within science?

To answer this question, let us turn it around and ask instead Why shouldn't we want to reinstate design within science? What's wrong with explaining something as designed by an intelligent agent? Certainly there are many everyday occurrences that we explain by appealing to design. Moreover, in our workaday lives it is absolutely crucial to distinguish accident from design. We demand answers to such questions as, Did she fall or was she pushed? Did someone die accidentally or commit suicide? Was this song conceived independently or was it plagiarized? Did someone just get lucky on the stock market or was there insider trading?

Not only do we demand answers to such questions, but entire industries are devoted to drawing the distinction between accident and design. Here we can include forensic science, intellectual property law, insurance claims investigation, cryptography and random number generation—to name but a few. Science itself needs to draw this distinction to keep itself honest. In a recent issue of *Science*, a Medline Web search uncovered a "paper published in *Zentralblatt für Gynäkologie* in 1991 [containing] text that is almost identical to text from a paper published in 1979 in the *Journal of Maxillofacial Surgery*."[6] Plagiarism and data falsification are far more common in science than we would like to admit. What keeps these abuses in check is our ability to detect them.

If design is so readily detectable outside science, and if its detectability is one of the key factors keeping scientists honest, why should design be

---

[6]Eliot Marshall, "Medline Searches Turn Up Cases of Suspected Plagiarism," *Science* 23 (January 1998): 473-74.

barred from the content of science? With reference to biology, why should we have to constantly remind ourselves that biology studies things that only appear to be designed but that in fact are not designed? Isn't it at least conceivable that there could be good positive reasons for thinking biological systems are in fact designed?

The biological community's response to these questions has been to resist design resolutely. The worry is that for natural objects (unlike human artifacts) the distinction between design and nondesign cannot be reliably drawn. Consider, for instance, the following remark by Darwin in the concluding chapter of his *Origin of Species*: "Several eminent naturalists have of late published their belief that a multitude of reputed species in each genus are not real species; but that other species are real, that is, have been independently created. . . . Nevertheless they do not pretend that they can define, or even conjecture, which are the created forms of life, and which are those produced by secondary laws. They admit variation as a vera causa in one case, they arbitrarily reject it in another, without assigning any distinction in the two cases."[7] It is this worry of falsely attributing something to design (here identified with creation) only to have it overturned later that has prevented design from entering science proper.

This worry, though perhaps justified in the past, is no longer tenable. There does in fact exist a rigorous criterion for distinguishing intelligently caused objects from unintelligently caused ones. Many special sciences already use this criterion, though in a pretheoretic form (e.g., forensic science, artificial intelligence, cryptography, archeology and the search for extraterrestrial intelligence). The great breakthrough of the intelligent design movement has been to isolate and make precise this criterion. Michael Behe's criterion of irreducible complexity for establishing the design of biochemical systems is a special case of this general criterion for detecting design.[8]

The Complexity-Specification Criterion

What does this criterion look like? Although a detailed explanation and justification of this criterion is fairly technical,[9] the basic idea is straight-

---

[7]Charles Darwin, *On the Origin of Species*, facsimile 1st ed. (Cambridge, Mass.: Harvard University Press, 1964), p. 482.

[8]Michael Behe, *Darwin's Black Box* (New York: Free Press, 1996).

[9]For a full account see my book *The Design Inference* (Cambridge: Cambridge University Press, 1998).

forward and easily illustrated. Consider how the radio astronomers in the movie *Contact* detected an extraterrestrial intelligence. This movie, based on a novel by Carl Sagan, was an enjoyable piece of propaganda for SETI —the search for extraterrestrial intelligence. To make the movie interesting the SETI researchers actually had to find an extraterrestrial intelligence (the nonfictional SETI program has yet to be so fortunate).

How then did the SETI researchers in *Contact* find an extraterrestrial intelligence? To increase their chances SETI researchers monitor millions of radio signals from outer space. Many natural objects in space produce radio waves (e.g., pulsars). Looking for signs of design among all these naturally produced radio signals is like looking for a needle in a haystack. SETI researchers sift through the signals they monitor using computers programmed with pattern matchers. So long as a signal doesn't match one of the preset patterns, it will pass through the pattern-matching sieve (and that even if it has an intelligent source). If it does match one of these patterns, then depending on the pattern matched, the SETI researchers may have cause for celebration.

The SETI researchers in *Contact* did find a signal worthy of celebration:

```
11011101111101111110111111111101111111111111011111111111111
11101111111111111111111011111111111111111111111101111111111111
11111111111111110111111111111111111111111111111111011111111111111
11111111111111111111111011111111111111111111111111111111111111
11111101111111111111111111111111111111111111111111101111111111
11111111111111111111111111111111111110111111111111111111111111
11111111111111111111111111111110111111111111111111111111111111
11111111111111111111111111111110111111111111111111111111111111
11111111111111111111111111111111111110111111111111111111111111
11111111111111111111111111111111111111111111111101111111111
11111111111111111111111111111111111111111111111111111111111
10111111111111111111111111111111111111111111111111111111111111
11111111111111111110111111111111111111111111111111111111111111
11111111111111111111111111111111111111111111101111111111111111
11111111111111111111111111111111111111111111111111111111111111
11111111110111111111111111111111111111111111111111111111111
11111111111111111111111111111111111111111111111101111111111
11111111111111111111111111111111111111111111111111111111111
11111111111111111111111111111
```

In this sequence of 1126 bits, 1's correspond to beats and 0's to pauses. This sequence represents the prime numbers from 2 to 101, where a given prime number is represented by the corresponding number of beats (i.e., 1's), and the individual prime numbers are separated by pauses (i.e., 0's).

The SETI researchers in *Contact* took this signal as decisive confirmation of an extraterrestrial intelligence. What is it about this signal that decisively implicates design? Whenever we infer design, we must establish two things—*complexity* and *specification*. Complexity ensures that the object in question is not so simple that it can readily be explained by chance. Specification ensures that this object exhibits the type of pattern that is the trademark of intelligence.

To see why complexity is crucial for inferring design, consider the following sequence of bits:

110111011111

These are the first twelve bits in the previous sequence representing the prime numbers 2, 3 and 5 respectively. It is a sure bet that no SETI researcher, if confronted with this twelve-bit sequence, is going to contact the science editor at the *New York Times*, hold a press conference and announce that an extraterrestrial intelligence has been discovered. No headline is going to read, "Extraterrestrials Have Mastered the First Three Prime Numbers!"

The problem is that this sequence is much too short (i.e., has too little complexity) to establish that an extraterrestrial intelligence with knowledge of prime numbers produced it. A randomly beating radio source might by chance just happen to output the sequence "110111011111." A sequence of 1126 bits representing the prime numbers from 2 to 101, however, is a different story. Here the sequence is sufficiently long (i.e., has enough complexity) to confirm that an extraterrestrial intelligence could have produced it.

Even so, complexity by itself is not enough to eliminate chance and implicate design. If I flip a coin one thousand times, I'll participate in a highly complex (or what amounts to the same thing, highly improbable) event. Indeed, the sequence I end up flipping will be one in a trillion trillion trillion, . . . (where the ellipsis needs twenty-two more "trillions"). This sequence of coin tosses won't, however, trigger a design inference. Though complex, this sequence won't exhibit a suitable pattern. Contrast this with the previous sequence representing the prime numbers from 2 to 101. Not only is this sequence complex, but it also embodies a suitable pattern. The SETI researcher who in the movie *Contact* discovered this sequence put it this way: "This isn't noise; this has structure."

What is a *suitable* pattern for inferring design? Not just any pattern will do. Some patterns can legitimately be employed to infer design whereas others cannot. The basic intuition underlying the distinction between patterns that alternately succeed or fail to implicate design is, however, easily motivated. Consider the case of an archer. Suppose an archer stands 50 meters from a large wall with bow and arrow in hand. The wall, let's say, is sufficiently large that the archer can't help but hit it. Now suppose each time the archer shoots an arrow at the wall, the archer paints a target around the arrow so that the arrow sits squarely in the bull's-eye. What can be concluded from this scenario? Absolutely nothing about the archer's ability as an archer. Yes, a pattern is being matched, but it is a pattern fixed only after the arrow has been shot. The pattern is thus purely ad hoc.

But suppose instead the archer paints a fixed target on the wall and then shoots at it. Suppose the archer shoots a hundred arrows, and each time hits a perfect bull's-eye. What can be concluded from this second scenario? Confronted with this second scenario we are obligated to infer that here is a world-class archer, one whose shots cannot legitimately be referred to luck but rather must be referred to the archer's skill and mastery. Skill and mastery are of course instances of design.

The type of pattern where the archer fixes a target first and then shoots at it is common to statistics, where it is known as setting a *rejection region* prior to an experiment. In statistics, if the outcome of an experiment falls within a rejection region, the chance hypothesis supposedly responsible for the outcome is rejected. Now a little reflection makes clear that a pattern need not be given prior to an event to eliminate chance and implicate design. Consider the following cipher text:

nfuijolt ju jt mjlf b xfbtfm

Initially this looks like a random sequence of letters and spaces—initially you lack any pattern for rejecting chance and inferring design.

But suppose next that someone comes along and tells you to treat this sequence as a Caesar cipher, moving each letter one notch down the alphabet. Behold, the sequence now reads:

methinks it is like a weasel

Even though the pattern is now given after the fact, it still is the right sort of pattern for eliminating chance and inferring design. In contrast to statistics, which always tries to identify its patterns before an experiment is performed, cryptanalysis must discover its patterns after the fact. In both instances, however, the patterns are suitable for inferring design.

Patterns divide into two types, those that in the presence of complexity warrant a design inference and those that despite the presence of complexity do not warrant a design inference. The first type of pattern is called a *specification*, the second a *fabrication*. Specifications are the non-ad hoc patterns that can legitimately be used to eliminate chance and warrant a design inference. In contrast, fabrications are the ad hoc patterns that cannot legitimately be used to warrant a design inference. This distinction between specifications and fabrications can be made with full statistical rigor.[10]

Why the Criterion Works

Why does the complexity-specification criterion reliably detect design? To see why this criterion is exactly the right instrument for detecting design, we need to understand what it is about intelligent agents that makes them detectable in the first place. The principal characteristic of intelligent agency is choice. Whenever an intelligent agent acts, it chooses from a range of competing possibilities.

This is true not just of humans but of animals as well as of extraterrestrial intelligences. A rat navigating a maze must choose whether to go right or left at various points in the maze. When SETI researchers attempt to discover intelligence in the extraterrestrial radio transmissions they are monitoring, they assume an extraterrestrial intelligence could have chosen any number of possible radio transmissions, and then attempt to match the transmissions they observe with certain patterns as opposed to others. Whenever a human being utters meaningful speech, a choice is made from a range of possible sound combinations that might have been uttered. Intelligent agency always entails discrimination, choosing certain things, ruling out others.

Given this characterization of intelligent agency, the crucial question is

---

[10]Ibid., chap. 5.

how to recognize it. Intelligent agents act by making a choice. How then do we recognize that an intelligent agent has made a choice? A bottle of ink spills accidentally onto a sheet of paper; someone takes a fountain pen and writes a message on a sheet of paper. In both instances ink is applied to paper. In both instances one among an almost infinite set of possibilities is realized. In both instances a contingency is actualized, and others are ruled out. Yet in one instance we ascribe agency, in the other chance.

What is the relevant difference? Not only do we need to observe that a contingency was actualized, but we ourselves need also to be able to specify that contingency. The contingency must conform to an independently given pattern, and we must be able independently to formulate that pattern. A random ink blot is unspecifiable; a message written with ink on paper is specifiable. Ludwig Wittgenstein in *Culture and Value* made the same point: "We tend to take the speech of a Chinese for inarticulate gurgling. Someone who understands Chinese will recognize *language* in what he hears. Similarly I often cannot discern the *humanity* in man."[11]

In hearing a Chinese utterance, someone who understands Chinese not only recognizes that one from a range of all possible utterances was actualized but is also able to specify the utterance as coherent Chinese speech. Contrast this with someone who does not understand Chinese. In hearing a Chinese utterance, someone who does not understand Chinese also recognizes that one from a range of possible utterances was actualized, but this time, because lacking the ability to understand Chinese, is unable to specify the utterance as coherent speech.

To someone who does not understand Chinese, the utterance will appear gibberish. Gibberish—the utterance of nonsense syllables uninterpretable within any natural language—always actualizes one utterance from the range of possible utterances. Nevertheless, gibberish, by corresponding to nothing we can understand in any language, also cannot be specified. As a result, gibberish is never taken for intelligent communication but always for what Wittgenstein calls "inarticulate gurgling."

This actualizing of one among several competing possibilities, ruling out the rest and specifying the one that was actualized, encapsulates how we recognize intelligent agency or, equivalently, how we detect design. Experimental psychologists who study animal learning and behavior have

---

[11]Ludwig Wittgenstein, *Culture and Value*, ed. G. H. von Wright, trans. P. Winch (Chicago: University of Chicago Press, 1980), p. 1e.

known this all along. To learn a task an animal must acquire the ability to actualize behaviors suitable for the task as well as the ability to rule out behaviors unsuitable for the task. Moreover, for a psychologist to recognize that an animal has learned a task, it is necessary not only to observe the animal making the appropriate discrimination but also to specify this discrimination.

Thus to recognize whether a rat has successfully learned how to traverse a maze, a psychologist must first specify which sequence of right and left turns conducts the rat out of the maze. No doubt a rat randomly wandering a maze also discriminates a sequence of right and left turns. But by randomly wandering the maze the rat gives no indication that it can discriminate the appropriate sequence of right and left turns for exiting the maze. Consequently, the psychologist studying the rat will have no reason to think that the rat has learned how to traverse the maze.

Only if the rat executes the sequence of right and left turns specified by the psychologist will the psychologist recognize that the rat has learned how to traverse the maze. It is precisely the learned behaviors we regard as intelligent in animals. Hence it is no surprise that the same scheme for recognizing animal learning recurs for recognizing intelligent agency generally, to wit: actualizing one among several competing possibilities, ruling out the others and specifying the one chosen.

Note that complexity is implicit here as well. To see this, consider again a rat traversing a maze but now take a very simple maze in which two right turns conduct the rat out of the maze. How will a psychologist studying the rat determine whether it has learned to exit the maze? Just putting the rat in the maze will not be enough. Because the maze is so simple, the rat could by chance just happen to take two right turns and thereby exit the maze. The psychologist will therefore be uncertain whether the rat actually learned to exit this maze or whether the rat just got lucky.

But contrast this now with a complicated maze in which a rat must take just the right sequence of left and right turns to exit the maze. Suppose the rat must take one hundred appropriate right and left turns, and any mistake will prevent the rat from exiting the maze. A psychologist who sees the rat take no erroneous turns and in short order exit the maze will be convinced that the rat has indeed learned how to exit the maze and that this was not dumb luck.

This general scheme for recognizing intelligent agency is but a thinly disguised form of the complexity-specification criterion. In general, to recognize intelligent agency we must observe a choice among competing possibilities, note which possibilities were not chosen and then be able to specify the possibility that was chosen. What's more, the competing possibilities that were ruled out must be live possibilities and sufficiently numerous so that specifying the possibility that was chosen cannot be attributed to chance. In terms of complexity, this is just another way of saying that the range of possibilities is complex.

All the elements in this general scheme for recognizing intelligent agency (i.e., choosing, ruling out and specifying) find their counterpart in the complexity-specification criterion. It follows that this criterion formalizes what we have been doing right along when we recognize intelligent agency. The complexity-specification criterion pinpoints what we need to be looking for when we detect design.

As a postscript it's worth pondering the etymology of the word *intelligent*. The word *intelligent* derives from two Latin words: the preposition *inter*, meaning between, and the verb *lego*, meaning to choose or select. Thus according to its etymology, intelligence consists in *choosing between*. It follows that the etymology of the word intelligent parallels the formal analysis of intelligent agency inherent in the complexity-specification criterion.

Application to Biology

Perhaps the most compelling evidence for design in biology comes from biochemistry. In a recent issue of *Cell* Bruce Alberts, president of the National Academy of Sciences, remarked, "The entire cell can be viewed as a factory that contains an elaborate network of interlocking assembly lines, each of which is composed of large protein machines. . . . Why do we call the large protein assemblies that underlie cell function *machines*? Precisely because, like the machines invented by humans to deal efficiently with the macroscopic world, these protein assemblies contain highly coordinated moving parts."[12]

Even so, Alberts sides with the majority of biologists in regarding the cell's marvelous complexity as only apparently designed. The Lehigh University biochemist Michael Behe disagrees. In *Darwin's Black Box* Behe presents a powerful argument for actual design in the cell. Central to his argument is his notion of *irreducible complexity*. A system is irreducibly

---

[12]Bruce Alberts, "The Cell as a Collection of Protein Machines: Preparing the Next Generation of Molecular Biologists," *Cell* 92 (February 1998): 291.

complex if it consists of several interrelated parts so that removing even one part completely destroys the system's function. As an example of irreducible complexity Behe offers the mousetrap. A mousetrap consists of a platform, a hammer, a spring, a catch and a holding bar. Remove any one of these five components, and it is impossible to construct a functional mousetrap.[13]

Irreducible complexity needs to be contrasted with *cumulative complexity*. A system is cumulatively complex if the components of the system can be arranged sequentially so that the successive removal of components never leads to the complete loss of function. An example of a cumulatively complex system is a city. It is possible successively to remove people and services from a city until you are down to a tiny village—all without losing the sense of community, which in this case constitutes function.

From this characterization of cumulative complexity it is clear that the Darwinian mechanism of selection and mutation can readily account for cumulative complexity. Indeed, the gradual accrual of complexity via selection mirrors the retention of function as components are successively removed from a cumulatively complex system.

But what about irreducible complexity? Can the Darwinian mechanism account for irreducible complexity? Certainly, if selection acts with reference to a goal, it can produce irreducible complexity. Take Behe's mousetrap. Given the goal of constructing a mousetrap, a person can specify a goal-directed selection process that in turn selects a platform, a hammer, a spring, a catch and a holding bar and at the end puts all these components together to form a functional mousetrap. Given a prespecified goal, selection has no difficulty producing irreducibly complex systems.

But the selection operating in biology is Darwinian natural selection. And this form of selection operates without goals, has neither plan nor purpose and is wholly undirected. The great appeal of Darwin's selection mechanism was, after all, that it would eliminate teleology from biology. Yet by making selection an undirected process, Darwin drastically abridged the type of complexity biological systems could manifest. Henceforth biological systems could manifest only cumulative complexity, not irreducible complexity.

Why is this? Behe explains in *Darwin's Black Box*:

---

[13]Behe, *Darwin's Black Box*, pp. 39-45.

An irreducibly complex system cannot be produced . . . by slight, successive modifications of a precursor system, because any precursor to an irreducibly complex system that is missing a part is by definition nonfunctional. . . . Since natural selection can only choose systems that are already working, then if a biological system cannot be produced gradually it would have to arise as an integrated unit, in one fell swoop, for natural selection to have anything to act on.[14]

For an irreducibly complex system, function is attained only when all components of the system are in place simultaneously. It follows that natural selection, if it is going to produce an irreducibly complex system, has to produce it all at once or not at all. This would not be a problem if the systems in question were simple. But they are not. The irreducibly complex biochemical systems Behe considers are protein machines consisting of numerous distinct proteins, each indispensable for function and together beyond what natural selection can muster in a single generation.

One such irreducibly complex biochemical system that Behe considers is the bacterial flagellum. The flagellum is a whiplike rotary motor that enables a bacterium to navigate through its environment. The flagellum includes an acid powered rotary engine, a stator, O-rings, bushings and a drive shaft. The intricate machinery of this molecular motor requires approximately fifty proteins. Yet the absence of any one of these proteins results in the complete loss of motor function.[15]

The irreducible complexity of such biochemical systems counts powerfully against the Darwinian mechanism and indeed against any naturalistic evolutionary mechanism proposed to date. Moreover, because irreducible complexity occurs at the biochemical level, there is no more fundamental level of biological analysis to which the irreducible complexity of biochemical systems can be referred and at which a Darwinian analysis in terms of selection and mutation can still hope for success. Undergirding biochemistry is ordinary chemistry and physics, neither of which can account for biological information. Also, whether a biochemical system is irreducibly complex is a fully empirical question: individually knock out each protein constituting a biochemical system to

---

[14]Ibid., p. 39.
[15]Ibid., pp. 69-72.

determine whether function is lost. If so, we are dealing with an irreducibly complex system. Mutagenesis experiments of this sort are routine in biology.[16]

The connection between Behe's notion of irreducible complexity and my complexity-specification criterion is now straightforward. The irreducibly complex systems Behe considers require numerous components specifically adapted to each other and each necessary for function. On any formal complexity-theoretic analysis they are complex in the sense required by the complexity-specification criterion. Moreover, in virtue of their function, these systems embody patterns independent of the actual living systems. Hence these systems are also specified in the sense required by the complexity-specification criterion.

Biological specification always denotes function. An organism is a functional system comprising many functional subsystems. The functionality of organisms can be cashed out in any number of ways. Arno Wouters cashes it out globally in terms of the *viability* of whole organisms.[17] Michael Behe cashes it out in terms of the *minimal function* of biochemical systems.[18] Even the staunch Darwinist Richard Dawkins will admit that life is specified functionally, cashing out functionality in terms of the *reproduction* of genes. Thus in *The Blind Watchmaker* Dawkins writes, "Complicated things have some quality, specifiable in advance, that is highly unlikely to have been acquired by random chance alone. In the case of living things, the quality that is specified in advance is . . . the ability to propagate genes in reproduction."[19]

So What?

There exists a reliable criterion for detecting design. This criterion detects design strictly from observational features of the world. Moreover, it belongs to probability and complexity theory, not to metaphysics and the-

---

[16]See, for example, Nicholas Gaiano et al., "Insertional Mutagenesis and Rapid Cloning of Essential Genes in Zebrafish," *Nature* 383 (1996): 829-32; Carolyn K. Suzuki et al., "Requirement for the Yeast Gene *LON* in Intramitochondrial Proteolysis and Maintenance of Respiration," *Science* 264 (1994): 273-76; Qun-Yong Zhou, Carol J. Qualfe and Richard D. Palmiter, "Targeted Disruption of the Tyrosine Hydroxylase Gene Reveals That Catecholamines Are Required for Mouse Fetal Development," *Nature* 374 (1995): 640-43.

[17]Arno Wouters, "Viability Explanation," *Biology and Philosophy* 10 (1995): 435-57.

[18]Behe, *Darwin's Black Box*, pp. 45-46.

[19]Dawkins, *Blind Watchmaker*, p. 9.

ology. And although it cannot achieve logical demonstration, it does achieve statistical justification so compelling as to demand assent. This criterion is relevant to biology. When applied to the complex, information-rich structures of biology, it detects design. In particular, the complexity-specification criterion shows that Michael Behe's irreducibly complex bio-chemical systems are designed.

What are we to make of these developments? Many scientists remain unconvinced. So what if we have a reliable criterion for detecting design, and so what if that criterion tells us that biological systems are designed? How is looking at a biological system and inferring it is designed any better than shrugging our shoulders and saying God did it? The fear is that design cannot help but stifle scientific inquiry.

Design is not a science stopper. Indeed, design can foster inquiry where traditional evolutionary approaches obstruct it. Consider the term "junk DNA." Implicit in this term is the view that because the genome of an organism has been cobbled together through a long, undirected evolutionary process, the genome is a patchwork of which only limited portions are essential to the organism. Thus on an evolutionary view we expect a lot of useless DNA. If, on the other hand, organisms are designed, we expect DNA, as much as possible, to exhibit function. And indeed, the most recent findings suggest that designating DNA as "junk" merely cloaks our current lack of knowledge about function. For instance, in a recent issue of the *Journal of Theoretical Biology* John Bodnar describes how "non-coding DNA in eukaryotic genomes encodes a language which programs organismal growth and development."[20] Design encourages scientists to look for function where naturalistic evolution discourages it.

Or consider vestigial organs that later are found to have a function after all. Evolutionary biology texts often cite the human coccyx as a "vestigial structure" that hearkens back to vertebrate ancestors with tails. Yet if you look at a recent edition of *Gray's Anatomy*, you find that the coccyx is a crucial point of contact with muscles that attach to the pelvic floor. Now anatomy is nothing else than an exercise in design, studying the large-scale design plans/blueprints for bodies. Thus here again we find design encouraging scientists to look for function where evolution discourages it. Examples where the phrase "vestigial structure" merely cloaks our current

---

[20]John W. Bodnar et al., "Deciphering the Language of the Genome," *Journal of Theoretical Biology* 189 (1997): 183.

lack of knowledge about function can be multiplied. The human appendix, formerly thought to be vestigial, is now known to be a functioning component of the immune system.[21]

Reinstating design within science can only enrich science. All the tried and true tools of science will remain intact. But design also adds a new tool to the scientist's explanatory tool chest. Moreover, design raises a whole new set of research questions. Once we know that something is designed, we will want to know how it was produced, to what extent the design is optimal and what its purpose is. Note that we can detect design without knowing what something was designed for. There is a room at the Smithsonian filled with obviously designed objects for which no one has a clue about their purpose.[22]

Design also implies constraints. An object that is designed functions within certain design constraints. Transgress those constraints and the object functions poorly or breaks. Moreover, we can discover those constraints empirically by seeing what does and does not work. This simple insight has tremendous implications not just for science but also for ethics. If humans are in fact designed, then we can expect psychosocial constraints to be hardwired into us. Transgress those constraints and we personally as well as our society will suffer. There is plenty of empirical evidence to suggest that many of the attitudes and behaviors our society promotes undermine human flourishing. Design promises to reinvigorate that ethical stream running from Aristotle through Aquinas known as natural law.[23]

By reinstating design within science we do much more than simply critique scientific reductionism. Scientific reductionism holds that everything is reducible to scientific categories. Scientific reductionism is self-refuting and easily seen to be self-refuting. The existence of the world, the laws by which the world operates, the intelligibility of the world and the unreasonable effectiveness of mathematics for comprehending the world are just a few of the questions that science raises but that science is incapable of answering.

---

[21]See Percival Davis and Dean Kenyon, *Of Pandas and People*, 2nd ed. (Dallas: Haughton, 1993), p. 128.

[22]See Del Ratzsch, "Design, Chance & Theistic Evolution," in *Mere Creation*, ed. William A. Dembski (Downers Grove, Ill.: InterVarsity Press, 1998).

[23]See J. Budziszewski, *Written on the Heart: The Case for Natural Law* (Downers Grove, Ill.: InterVarsity Press, 1997).

Simply critiquing scientific reductionism, however, is not enough. Critiquing scientific reductionism does nothing to change science. And it is science that must change. By eschewing design, science has for too long operated with an inadequate set of conceptual categories. This has led to a constricted vision of reality, skewing how science understands not just the world but also ourselves. Evolutionary psychology, which justifies everything from infanticide to adultery, is just one symptom of this inadequate conception of science. Barring design from science distorts science, making it a mouthpiece for materialism instead of a search for truth.

Martin Heidegger remarked in *Being and Time*, "A science's level of development is determined by the extent to which it is *capable* of a crisis in its basic concepts."[24] The basic concepts with which science has operated these last several hundred years are no longer adequate, certainly not in an information age, certainly not in an age where design is empirically detectable. Science faces a crisis of basic concepts. The way out of this crisis is to expand science to include design. To reinstate design within science is to liberate science, freeing it from restrictions that were always arbitrary and now have become intolerable.

---

[24]Martin Heidegger, *Being and Time*, in *Basic Writings*, ed. D. F. Krell (New York: Harper & Row, 1977), p. 51.

15

THE CHALLENGE OF THE HUMAN SCIENCES

The Necessity of an Interactive & Dualistic Ontology

MATTHEW FRAWLEY

D URING MY FRESHMAN YEAR IN COLLEGE I WOULD OFTEN SPEND TIME AT night out on the sun deck of my dorm. As I laid there on one of the beach chairs and stared up at the night sky, a feeling of insignificance often overwhelmed me. It seemed I was a mere speck of dust in the great expanse of the cosmos and a mere blink in the great timeline of universal existence. Despite this sense of being swallowed by the universe, I always steadied myself with the conviction that my existence did have meaning and value. I had submitted my life to Christ the year before I entered college, and now within the midst of the chaos of college life and the apparent meaningless of my life in the universe, the Holy Spirit was continually challenging me to affirm the truth that in Christ alone my life had substance. Jesus' death and resurrection not only secured my salvation but also demonstrated

God's love for me. Consequently, the value I have derives from God and not from some self-imposed delusion.

But how can I be sure? Certainly the Bible and Christian tradition celebrate my testimony because they affirm the existence of a transcendent reality that is independent of the contingencies of space and time. Yet many in the human sciences offer a different opinion. While they might applaud my apparent healthy self-image and strong self-esteem, these scientists would suggest that there are theories of human understanding, motivation and interaction that completely explain religious experience apart from any appeal to a dualistic ontology that a belief in a transcendent God necessarily entails.

To understand the "challenge of human sciences" and to formulate a Christian response to the naturalistic perspective they adopt, I have divided this chapter into three sections. I will first examine Freud's theory of the genesis of religion, because even though the scientific community has rejected his overtly antagonistic approach to religion, many still operate within the same paradigm as Freud. Consequently, as I will show at the end of the first section, they fall prey to the same limitations inherent in any closed-world approach to religion. This exposition will lead into the second section, where I discuss the possible relativistic and reductionistic ramifications of an uncritical incorporation of these sciences into theology. The third and last section will be "reconstructive": theology has an obligation and divine duty to engage these sciences because we are part of creation. Christianity holds that God's inherent rationality is reflected in creation so that through a proper theological perspective, the interpretations of human behavior and interaction that the human sciences offer can be reinterpreted to render more intelligible the theories themselves. I will therefore offer some suggestions for the proper interaction between theology and the human sciences.

Freud's Theory of Religion

In his book *Theories of Primitive Religion* E. E. Evans-Pritchard emphasizes that a lack of reliable data makes it scientifically impossible to discover the origin of religion. This fact, however, was not an impediment to researchers in the late 1800s and early 1900s. For most pursuing this grail, a cogent explanation of the phenomena of religion held great power. It was believed that religion was a phase in the evolutionary progression of society so that the source or origin of religion would yield the essence of its character. If it could be demonstrated that its causal factor was either psychological or sociological, a naturalistic explanation would, according to Max Muller, justify qualifying religion as "a hallucination or an infantile disease."[1] Through this evolutionary approach theorists conceived religion not as the institution that most fully defines the essence of our activity but confined it to a paradigmatic stage that will be surpassed in humanity's progression toward its true essence exemplified at that time in the burgeoning of science.

No one theorist better represents this perspective than Sigmund Freud. In *The Future of an Illusion* he argued that while religion has alleviated some of the problems of society, it has in general failed to satisfy its grand expectations. Religion was created and perpetuated as an institution of society in order first to exorcise the mystery and cruelty of nature, second to create hope and purpose in the presence of the cruel indifference of fate, and third to provide meaning in the midst of suffering that communal living has imposed upon every individual.[2] Nevertheless, according to Freud, science has demythologized nature by revealing its cause-and-effect machinations and a prevailing sense of skepticism persists that the existential condition of humanity is beyond salvation. Consequently, these first two emphases have faded so that religion now only serves to socialize people by pacifying the tension created by instinctual restrictions necessary for communal living.

Yet even in this area, religion has proved wanting. According to Freud people are not happier now than they were hundreds of years ago when religion enjoyed cultural hegemony. Therefore Freud states, "If the achievements of religion in promoting men's happiness, in adapting them to civilization, and in controlling them morally, are no better, then the question arises whether we are right in considering it necessary for mankind, and whether we do wisely in basing the demands of our culture upon it."[3] Freud's answer was a resounding no. He thought that the historical, or evolutionary, progression of humanity resembles the ego development of a child in an Oedipus/Electra complex and thus correlated the father-complex of the child with society's fascination with religion. Just as

---

[1] E. E. Evans-Pritchard, *Theories of Primitive Religion* (Oxford: Clarendon, 1965), p. 100.
[2] Sigmund Freud, *The Future of an Illusion*, trans. W. D. Robson-Scott (London: Hogarth, 1925), p. 30.
[3] Freud, *Future of an Illusion*, p. 67.

the child works out his or her sexual tensions and resultant ambivalence to the same sex parent, society must progress through religion to a more scientific and optimistic perspective on reality.

In his book *Totem and Taboo: Resemblances Between the Psychic Lives of Savages and Neurotics*, Freud specifically endeavors to show this correlation between his theories of ontogenetic development and phylogenetic progression. Between the ages of three and five, children begin to confront instinctual frustration and guilt, which Freud entitled an Oedipus complex. Freud's terminology derives from Sophocles's *Oedipus Rex*, which describes the emotional trials of a young man who learns after the fact that the man he has killed and the woman he has married are actually his biological parents. Freud argues that a young boy during this time confronts both his growing sexual attraction to his mother and his resultant jealously of the father. Due to incest taboos and his own physical limitations, the son will eventually sublimate this jealousy and begin to identify with the father and endeavor to emulate his persona. This process of sublimation is a defensive move of the ego and serves to alleviate the tension the child feels through his ambivalence to the father. The son hates the father because he is a threat to the child's desire for the mother. Yet, more importantly, the child needs security and affirmation from his father. Therefore through identification with the father, the son allows the more positive emotions to gain expression over the negative and destructive feelings.

Freud suggests that a similar process occurred in primitive society. To correlate the struggle over guilt that every child experiences during the oedipal crisis, Freud cashed out humanity's Oedipus complex in terms of religious development. Because he was convinced that psychoanalytic interpretations could fully explain any phenomena of behavior, Freud felt justified in creating a story of primitive humanity that would explain the genesis of religion in terms of totemism, a system of rituals and group identification based on animal representation. He suggests that a group of primitive brothers were jealous of their father, who kept their respective mothers to himself for his own libidinal satisfaction. The mounting frustration over their inability to satiate their sexual desires eventually burst forth in collective rage, which ended in the murder of the father. Although they subsequently ate the father, hoping to gain his physical prowess, their optimism soon gave way to emergent feelings of guilt. In an effort to placate their discomfort, the brothers resigned not to touch their mothers (incest taboo) and not to kill the father substitute (the totem animal). Only in times of celebration is the totem animal eaten for rituals of solidarity among the totem group and the immortalized father projection. From this external outworking of the oedipal crisis, argues Freud, all historical religious practices developed.

In general then, religion is simply our continual struggle with the oedipal crisis, and as a child resolves these internal conflicts, so too will society. Consequently, Freud reduces religion to a mere phase of communal growth and through the scientific efforts and research of psychotherapy, society will be able to rid itself of its maladaptive dependence on God because religion is nothing more than psychological projections of internal conflict.

According to Evans-Pritchard, in determining the historical origin of religion Freud's theory has been "as dead as mutton" for quite some time.[4] The main reason for this is that Freud could not offer one bit of historical proof to validate his claim—it was sheer speculation. Nonetheless, while current theorists in human sciences have seen the futility of Freud's endeavor, and therefore study religion as an entity in itself, their efforts are still no less antagonistic to Christianity. Even though current scientists do not overtly strive to remove religion, and even at times believe themselves to support the practice of religion, they still operate under the same naturalistic perspective as Freud so that they often reduce religion to a form of human behavior that psychological and sociological theories can accurately and exhaustively interpret.

For example, Ana-Maria Rizzuto in *Birth of the Living God* rejects Freud's phylogenetic speculations and strives to reformulate his theory to account for maternal influences on children and God imagery in young girls. She argues that pre-oedipal conflicts are critical for development of God imagery and that this original God image is developed and reworked as an individual confronts situations later in life that jeopardize ego defenses. She writes, "Those who are capable of mature religious belief renew their God representation to make it compatible with their emotional, conscious, and unconscious situation."[5] Specifically in times of "felt disharmony," latent images of God are brought to the surface and reformulated so as to regain a sense of normalcy in the real world. She

---

[4]Evans-Pritchard, *Theories of Primitive Religion*, p. 100.

[5]Ana-Maria Rizzuto, *The Birth of the Living God* (Chicago: University of Chicago Press, 1979), p. 46.

concludes then that there is a "constant dialectical process" between the primacy of object representation and the sense of self, which brings the pre-oedipal child to form some representation of the parent who becomes supreme being over all creation. This being subsumes all reality unto itself and thereby satisfies our emotional needs.

The consequences of Rizzuto's model for Christianity is obvious. Implied in Rizzuto's conclusion is that the true author of God is ourselves, and when this image is radically redefined in personal events such as conversion, a transcendent deity does not cause this transformation. Instead, it is our ego defenses that triumph over threats to our feelings of security and harmony by reworking our projected image of God so that he or she or it can subsume and conquer the source of the psychic disturbance. If Rizzuto's analysis is correct, we cannot hold a dualistic interpretation of God's interaction with the world. Rather we must collapse this perspective into a naturalistic paradigm so that all testimonies of fellowship with God are reinterpreted as examples of the miraculous power of ego defenses. We can therefore take biblical criticism to a new level and speculate, for example, that Isaiah's confrontation with God in Isaiah 6 was probably just a bad case of low self-esteem.

Rizzuto's analysis relies on her belief in humanity's evolutionary drive toward adaptation. Rizzuto limits herself to the belief that God is only a transitional object engendered by the psyche, thereby maintaining a closed-world, naturalistic interpretation of religion. The reality of God in people's lives therefore follows "the dynamic laws of psychic defense, adaptation, and synthesis, as well as the need for meaningful relations with oneself, others, and the world at large."[6] While this is certainly true in a limited sense, it cannot capture the rich complexities of human nature. The Bible declares that we are not only our socialized egos but also creatures who have the capacity to interact with God through the Holy Spirit and by his grace. Therefore, Rizzuto's analysis, as well as any psychological analysis, can only capture the psychological effects of this spiritual interaction. Consequently, while Rizzuto may show how people construct images of God, it may be these very projections of God that the Lord often has to destroy, or at least overcome, in order for people to know his true and merciful nature.

While the human sciences certainly have a legitimate role in the analy-

---

[6]Ibid., p. 179.

sis of religion, they overstep their inherent bounds when they endeavor to explain all the dynamics of religious experience. This is simply a closed-world, naturalistic perspective that is the progeny of a mechanistic cosmology. While the human sciences have tempered their initial zeal for explaining away religion, they now keep the institution of religion alive in name only. Because there is no reference to the transcendent reality that Christianity demands for proper interpretation, Christian faith is reduced to a mere form of personal experience apart from the content of that faith actually decisive for the individual. Rizzuto exemplifies this approach in her methodology. She bases her theories of God imagery on the commonalities she discovers among the people she studies. To her it does not matter if you are a Christian, Buddhist, Muslim or New Age spiritualist because psychoanalysis can show the deeper commonalities between all forms of religious experience. To call it a Christian or Muslim experience is simply a nominalistic appendage that Rizzuto tolerates.

However, Christian faith resists reduction to any neat category. There is true and false religious experience, and the way to discern the difference is not by wooden-headedly asking whether the experience reduces tension and promotes adaptation. Scripture affirms that we are spiritual beings who are created for fellowship with God and will not find rest until we are in union with God. Therefore, the anxiety we experience in life is not inherently something we should avoid. Rather anxiety may be the result of our futile attempts to create meaning apart from the Holy Spirit. The breakdown of ego defenses exemplified in the experience of a teenage identity crisis or middle-age crisis is actually truth-producing error that shows the inevitable limitation of adaptational theories, and it signals that we need to find another, higher level of interpretation for our existence. Furthermore, if this anxiety is allowed to intensify, it will not rest until it finds true and eternal satisfaction.

A person in the throes of such an existential crisis in which all life seems utterly meaningless will therefore not settle for paltry, humanistic theories of life but will find lasting and true meaning that negates this crisis only in Jesus Christ. That is the hope and message of Christianity. Moreover, if there is a transcendent reality, the spiritual realm of human experience remains a viable category that does not disintegrate through psychological reductionism. Nevertheless, while this shows that theology is indispensable to the human sciences, ironically, many theologians have capitulated to the closed-world perspective adopted by the human sciences.

Theological Appropriation of Reductive Human Sciences

Contextualism is the key characteristic of postmodernism. According to postmodernism, because we are the socialized products of our specific environment, our views of reality are contextual, localized and preconditioned. Accordingly, postmodernists conclude that any form of foundational epistemology is impossible. Because our beliefs are the products of inculcation, we can never shed these contextual influences. As a result, it is impossible to attain objectivity. Subjectivity invariably skews our reasoning and obstructs our access to whatever objective truths there might be. Consequently, to espouse universal claims within communities and cultures outside our specific context constitutes imperialism.

For example, in *Remembering Esperanza* Mark Taylor decries the oppressiveness of foundational theologies. According to him, theologians face a "trilemma."[7] Within the matrix of pluralism the theologian must first secure some sense of tradition. But instead of acting as an institution of authority, tradition locates us within a particular context. Every individual grows up within a particular context in which the veracity of cultural norms are initially assumed and universalized.

Nevertheless, because we cannot in good conscience impose our rules and beliefs on another without proper justification, we must respect different perspectives no matter how divergent they are from our own. Yet this position is problematic for Taylor because the third component of the trilemma is the need to espouse a theology that will denounce and resist all attempts at oppression. If justification for any particular set of beliefs remains elusive, no one can legitimately criticize another. While Taylor believes that he can overcome this paradox through his "radical revisioning" of the Christian message, he fails to appreciate that any contextual theology that does not appeal to a transcendent order will remain relative to its particular context as well.

Taylor repeatedly emphasizes throughout his book that his particular context influences the presentation of his theory. He writes that his book is not for everyone. But does this mean that those who disagree with him should ignore him? By overemphasizing his context Taylor limits the scope of his argument to the extent that those who disagree with his position may classify Taylor's pleas for emancipation of the oppressed as merely the product of his particular culture and thereby discard his declarations.

---

[7]Mark Kline Taylor, *Remembering Esperanza* (Maryknoll, N.Y.: Orbis, 1990), p. 23.

Furthermore, Taylor never establishes the criteria for determining which psychological and sociological variables determine a person's context. Taylor, for example, describes his context as white, middle-class male. Yet is this an exhaustive account of his context, or are there other variables not included that define his context better? To limit context to sex, race and financial status is arbitrary. Without proper criteria I can just as easily substitute my shoe size, love of graham crackers and abhorrence of disco music as the determinative influences of my context.

Moreover, if we could completely define the myriad factors that make up a person's context, we would, as Roger Trigg writes, "be inexorably driven in a downward spiral to ever smaller groups, searching for a firmer spread of agreement. The trouble is that we could reach a stage . . . where it appears that a form of life has only one member."[8] Every individual would remain isolated in his or her particular context with little hope of constructive dialogue with others. To celebrate pluralism in the name of contextualism is ultimately to commit epistemological suicide because the relativism that pluralism engenders erodes all foundations of commonality that are necessary for identifying with other people. Christianity, on the other hand, states that this foundation is found in our status as creatures of God so that true and lasting respect for others is gained only through fellowship with God.

Besides encouraging epistemological suicide, contextualism also underwrites a psychosocial reductionism of theology. Postmodern theologians like Sallie McFague argue from the epistemological limitations inherent in contextualism that objective appropriation of divine truth is impossible and defies symbolic representation. The symbols of our faith are not signs that point us to another reality (which has been traditionally held to give these symbols meaning) but are simply the products of our own community's experience.

Implicit here is that we cannot have an experience of God that transcends our symbolic constructions, because the symbols themselves engender and direct religious experience. McFague, then, as well as Taylor and naturalistic researchers in the human sciences, may believe in the existence of God, but their commitment to contextualism causes them to reject a traditional understanding of God's interaction with the world. Given our

---

[8]Roger Trigg, *Rationality and Science: Can Science Explain Everything?* (Cambridge, Mass.: Blackwell, 1993), pp. 160-61.

apparent inability to attain an objective perspective, McFague believes she is justified in reconceptualizing God in accord with our subjective needs and desires.

Instead of despairing at the obvious loss of hope implied by this conclusion, theologians like McFague and Taylor press forward their pragmatic interests. They believe that because there is no accessible transcendent reality that constrains theological inquiry, the precious symbols of the Christian tradition can be manipulated to redirect social behavior deemed destructive and oppressive (traditional Christian moral behavior being one of the worst offenders).

McFague, in *The Body of God: An Ecological Theology,* continues her project from the previous book, *Models of God,* reconceptualizing the transcendence of God in terms of immanence. In the end McFague leaves no transcendence at all. For McFague, the lack of a guiding interactive and dualistic ontology frees her to construct an organic conception of God that, she claims, will help the church lead the way in society's effort to resolve the present ecological crisis. She develops a panentheistic worldview, where incarnation comes to include the whole world and not simply Jesus Christ.[9] Through this reworking of our conception of God, McFague hopes that we will interact with each other and with the world in ways that are more tolerant and ecologically responsible.

Likewise, Taylor employs anthropological, sociological and psychological studies to show how sexism occurs and how cultural myths of gender inequality invite racism, heterosexism and classism. He notes how at certain times in the history of the church the "Christ symbol" has implicitly and explicitly fostered gender oppression. He therefore advocates that the mythic symbol of Christ should be changed to move beyond the person of Christ and locate the work of Christ in a broader cultural framework. Jesus can then be viewed as a person who worked for emancipation without specific appeal to his gender.

The question now for McFague, Taylor and others who seek to reconceptualize God is whether they aren't in fact imposing their theological models on a general populace that still largely ascribes to a dualistic ontology. If so, then their projects are reminiscent of B. F. Skinner's "technology of behavior." Skinner believed that we could eradicate social ills through

---

[9]Sallie McFague, *The Body of God: An Ecological Theology* (Minneapolis: Fortress, 1993), p. 149.

proper conditioning. To produce socially desirable behavior we need only change the stimuli to which people are exposed, say by operant or classical conditioning. Likewise, for Taylor we need to strip the Christ metaphor of all oppressive, patriarchal imagery, and for McFague we need to alter our view of God so that we treat the world more responsibly.

Although McFague and Taylor present their respective projects in altruistic clothing, the implications of their methodology are frightening. Skinner argued that humanity did not possess free will or self-reflective consciousness. Instead we are simply automatons who are socially conditioned by external stimuli. There is no internal locus, no "I," that ponders alternatives and selects actions. We are only response mechanisms (and that includes Skinner himself) under the control of circumstances that manipulate our behavior. Similarly, Taylor and McFague advocate reorienting our God imagery to change our behavior. The power over society thus resides in their hands, but the direction they propose conforms only to their pragmatic and unjustifiable interests because they reject any appeal to a transcendent reality.

McFague, Taylor and their colleagues are in no position to set the direction of the church, because pragmatism depends on a personal, or agreed upon, agenda. That's why Taylor and McFague write about political oppression and ecology at a time when those issues are relevant and easily discussed in our cultural climate. Christianity, however, does not depend on the transient concerns of the late twentieth century. While ecology and political oppression are important issues for the social mission of the church, these issues are subsumed within a larger framework that includes our personal participation in God's reality. Within that broader framework, political and ecological concerns are properly interpreted in terms of human sin and transformation. We therefore do not fight "the system" but engage the world as God's creatures desperately needing his love and transforming power.

Proper Christian Appropriation of the Human Sciences
The previous section showed the deleterious consequences of contextualism in theology. In line with psychosocial theories, contextualism maintains that all religious experience is reducible to human behavior broadly construed. Instead of taking seriously the danger of relativism and its concomitant reductionism, postmodernists find in contextualism a source of freedom. No longer obligated to treat the biblical witness as determinative

and authoritative, they hold that the theories of the human sciences show the correlations between certain perspectives (which are contextually determined) and our resultant activity. Therefore, we need only to change our perspectives to achieve the desired behavior in the church and society.

While the postmodernists have uncritically embraced the human sciences and a prevalent closed-world ontology, the church should not react to their excesses by denying any connection between the human sciences and theology. The human sciences have certainly revealed aspects of our being that undoubtedly can help Christians better understand such theological doctrines as sin, reconciliation and transformation. The goal is to establish a relationship between God's revelation and the human sciences that preserves the integrity of both.

Perhaps the most impressive attempt to achieve such a relationship is Wolfhart Pannenberg's *Anthropology in Theological Perspective*. He is aware of the reductionistic threat of those who operate under a naturalistic perspective like Freud and Skinner, but he refuses to assert the priority of Christian revelation up front in his discussion of the various psychological theories of humanity. His approach is to legitimate the role of theology in elucidating human nature through an examination of anthropology itself. He writes, "Theologians will be able to defend the truth precisely of their talk about God only if they first respond to the atheistic critique of religion on the terrain of anthropology."[10]

Theologians can tread down this path even though the human sciences are biased against Christianity precisely because God is the creator of all reality, and therefore secular and religious understandings, if faithful to reality, must be consonant. Pannenberg therefore believes that he can show that Christianity is impervious to any reductionism principally because the human sciences show the necessity of considering the religious dimension of our being. Using this strategy Pannenberg accepts secular descriptions of human nature as "a provisional version of the objective reality, a version that needs to be expanded and deepened by showing that the anthropological datum itself contains a further and theologically relevant dimension."[11]

Pannenberg believes that his methodology is valid because it fully

---

[10]Wolfhart Pannenberg, *Anthropology in Theological Perspective*, trans. Matthew J. O'Connell (Edinburgh: T & T Clark, 1985), p. 16.

[11]Ibid., p. 19.

engages the secular critique of religion without jeopardizing the integrity of human sciences. Nonetheless, the relevant issue now becomes whether he has maintained the integrity of the Christian revelation. In accepting the secular interpretations of human behavior Pannenberg has committed himself to dialogue on the level of that perspective. Yet, if knowledge of ourselves is dependent upon our knowledge of God, we cannot rely upon secular understandings of human nature to provide an exhaustive account of the dynamics of human experience. While Pannenberg endeavors to prove this very point, his project suffers by considering our spiritual reality last instead of first.

Indeed, the inherent defect in Pannenberg's "bottom-up" approach becomes clear from his over-reliance upon Erik Erikson's concept of "basic trust." Erikson shifts Freud's emphasis from libido and destrudo interaction to the development of the ego in terms of autonomy and adaptation. He argues instead that a person's existence is dependent on three processes of organization that are mutually complementary. There is the biological process of growth *(soma)*, the psychic process organizing individual experience *(psyche)* and the communal process of the cultural organization *(ethos)*.[12] Throughout life these three systems interact to give rise to new levels of ego adaptation and competence that reorganize perceptions and develop ego strengths.

From birth until eighteen months the baby engages in a time of bonding with the maternal other who acts as a centering whole for the child. It is this influence that provides security for the baby and tells it that the world is basically trustworthy. Conversely, the maternal other may convey the message that the world is dangerous so that the rest of the child's development may tend toward the pathological. The desired ego strength that develops from this stage is hope, because the child sees that the world is trustworthy and that all human efforts are worth the risk. Any anxiety at a later stage of development is simply nostalgia for the symbiotic unity previously enjoyed. Consequently, ego balance becomes the primary task throughout life.[13] The adaptational adequacy of the ego is thus determined by its ability to suppress any tinge of anxiety that threatens developmental stability.

Yet from the spiritual-existential perspective this endeavor of the ego is

---

[12]Erik H. Erikson, *The Life Cycle Completed* (New York: W. W. Norton, 1982), pp. 25-26.
[13]Erik H. Erikson, *Childhood and Society* (New York: W. W. Norton, 1963), p. 250.

driven by despair and is ultimately doomed to fail. While at first the child's center of meaning is located outside itself in the maternal other (an analogy of a properly posited self), in that moment when the child separates itself from a state of integration, it falls back on itself to avoid the threat of the void of nonexistence. The child senses a cosmic, infinite nothingness that can swallow up his or her perceived reality. The development of the ego is therefore not just a structural component of humanity as Erikson believed. Instead the ego is the work of the human spirit in its fight to stave off the existential threat of the void of nonexistence. Erikson thus accurately describes the work of the self to some degree, but because he does not see the true existential import of the ego defenses, his developmental theory cannot capture the full extent of human behavior.

It is telling, then, that Pannenberg incorporates Erikson's category of basic trust into his perception of the *imago Dei*. He likes the way Erikson captured the expansion of the ego out into greater and greater realms of reality. Pannenberg employs that idea and expands it to include the spiritual presence as the last and final movement of the ego. Consequently, the child moves from the symbiotic unity of the mother to the family and then on into society. The ego continues to progress exocentrically out beyond all finite reality until it ultimately rests in the ground of all being. However, because Erikson does not capture the true essence of humanity as spirit, Pannenberg's theological anthropology proves overly optimistic because it does not develop the true extent of despair.

In order to understand despair psychologically, Søren Kierkegaard knew that he could not reduce the human spirit to psychology; he could only capture the movement of the spirit as it affected the psychological aspects of personal reality. Therefore, Kierkegaard's approach to understanding human activity is markedly different from that of Pannenberg. While Kierkegaard respected the limitations of human perspectives of knowing, Pannenberg, in his apologetic endeavor, inappropriately restricts the activity of the human spirit. His methodology for a theological anthropology therefore proves ultimately inadequate. It is admirable that he wishes to engage the human sciences and strive to disprove their attempts to reduce religion to a subcategory of their respective discipline. However, by starting in the scientific paradigm and moving through them to theology, Pannenberg fails to account for the whole of the kerygma. He is forced instead to reinterpret the traditional Christian doctrines to fit the modern perspective. Consequently, his interpretation of humanity does not capture our true spiritual essence.

The inherent limitations of Pannenberg's approach hold for bottom-up methodologies generally. Because their ontological perspective and resultant realm of discussion are predetermined, they are overly dependent upon the secular disciplines to decide the bounds of human activity, including our interaction with God. In contrast, T. F. Torrance argues in *Space, Time, and Incarnation* that God's revelation does not conform to any one paradigmatic view of reality but affects all facets of existence in ways that can only be fully understood through God's revelation in Jesus Christ.[14] This does not mean that the sciences are useless; rather it means that no matter how much we try to understand ourselves scientifically, we can only learn so much. Full interpretation of our behavior only becomes intelligible through Jesus Christ.

For example, the human sciences can detail the benevolent psychological and sociological effects of God's presence within a community and an individual, but they cannot decipher the connection between the human spirit and the Holy Spirit. This means that the Christian perspective actually captures a broader view of our experience, while psychology and sociology pick up on one facet of this spiritual dynamic. Consequently, we must begin first with the theological interpretation of humanity and then engage the human sciences. Only in this way do we maintain the integrity of the gospel. Even so, this does not mean that the secular disciplines are compromised in any way. We can still respect their level of interpretation and actually bring insights to them which they were not able to attain on their own. This is one of the great achievements of Kierkegaard's work.[15]

Only theology can fully appropriate the dynamics of God's interaction with the world. Theology must therefore not succumb to the naturalistic perspective of the human sciences. Instead theology, and more specifically practical theology, must maintain the transcendence of God. Divine transcendence reinterprets these psychosocial theories and thereby appropriates the full extent of human activity. On a practical level this means that the church should engage these disciplines to understand more fully how people perceive reality. Rizzuto, for example, may be right about how peo-

---

[14]Thomas F. Torrance, *Space, Time, and Incarnation* (London: Oxford University Press, 1969).

[15]See James E. Loder and W. Jim Neidhardt, *The Knight's Move* (Colorado Springs, Colo.: Helmers & Howard, 1992); and James E. Loder, *The Transforming Moment* (Colorado Springs, Colo.: Helmers & Howard, 1989).

ple come to view God through parental images. Many churchgoers may indeed maintain a false parental-induced view of God's activity in their lives. This may explain why some people believe that God has no time for them or that God will always condemn them no matter how much we preach God's love for them. If we can gain a better understanding of how people come to a false belief in God, we will be better equipped to assist the Holy Spirit in breaking these erroneous perceptions and to lead people to an authentic, fulfilling and worshipful relationship with God.

Now therefore and always be ascribed as is most justly due all might, dominion, majesty and power to the Unity indivisible, the Trinity of sovereign love, God the Father, Son and Holy Spirit. Amen.

AFTERWORD

JAMES PARKER III

ANEW WAVE IS BREAKING UPON THE AMERICAN CHURCH. AT A TIME when the mainline denominational churches are dismissed by the secular society, and their numbers are shrinking at an alarming rate, new life is rising up from a parched land. The young scholars from the Charles Hodge Society who contributed to this volume represent a new and rising generation of top-drawer evangelical scholars who promise to renew and revolutionize theological education in our country. They have engaged and held their ground against the false ideologies that have decimated the old mainline denominations. Whether it will be possible for the old seminaries to become rejuvenated and return to Christian orthodoxy, only time will tell. But if it happens, an intellectual renewal like the one outlined in this volume will have to occur.

In my own experience, both as a seminary student and as a seminary professor, I have seen scores if not hundreds of eager, fresh-faced seminary students begin their studies with enthusiasm and vibrancy, only to abandon anything remotely resembling traditional Christian orthodoxy, or what C. S. Lewis called "mere Christianity." A typical seminary education takes three years, but the change often happens in the first year. Why do so many seminary students lose their faith? After all, many of these bright people did their undergraduate degrees in very difficult fields at prestigious universities where they survived and even flourished. How did they succumb in seminary to an anemic and secularized imitation of the Christian faith?

They survived university studies because they understood the pervasive influence of naturalism at the university. Naturalism, the view that nature is ultimately ruled not by God but by the unthinking and uncaring forces of nature, was explicitly presupposed throughout their university curriculum. Consequently these students had no illusions about the secular university and its opposition to Christian belief. However, they thought seminary would be different. They expected to study at a seminary where their most cherished beliefs would not be under constant attack but would be nourished and encouraged.

Thus when they arrive at their required New Testament class at seminary, they are perplexed when their professor assures them that the miracles of Jesus are legends and do not belong to actual history. Their guard is down. They do not know how to react. They were prepared to challenge their atheist philosophy professors at the state university when they argued against miracles. But their own church sent them to this seminary. Their denomination financially supports this seminary. They have been sent to this seminary expressly to be tutored and mentored by this professor. How then can this professor be wrong? Perhaps the Christian faith needs to be radically reinterpreted? And so proceeds the slide into spiritual oblivion.

Several years ago I arrived as a junior faculty member at a mainline seminary on the East Coast (not Princeton). I was young at the time, and people couldn't tell whether I was a student or a professor. Most people initially assumed I was a student. My first day on campus I just wandered around the place incognito to meet people at random. I stumbled upon a Th.M. student who was mopping the floor in the administration building. We chatted, and he gave me some candid information about the school where I would begin teaching the next day. He told me how he had graduated from a major state university, had been very active in his church and in an evangelical student group on campus. He also told me that the very first night in his seminary dorm room he got down on his knees and poured out his heart to God, committing and dedicating his time of study to God.

Time went by and he took courses like the New Testament course I described. He told me how his confidence in the truthfulness of Scripture gradually eroded. He reinterpreted his former faith as a "mindless fundamentalism" to be discarded. He remembers the exact turning point: one day he realized that he was no longer sure a person could know anything about Jesus from reading the Gospels. That uncertainty eventually led to a loss of faith. Throughout the time his faith was disintegrating no one ever attempted to answer his doubts by directing him to sound evangelical scholarship.

If every seminary student read just one paper to understand the fundamental problem in contemporary theological studies, it should be Jay Richards's essay "Naturalism in Theology & Biblical Studies" in this volume. This essay should be required reading for anyone who wants to pursue academic study in theology. Mainstream academic theology can be extremely dangerous to a student's spiritual health if he or she wanders into these hoary woods unwarned and unprepared.

Most of the papers in this volume were written by a group of Princeton Seminary students organized as the Charles Hodge Society. The Charles Hodge Society is part of a larger international movement of theological students known as the Religious and Theological Students Fellowship or RTSF for short. RTSF is in turn part of the graduate student ministry of InterVarsity Christian Fellowship or IVCF. IVCF began in England and through various ancillary organizations (the Religious and Theological Students Fellowship, the Tyndale Fellowship for Biblical Research and so on) has revolutionized theological study in the United Kingdom.

Forty years ago you could count the evangelical biblical scholars at British universities on one hand. Today they are everywhere in the United Kingdom. How did this turn-around happen? The concerted, coordinated efforts of evangelical scholars throughout that country proved decisive. A major factor here was the Religious and Theological Students Fellowship of the British IVCF. Chapters were established at faculties of theology at major institutions. Here the students could have fellowship, which is very important when you are in an environment that is not sympathetic to your most deeply held beliefs. Equally important, they were given access to scholarly literature, visiting lecturers and bibliographic references that enabled them to answer the objections to their faith that they were daily encountering.

This same movement is growing and influencing seminary students today in the United States. Among its tangible fruits is this volume of essays. As in the United Kingdom the goal this side of the Atlantic is to provide a context for pastoral nurture and encouragement, and to provide information so that theological students can face the intellectual challenges placed before them. It is a challenge to be an evangelical student at a mainline theological seminary. If you are theologically conservative, you must learn the orthodox position that you yourself hold, the liberal position that is being taught but which you reject and finally how the orthodox position engages the liberal position. This means a lot of extra effort. Going with the liberal flow is easier. Indeed, liberal theologians rarely bother to investigate conservative evangelical scholarship, either ignoring it or stereotyping it.

The number of local chapters of the Religious and Theological Students Fellowship is growing, and the Charles Hodge Society belongs to it. This movement has a quarterly theological journal called *Foundations*, of which I am the editor. It presents theological students with essays, book reviews and bibliographic tools to help them respond substantively and thoughtfully to the intellectual challenges they face in their theological education. For more information about *Foundations*, or for information about starting a local RTSF chapter, contact me at Southern Baptist Theological Seminary <jparker@sbts.edu>. Other academic resources that deal directly with the academic challenges described here are available through the Trinity Institute (P.O. Box 100, Tehuacana, Texas 76686-0100, telephone: 254-395-4444), a residential Christian study center of which I am the director.

I close with a lesson from Gilbert Tennent, who, like the contributors to this volume, had close connections to Princeton. In 1742 while he was a minister in New Brunswick, New Jersey, he preached and published a sermon titled "The Danger of an Unconverted Ministry, Considered in a Sermon on Mark 6:34." The dangers he warned of back then are even more pertinent today. Never let us forget that the first requirement for ministers of Christ is their own conversion to the Christian faith—and that means the conversion of the heart as well as the mind.

CONTRIBUTORS

Michael D. Bush, Ph.D. candidate in history of doctrine (Princeton Theological Seminary), STM (Yale University Divinity School), M.Div. (Union Theological Seminary in Virginia). The Reverend Bush is senior pastor at First Presbyterian Church in Mobile, Alabama (PCUSA).

Raymond D. Cannata, Th.M. and M.Div. (Princeton Theological Seminary). The Reverend Cannata has written articles and reviews for several theological journals (including *Perspectives in Religious Studies* and *Foundations*). He helped found the Charles Hodge Society at Princeton Theological Seminary, writing the lead article for the revived *Princeton Theological Review* in September 1994. He is an ordained minister in the Presbyterian Church in America (PCA) and is senior pastor of Grace Church in Bridgewater, New Jersey.

Gary W. Deddo, Ph.D. (systematic theology under James B. Torrance, University of Aberdeen), M.Div. (Fuller Theological Seminary). Dr. Deddo is an acquisitions editor for InterVarsity Press. Before that he was an associate director for InterVarsity Christian Fellowship's ministry to graduate students, with national, regional and local campus responsibilities (locally at Princeton University). Dr. Deddo is an ordained Presbyterian minister (PCUSA) and has also served as campus chaplain at two universities. During the past six years he has taught systematic theology as an adjunct professor for Fuller Theological Seminary, Eastern Baptist Theological Seminary and also at Eastern College. He has written a number of articles for journals such as *The Scottish Journal of Theology* and *The Evangelical Quarterly.* His book *Karl Barth's Theology of Relations: Trinitarian, Christological and Human: Towards an Ethic of the Family* is published with Peter Lang. Dr. Deddo with his wife, Cathy, wrote *George MacDonald: A Devotional Guide to His Writings with Selections* (St Andrew Press, 1996).

William A. Dembski, Ph.D. (mathematics, University of Chicago), Ph.D.

(philosophy, University of Illinois at Chicago), M.Div. (Princeton Theological Seminary). Dr. Dembski is a writer, lecturer, author of *The Design Inference* (Cambridge University Press, 1998) and *Intelligent Design: The Bridge Between Science and Theology* (InterVarsity Press, 1999), also the editor of *Mere Creation: Science, Faith and Intelligent Design* (InterVarsity Press, 1998). He has done postdoctoral work at MIT, University of Chicago, Northwestern, Princeton, Cambridge and Notre Dame. He has been a National Science Foundation doctoral and postdoctoral fellow. Dr. Dembski's publications range from mathematics *(Journal of Theoretical Probability)* to philosophy *(Nous)* to theology *(Scottish Journal of Theology)*. As students at Princeton Theological Seminary, he and Richard Gardiner founded the Charles Hodge Society and reinstituted the *Princeton Theological Review*. Dr. Dembski is a fellow of the Discovery Institute's Center for the Renewal of Science and Culture, Seattle.

Matthew Frawley, teaching fellow and Ph.D. candidate in theology (Princeton Theological Seminary), Th.M and M.Div. (Princeton Theological Seminary). Mr. Frawley is currently serving as the associate editor of the *Princeton Theological Review* and was formerly cochair of the Theological Students' Fellowship, which is associated with the Charles Hodge Society. He has published articles in the *Princeton Theological Review* as well as presented papers for the Princeton Apologetics Seminar. His dissertation examines the dialectic between Søren Kierkegaard's understanding of human nature and revelation.

Phillip E. Johnson, J.D. (University of Chicago), Jefferson Peyser Professor of Law at the University of California at Berkeley, well-known speaker on the cultural impact of Darwinism, author of *Darwin on Trial, Reason in the Balance, Defeating Darwinism by Opening Minds, Objections Sustained* and *The Wedge of Truth* (all InterVarsity Press). After completing his law degree at the University of Chicago, Professor Johnson was a law clerk for Chief Justice Earl Warren of the United States Supreme Court. He has taught law for thirty years at the University of California at Berkeley. He is the author of two massive textbooks on criminal law: *Criminal Law: Cases, Materials, and Text*, 4th ed. (West Publishing, 1990) and *Cases and Materials on Criminal Procedure*, 2nd ed. (West Publishing, 1994). He entered the creation-evolution controversy because he found the books defending Darwinism dogmatic and unconvincing. Professor Johnson is an advisor to the Discovery Institute's Center for the Renewal of Science and Culture, Seattle.

James Parker III, D.Theol. (New Testament, University of Basel, Basel, Switzerland), M.Div., Th.M. (Princeton Theological Seminary), M.A. (Trinity Evangelical Divinity School), postdoctoral fellow (Johns Hopkins University). Professor Parker is the academic dean at Southern Baptist Theological Seminary in Louisville, Kentucky, and is responsible for Christian apologetics. He also directs the Trinity Institute, a residential Christian study center located in Tehuacana, Texas. He serves as the national coordinator for the Religious and Theological Studies Fellowship, a branch of the graduate ministry of InterVarsity Christian Fellowship. He is editor-in-chief of *Foundations*, an international theological journal aimed especially at seminary students and faculty.

Jay Wesley Richards, Ph.D. (theology, Princeton Theological Seminary), Th.M. (Calvin Theological Seminary), M.Div. (Union Theological Seminary). During his time at Princeton Theological Seminary, Dr. Richards was a teaching fellow in theology as well as executive editor of the *Princeton Theological Review* (to which he contributed frequently). He was president of the Charles Hodge Society from 1996 to 1998 and has published articles in philosophy of religion *(Religious Studies)*, theology *(Christian Scholars' Review)* and science *(Perspectives on Science and the Christian Faith)*. He is currently a fellow and program director of the Discovery Institute's Center for the Renewal of Science and Culture, Seattle.

Leslie Zeigler, Th.D. (theology, Pacific School of Religion, Graduate Theological Union, Berkeley). Professor Zeigler is a professor emerita at Bangor Theological Seminary in Maine. Before joining the faculty at Bangor Theological Seminary, she also taught at Oregon State University and the Pacific School of Religion. She has published on Buber and Kierkegaard. She is a contributor to Alvin Kimel's *Speaking the Christian God: The Holy Trinity and the Challenge of Feminism* (Eerdmans, 1992).